BOOKS BY THE SAME AUTHOR

1. Scattered Matherticles: Mathematical Reflections, Volume I (2010)
2. Vectors in History: Main Foci; India and USA, Volume I (2012)
3. Epsilons and Deltas of Life: Everyday Stories, Volume I (2012)
4. My Hindu Faith & Periscope, Volume I (2012)
5. Via Bhatinda: A Braid of Reflected Memoirs, Volume I (2013)
6. Swami Deekshanand Saraswati: My Swami Mama Ji (2014)
7. Darts on History of Mathematics, Volume I (2014)
8. Converging Matherticles: Mathematical Reflections, Volume II (2015)

Plums, Peaches and Pears of Education

Volume I

Satish C. Bhatnagar

Trafford PUBLISHING® www.trafford.com
North America & international
toll-free: 1 888 232 4444 (USA & Canada)
fax: 812 355 4082

DEDICATION
To
Narmada Shankar Bhatnagar
(July 01, 1908 - January 01, 1971)

Narmada Shankar Bhatnagar is my father and I dedicate this book to him gratefully, respectfully and lovingly. The last time I saw him was when he came to Delhi from Bathinda (BTI) to see me off on Aug 25, 1968, at the Palam (Indira Gandhi since 1986) airport for my flight to Bombay (Mumbai since 1995) - on the way to the US. It was with teary eyes, as I knew that it would be our last meeting. He wanted me to return home with a PhD and serve India. We had regular exchange of letters. His health was on decline.

Born to Jawala Sharan and Gopi Devi, father was younger than his three sisters, but older than his two brothers. He grew up in an ancient city of Firozabad (renaming in 1566 of the Hindu city, Chandwar Nagar). Being his ancestral town, we often visited Firozabad at least once a year. It remains famous for all kinds of decorative glass wares.

Father moved to Delhi and lived with his sister (19 years older than him) and brother-in-law, who was in the Indian Railways. He finished high school from a Delhi school and went to Agra, 40 KM from Firozabad to join Agra College. Started in 1823, it is the oldest college in North India. But, he quit it after getting a job in the Indian Railways. For years, he treasured his college books. It is a human tendency that unfulfilled dreams of the youth are either realized later in life or lived out through his/her off springs.

That is what my father did it with his seven children. BTI was/is the second largest railway junction of India and is located on the edge of the Thar Desert. However, he literally created an intellectual oasis as far as our home was concerned. Books, newspapers and magazines, unheard of in my circle of friends in BTI of the 1950s, were regularly subscribed to. I was around thirteen when he got me a membership of a one-room public library located in Kikkar Bazaar, which was moved to Nai Basti later on. At the age of 17, he put me on the daily diet of the *Hindustan Times* for developing English and global awareness.

Despite his brutal work schedule in the Railways, he took keen interest in the schooling of all the kids. Most importantly, he often talked about the achievements of Delhi's legendary intellectual, Lala Hardayal Mathur, breakthrough researches of a relative who did PhD in Physics before 1947, and of another who joined the elite Indian Administrative Services in 1950. On the annual Dussehra festival, we watched him doing ritual worship of our pens and inkpots. At times, pens are mightier than the swords!

His focus was on acquiring knowledge rather than on what was taught in the schools. He badly wanted me to go for an engineering degree, but I refused. He did support me for Math MA; second brother, Sanskrit MA. The third one had an educational detour, but got preference in joining the Indian Railways. He morally supported the fourth one for his shifting to vocational education. But he gave his little savings to the fifth brother for investing in an electrical shop. By the time the last two siblings turned teens, he had retired in 1966. Their responsibilities became that of the older siblings too, as per the family tradition. It may be paradoxical to say that he spent more money on the education of his children than he earned it.

It is partly due to his legacy that I let my kids pursue the studies and careers, as they wanted. I gently steered them. My wife often talks of our 'failures' as parents in that we did not push our kids to become money-making professionals – like, physicians, attorneys and CPAs. My rationale is that I have largely made and lived my life of fulfillment starting it from BTI. The world is open for my kids to be what they want to be. The US is acclaimed as a land of opportunities, though I have started doubting it lately.

Long live the legacy of my father!

SELECTED COMMENTS

Thank you for sharing your reflections. They are wonderful – detailed, principled, educational and politically astute. **Patrick Hayashi,** Retired Associate President, University of California System. (#13)

Thank you so much for sharing your observation and reflection. Will keep your advice in mind as I develop my career. Your friend, **YU/Philip XU. Late Professor of Nursing (#18)**

Satish, Thank you for sharing. Your comments are most thoughtful and appropriate. And by the way, I did read and enjoy your earlier reflections. *I can assure you they did influence my thinking and actions.* Best, **David (Ashley,** Ex-President UNLV) (#26)

Really interesting note Satish, and worth discussing. **Neal Smatresk,** UNLV President (#31)

Hello Satish: Many thanks for sharing the write-up. I enjoyed reading it. I agree that such projects or fair cultivate a culture of science in the minds of students. Best wishes,
Alok Kumar, Chairman Physics Dept, SUNY, Oswego (#37)

Congratulations on the respect and regard that you received. The trouble arises when the student thinks he is only a consumer whereas he is truly a product as well. Best regards, **Ajit Iqbal Singh (#63)**

Congratulations! Sure, we do as teachers make a great impact on our students. Your 'reflection' hits the nail on the heath, to use a cliché' for a change. Teaching is a fulfilling profession. **Moorty (#63)**

Dear Satish, While I was reading your fine composition it occurred to me that sex here in USA is much more open and exposed than in other parts of the world. And talking about sex at appropriate times and in appropriate places is much more fun than keeping it silent and hushed. Yes, it is titillating and exciting. Fun is the name of the game. **Dutchie (#65)**

Dyspareunia has both medical and psychological causes. It is a real medical condition and is not a crazy funded research product. **Rahul (#65)**

Dear Bhatnagar Sahib, First, your little essays have been so communicative that I have felt always in touch: what could I have said if I did call? Also, I have been busy doing some writing of my own - - though by no means as lively. With all this, I still manage to think of you; especially when I am reading your wonderful stuff! With Love, **Harbans (#77)**

I am appalled beyond doubt about the school policy. Is not honesty the best policy? Punishment beyond the bounds of so-called 'violation' school policy? Sherni stuck to her guns. She needs to be applauded; the school needs to be chided. **Moorty/Cedar City, Utah (professor) (#86)**

I fear I might sound naïve above and it may sound ironical, since I have mostly told you- the author about what you write about. LOL!! But if I were to sum it up then what stands out the most to me in your writings is the simplicity of the matter presented in a rather un-opinionated way, which is still up for a good healthy debate. **Rohan Bhatnagar**

DISTRIBUTION OF CONTENTS

II. EDUCATION–ADMINISTRATION

III.   NON-LINEAR EDUCATION

FRONT COVER
(HAIL MY GODDESS, *SARASTHENA!*)

Today, while small talking with my 24-year old grandson, I abruptly told him that I was going to 'create a new goddess'. His response was, "Yes, only you can do it, Nana!" That was quite an off-the cuff compliment from his generation. Off and on, he does read my **Reflections** and lately has started delving into some. He is a policy analyst with a national organization based in Washington DC – his first job after MA from the American University in the DC area.

The context of our conversation was the designing of the front cover of my forthcoming book, **PLUMS, PEACHES AND PEARS OF EDUCATION**. The front cover has to capture the title and contents of the book dealing with an entire enchilada of Education. For weeks, I wrestled with choosing a background color for the book cover (both front and back) - the first task. It is like the athletic colors of the US universities or like the colors of Las Vegas casinos, in which the exteriors are totally bathed in colorful lights at night – creating surreal sights.

The color of the book cover is going to be light green, which is a symbol of growth, vibrancy and fertility. It will be augmented with the images of Plums (purple color) Peaches (golden color), and Pears (light yellow). These fruits are to be shown all over in the front cover, but not on the back cover. In the center of the front cover is a kind of statue of the goddess **Sarasthena** in white marble with her left shoulder bare, as in the style of Greek women. Her right arm goes around a **veena**, an Indian musical instrument and in her left hand holding a book. The musical sound (**shabd**) symbolizes eternal knowledge, and the book, temporal knowledge. The Design Department of the Trafford Publishing has always been successful in recreating the front covers that I visualize in my mind.

A natural question is - where does the goddess **Sarasthena** come from? Google does not produce any link or reference! Well, here is a glimpse into its genesis. Athena is the Greek goddess of wisdom, courage, inspiration, strength, and war strategy. Goddess Athena became goddess Minerva after the Roman conquest of Greece. In Hindu Diaspora, Saraswati is the goddess of knowledge, music, arts, and wisdom. The goddess, Durga (has other names, like Kali, too) eliminates the sufferings of her devotees and projects strength in times of distress. The Greek Athena captures the attributes of both Saraswati and Durga. My conviction is that both the goddesses have showered their blessings on my writings. At this juncture, I would simply add that there is a long and sad history behind the separate identities of the goddess Saraswati and the goddess Durga in the Hindu pantheon.

Putting the pieces together: the part 'Saras' in *Sarasthena* is taken out from **Saras**wati and the part 'thena' from **Athena** – simple parsing and concatenation of strings such as in computer science.

A saying that man (gender neutral) is made in the image of God is as meritorious as the saying that gods are made in the images of man.

Feb 11, 2016

PS: Thanks to Namit, my nephew, for making the initial image of the front cover.

EDUCATION-AL PREFACE

GENESIS

In life, deadlines are generally set so that one does not go astray from an immediate task at hand. Likewise, the mental dams are built so that energies are fully harnessed. Still, we hate deadlines when they face us, but we appreciate them after the jobs are done on time. It just happened with me at 2 AM today, December the 16th!

Last May, after finishing my eighth book, the **Second Volume of Mathematical Reflections**, I spent two months overseas. Off and on, the idea of working on the next book would float into my mind; I wanted it to be something different - not the volume II or III of the ones already published. After returning to the US and while teaching during five weeks of intense summer session, a book on Education flashed through a crack in my mind. It was to be on Education – a kind of my longest journey of life. It partly came as educational legacy of my family at large.

Personally, this journey started from an elementary school in Bathinda to high school, to college, and to universities in India and USA – while also working as lecturer/professor in Bathinda, Shimla, Kurukshetra and Patiala - in India, US, Malaysia and Oman. As a matter of fact, the student mindset has never left me. I continue taking short/refresher/mini courses, workshops, various development courses, and lately going on study tours almost every year! Consequently, I remain fully engaged in the academic life of every place. My output is based on a simple principle of conservation- what goes in must come out – their forms at the points of entry and exit are naturally different.

By temperament, I am reactive - in the sense that I must take a stand on a topic or issue, whether I read or listen something. Public speaking was not my forte until I joined a toastmasters club at the age of 60. Thus, I poured out my views and ideas in writings. That took the form of thousands of long letters to my wife, friends, relatives, colleagues, and editors of newspapers and magazines. This rate and pace of writing kept going up with age and experiences. Fifteen years ago, when the old-fashioned letters morphed into **Reflections**, they were saved on a computer. Before the 1980s, I used to make carbon copies of only a few important letters.

These *Reflections*, more than a thousand in number, were naturally mined out of my mind - without any thought of ever publishing them into the book forms. Under a strange set of circumstances, the first book came out five years ago. It was truly a transformational moment! Meanwhile, I continued to write new *Reflections* - call it out of compulsion, addiction, or sheer outburst. In parallel, I kept on working on the next book.

The second kind of mining is from a pile of a thousand Word files. It involves sorting, which means reading a particular *Reflection* first, as I literally forget a previous *Reflection* the moment a new one grips over my mind. I enjoy this mental exercise in the sense that at the age of 70+ as I am impressed with my own ideas penned down 10-20 years ago. It may be viewed as a kind of intellectual masturbation. Nevertheless, sorting, compiling, editing and formatting do not weigh on my mind at all. On the other hand, this entire process becomes a vehicle of my inward journey. It may be leading to my own brand of Self-Realization!

Six weeks ago, I resolved to finish this task before Dec 16, when my birthday falls on it. At times, the job would appear overwhelming and head reeling. It did slow me down, but I did not extend the date. Instead, I added more time. Also, I wanted to start on the Preface of the book on Dec 16, 2015, as I complete 76 years on the Planet Earth. The title of the forthcoming book is *PLUMS, PEACHES AND PEARS OF EDUCATION.*

WHAT AND WHERE OF THE *PLUMS, PEACHES AND PEARS*
The title of a book is like the name of a person, which amongst the Hindus, in particular, is very significant. It is generally given in a *naam sanskar* (naming ceremony). A family astrologer or temple priest describes the characteristics of a newly born baby based upon the Zodiac signs or horoscope duly prepared. A propitious time and name are chosen accordingly. For me, this process is no less important even when it comes to choosing a title of my book or a *Reflection*. After having given titles to over a thousand *Reflections* and eight books, it still takes considerable amount of time and thought for the naming of a new one. The process involves frequent tinkering with both syntax and semantics.

Once it became clear that the next book was going be on the entire enchilada of Education, as it has pervaded my life, the next question was of choosing a title that would capture its contents. It was not easy as the kind of material that I have is very different from what a professor, say, in a US College of Education would have it. For example, typical titles of research papers in education read as: 1. *Education for Rural Transformation in Thailand: Perspectives on Policies and Practices.* 2. *A System Theory Perspectives on Education for Rural Transformation: In the Dialectic between Global Context and Local Conditions.*

The papers cited above are two of the many scholarly research papers of Dr. H S Bhola, Emeritus Professor of Education, Indiana University, Bloomington, and the winner of many awards - including the prestigious 2015 Nehru Literacy Award. We have been friends for 45 years. He wanted me to browse through these papers, but in all honesty, I just could not wade through them due to the 'heavy' terminology used. I want my book that is readable in bits and pieces - like taking bites of fruits or appetizers, sipping evening drinks, or relishing desserts. That is the divergence in my approach.

The material of this book has bubbled up in different settings. It is like preparing Indian homemade *ghee* – you start from unpasteurized milk, turn it into curd; then curd into *lassi* and churn the butter out from *lassi*. Finally, slow heat melts down the butter and is filtered into *ghee*. It involves various stages of bacterial and mechanical processes. This book material has grown out of 65 years of my being in education – both as a student and teacher – however, all based upon my experiences and observations. Yes, I feel blessed with my power to observe scenarios and uncanny ability to interpret them.

As I was sorting out the *Reflections*, the sheer variety suddenly grew out of control – obviously, no two *Reflections* are similar. Initially, the title of the book was *My Perspectives on Education*. After a few days it changed to *Perspectives of My Education*, as I am not talking about anybody else's experiences; I am not quoting anyone; there is no bibliography at the end. A few days later, the word 'perspective' started turning me off, as it is used so much in the vernacular these days – rather indiscriminately!

With the exception of my one book, every title has a subtitle. A couple of them were tried, but were eventually set aside. As the variety of *Reflections* kept passing before my eyes, a 'fruity' title, *Plums and*

Peaches of Education flashed into my mind. I wanted to get the names of three fruits (corresponding to three sections of the contents) all starting with the letter 'P'. In order to get some validation on the choice of such a title, I sent out an email to my children and grandchildren, always a reliable sample of nine. Within an hour, the title became *Plums, Peaches and Pears of Education*. Whoever, I mentioned it to, liked it. However, two weeks later, when I was telling this name, 'prunes' came out of my lips instead of 'pears'. I regularly eat prunes for its values as laxative and nutrient. Also, 'prunes' sounds crispier than 'pears'. The title became *Plums, Peaches and Prunes of Education.*

After nearly two months of the writing of the above para, I just discovered that **every prune is a plum – but, not conversely**! Hence, 'Pears' came back and replaced 'Prunes' in the title. What a title story, but it does not end here. Another question was to add or not to add 'Volume I', as a subscript to the title. Only two out of eight books were visualized ending in Volume I. However, a few months after the publication of the *Darts on History of Mathematics*, I have written many *Reflections* during 2015 that in two years, there would be enough matter for its sequel, Volume II – God willing (*Inshallah*)! Thus, I decided to add 'Volume I' to the title, though I do not see its Volume II on the horizon at this moment! That is the story of the title, *PLUMS, PEACHES AND PEARS OF EDUCATION, VOLUME I.*

ORGANIZATION
There is a total of 98 *Reflections* and articles going back to 1987 and written through 2014. Let me add at the outset that there were no *Reflections* worthy of being labeled as 99th, and the 100th, a standout number in life! However, there are a few pieces written before 1987 too, but those files could not be easily tracked. Besides, they were done on a different software. In my first book, all the *Reflections* were lumped together, but soon after publication, it was realized that they could be categorized into 3-4 sections for convenience. With the result, the second book had four sections. However, it turned out that four sections were a bit too much for any sorting of the numerous *Reflections*, as there is a natural overlapping of sub-ideas in most *Reflections*. Since then, three sections have proved effective.

The first section, called **EDUCATION CO-ORDINATES**, includes thirty-one *Reflections* on the fundamentals of education, institution and administration. Historically, all great men and women had visions of private and public education in the making of their families and societies. Gandhi experimented with early education in his ashram in South Africa, and subsequently gave a model of *Nai Taleem* (means New Education) to independent India. The Nobel Laureates, Bertrand Russell and Rabindranath Tagore experimented with education too. Tagore's Shantiniketan (Vishwa Bharati) has already survived 100 years. Of course, all the despots - Hitler, Stalin and Mao had full control on the mental development of their citizenry - from infancy to adulthood - through education imparted in schools and colleges.

The second section of the book is titled as, **EDUCATION – ADMINISTRATION**. It has forty-one *reflections*. Most of the *Reflections* were written when I was the Associate Dean of the College of Sciences (2003-2006). In that position, I dealt with the students, faculty, administration, and tackled issues far beyond the confines of my experience as a mathematics faculty member. I often represented the Dean and the College at several functions and events. Being a toastmaster, I looked forward to such public opportunities, as they also provided me new material to write on. One of most important features of educational enterprise is its component of administration – how lean, speedy and responsive it is. Overall, *Reflections* in this section are directed on straightforward aspects of education.

In contrast to the *Reflections* in the Second section, the title of **NON-LINEAR EDUCATION** of Section III implies that educational substance and values are not clearly set on the surface. There is a total of twenty-six *Reflections* in this section. The term, Non-Linearity comes from mathematics. It means that various aspects of education are not seen right on the surface. One has to adjust one's lens to discern them. For example, my talks to middle school students have non-traditional educational value for them in a long run of their lives.

With regard to the organization of the matter in all of my books, a couple of things are like the fixed points of a mathematical function. Number one is the chronology of the *Reflections* – dating every *Reflection*; the second date in a few cases means significant revision since the first date. I am getting increasingly convinced of its value. It tells the reader where my thoughts are coming from – the reader does not have to probe around for it. Whenever, I read the writings of other authors, I always remain curious as to when and where this piece was written. Thus, my entire book opens out in an 'evolutionary' manner. The second feature is the spaces for **PERSONAL REMARKS** - spread over in 5-6 places. Furthermore, the last two pages are marked exclusively for comments in detail. Personally, I can't read a book without scribbling with a pencil along inside it!

ACKNOWLEDGEMENTS

This is the last part of any preface. I have seen the list of persons thanked going over one page, particularly, in the writing of a college textbook. Generally, it includes the name(s) of spouse(s), children, grandchildren, colleagues, friends, collaborators and editorial assistants from the publishers etc. For this book, there is absolutely no one to be acknowledged. This book has literally come out into its own existence like a baby to its parents when there was no planning for it! Yet, there is an exception.

Francis A. Andrew has been a fixed point in all my books. He is a professor of English in an Omani college, runs a school, and has authored nearly a dozen science fiction books. His study of Christian theology, computer science and astrobiology runs deep. He has provided me feedback to all the *Reflections*. In the seven years of our association, I have benefited a lot from his scholarship - including my newfound appreciation of the power of the English language!

I must confess that my command over Hindi, my mother language and over Punjabi, the language of Punjab where I grew up, are now second to English. In fairness, when you live in the US, Hindi and Punjabi are no longer in linguistic circulation on a regular basis. At the age of 76, I want to have mastery over one language, and that is English. Thank you Francis for being a part of this intellectual journey!

Finally, my e-readers, e-mail (viabti1968@gmail.com) any comments and feedback. They would be gratefully acknowledged.

Dec 16, 2015 - Feb 14, 2016

SECTION I
EDUCATION CO-ORDINATES

There are thirty-one articles and *Reflections* in this section. A few were written when I was in Southeast Asia, India and Middle East for an extended period as a visitor or on faculty while on leave from UNLV. The one main idea that percolates in most *Reflections* is akin to the one seen in analytic geometry, where an equation of curve or surface is understood by the choice of coordinates. Likewise, there are choices of coordinates in education, which shape its products. However, the education coordinates are not straight.

For example, in Dec, 2003, I propounded a theory on the foundations of education - rather revived it from India's ancient time (1000-2000 BC) of the Ramayana and Mahabharata era. It is based upon three cardinal principles - *Shaastra* (knowledge of national heritage including its classics and scriptures), *Shastra* (literary it means weaponry, but it also implies the defense of heritage - its knowledge) and *Shatru* (enemy within and without - this knowledge). The Islamic *madrassa* education is a corollary of the *gurukul* educational system of ancient India! The *madrassa* education hinges on deeper study of the Quran, militancy/*jihad* and *Shaitan* (the enemy of Islam).

This section opens with my 1988 article focusing on the teaching of mathematics – not from its pedagogical angle, but on its relative less importance to the research component in academia. There is a passionate denunciation of putting too much premium on traditional Research over Teaching, particularly, in the colleges and universities, which do not have even PhD programs in mathematics. Yes, the ideas can be modified to other disciplines. The second article, in a way, goes to the extreme for its relatively global scope. It is a mammoth effort to tackle the entire enterprise of education. Starting from the three Rs, the pillars of western public education, it encompasses the ancient Indian model of intimate education provided by the 60-year old grandfather like teachers to 8-year old grandson like students. It is encapsulated in a principle of early education, *athe aur sathe* (eight and sixty). I have heard it laid out by Swami Deekshanand Saraswati (1918-2003), a Vedic scholar – in his books and public discourses.

There are **reflections** on the flexibility of curriculum when compared with India (# 7, 10, 12, 19, 31). Religion factors into education in theocratic societies and nations (5, 10, 19, 27). Then there are **reflections** on a business side of education as well as education completely as business (4, 6, 19, 29). The US undergraduate education is delivered largely as a business product, but the graduate education is totally on merit. Academics and Athletics define the US education like the two sides of a coin. It is seamless - from schools to colleges (11). The rest of the world is miles 'behind'.

With the passage of time, I became conscious of the lack of representation of Indians in the administrative positions beyond the department chairs (13, 15, 18). For a short while, UNLV was embroiled in racial diversity (15, 16, 18) - largely concerned with Afro-Americans, women, and Hispanic in administration. Asians, Pacific Islanders, and Native Indians are of no consequence for their lack of any strong political organization at the state or national level.

Faculty governance is a hallmark of the US higher education. Generally, the administrators (except the presidents) rise from the ranks of faculty and come back to the faculty ranks when fired, removed, or they voluntarily step down. One rarely retires into an administrative position. Thus, communication between faculty and administration goes on through proper channels and otherwise. Over the years, I have suggested many ideas to the Chancellors, Presidents, Provosts, Deans and department chairpersons. They have welcomed it (17, 22, 26, 30).

In India, a university budget is never a public issue. But, in the US, it goes on for one full year at several levels. Due to the collapse of national economy in 2008, every public entity was affected. During UNLV's budget crisis, I passed on some suggestions from a faculty in the trenches (20, 23, 24, 25).

1. STATUS OF MATHEMATICS TEACHING

[**Note:** Written in 1988, my present style of reflected writing was still in the embryonic state! In order to give the entire book an evolutionary touch, this formal style is not changed. The formatting and editorial changes are kept to the minimum, and are done only to enhance the clarity of ideas. Nevertheless, its inclusion is justified as the ideas formulated twenty-seven years ago are still valid.]

Introduction
There is one essential difference between research in mathematics and mathematics/mathematical education. Generally, research in mathematics ends up in results that are basically linear in the sense that any one result is connected with the preceding ones. Research in mathematical education tends to be cyclic in nature too. The old ideas can be practiced with different emphasis in new situations.

The main ideas of this paper were included in another paper, *Why Should Anyone be a Teacher Professor?* Which I presented in a session, **Profession of Teaching** (5.7 Theme) during the **Sixth International Congress on Mathematical Education** (ICME-6) held in Budapest, Hungary, from July 27 to August 3, 1988. The title is indeed very catchy. After submitting its abstract in Jan 88, I learned that the **Magna Publications, Inc**. publishes a newsletter by a similar title, *The Teaching Professor* with the main purpose of reviving and boosting teaching in the US colleges and universities.

Most of the observations in this article are applicable to all disciplines; however, they are more pertinent to mathematics. It is necessary to narrow down the audience so that the paper could be properly related and understood in right context of institutions, specifically the ones which don't have PhD programs in mathematics.

In the US, the popular image of a professor, no matter, where she/he works, is one who is generally engaged in research activities, has nothing to do with undergraduates, and has little time even for his graduate students. There are three main components of the college/university academic profession: Teaching, Research and Service. Service means contributions to one's professional organization, institution, and the community at large. In a traditional sense, research means publishing in research journals.

Example of an Institution
It is pertinent to bring in focus the background of my experience and observations by telling about the type of institutions I am associated and concerned with. The University of Nevada Las Vegas (UNLV) is located in a metropolitan area having a population of nearly 500,000. There is no other 4-year college/university within a radius of 100 miles. On the average, every year, 4-5 undergraduate students, out of a population of 14,000, get their bachelor's degrees with major in mathematics. Some of them are engineering/computer science majors who pick up mathematics as a double major. There is small graduate program for master's degree, and on the average, one or two students finish it every year. This is a typical profile of scores of universities and hundreds of colleges in the US. Many colleges and universities in the developing countries can also identify with its size and program in mathematics.

Start of the Malaise
Since the early 1960s, when the federal money was pumped in for the improvement of math and science instruction in order to catch up with the Soviets in the sputnik race, high schools went for new math and colleges upgraded their graduate programs. The impact of whole scenario has been that in the academic profession, research became a byword. Publication of any sort started guaranteeing some kind of immortality on the top of all professional rewards.

Today, one witnesses a general apathy and neglect toward teaching at every level, and is prevalent in all disciplines [3]. The biggest contributory factor is that for all personnel considerations of tenure, promotion, merit, sabbatical leaves, and other benefits, traditional research carries nearly all the weight. This problem is not confined to the US alone. For seven years, I taught in India before migrating to the US in 1968. My erstwhile colleagues in India tell that conscientious teaching has almost disappeared from the colleges and universities. In the third world countries, the politicization of students and the faculty due to their respective powerful unions is another reason for the erosion of the teaching environment. The countries, which are introducing some of the US systems of higher education, are bound to confront these problems too.

After a couple of decades of neglect of the teaching component of the profession, professors just don't want to each anymore [3]. They perhaps know what it takes to do a good teaching, but they don't want to spend any time and energy on it. The administration has been largely responsible for it. They promote research far more that teaching, as big chunks of research grants of the faculty goes to the administration.

Besides, for varied evaluations of faculty during the year, it is much easier to compare research productivity even across different disciplines by simply counting the number of publications. This number game has not only relegated teaching, but it has now started damaging the quality of research too. When it comes to teaching, everyone is deemed to be a good teacher and faculty pat and patronize each other. The result is that one who does a conscientious job of teaching gets equated with ones who pay no attention to it.

Current National Status
A preliminary report of the **National Research Council** (NRC) project, MS 2000 [2] has brought out the dilemma between research and teaching by identifying the following two gaps:

1. Thinking and Teaching
2. Calculus

The nature of research in mathematics is such that it simply cannot be transferred into the classroom [5, 6]. Therefore, when a professor walks into the classroom, his upper mind is occupied with research problems, which are disconnected from his teaching chores. The head and heart are not together in the classroom. Such a teaching is counterproductive; students learn much less, and they develop a poor attitude toward teaching, particularly, if they opt for teaching profession.

The gap about calculus means that by and large, a student thinks that calculus would be the highest-level math course he/she is going to take, but the professor thinks that calculus is the lowest level course he is going to teach! In the universities, there is a perception of some loss of prestige in teaching a pre-calculus course. The fact is that at least 80% fulltime fee equivalency is generated by pre-calculus courses.

A touch of history is worth adding here. On the recommendations of an MAA committee [1] in Sept '66, it was resolved that no college credits would be given in four-year degree programs for courses in pre-calculus and trigonometry. Moreover, after Sept '68, these courses should, no longer, be offered in four-year colleges even on non-credit basis. What a collective vision of mathematicians!

A generation later, mathematics landscape is different. Something unforeseen has led to the decline in mathematics preparation. Today, even big and prestigious universities are offering remedial courses in arithmetic and algebra. Yet, the debate continues. The single most factor is that during the last two decades, teaching, no matter how excellently it is done, has become a poor second fiddle to research.

Most of the pre-calculus courses are taught either by the part-time instructors who are moonlighting in the teaching profession, or by the graduate teaching assistants, who are primarily there to finish their graduate degrees. The net effect is that the general performance of the US students in mathematics continues to decline by international standards according to several studies done by the Department of Education.

Another Negative Consequence
Such colleges and universities lie between high schools and PhD granting universities. Products of such institutions are like unwanted pregnancies in a sense that the children become burdensome to the society on one hand, and yet are in great demand for adoption due to high infertility rate amongst the US couples. Graduates of such colleges don't easily fit and excel anywhere.

If they go and teach in high schools, they are found incompetent. Some forty-eight states in the US have instituted some testing of math teachers at different stages despite the shortage of math and science teachers across the country. At the other end of the spectrum of college graduates, only a few go for PhD in mathematics (not Mathematics Education). Since as undergraduates, they are not well taught and prepared, they are much less competent to pursue PhD programs. This is also reflected by the data released by the American Mathematics Society, that in 1987, foreign students earned more than 50% of doctorates from the US institutions.

Therefore, if teaching is not properly rewarded, both high schools and the PhD granting universities are likely to suffer eventually.

Cultural Factor

In oriental countries like India and China, the loss is at another and higher level. Traditionally, teachers and professors have been accorded a very dignified status in the society. To mention a personal incident is not out of place here. In 1978, I arrived at Seoul airport, and was in line for my custom clearance. On my turn, I produced my passport and put my bags up for inspection. However, the inspector, on noticing from my passport that I was a professor, respectfully bowed in front of me and personally put my bags down without checking any one of them!

However, lately due to the transplantation of disinfectant Western models of education, there has been a deep erosion of the wholesome Eastern teaching in all ranks in colleges and universities. Indiscipline and even hooliganism have been at rampant. The politicization of institutions has made it all the worse. Net effect is that the students are not receiving the right education and the teachers in colleges are frustrated and losing respect. Moral values are also losing ground. Through conscientious teaching alone a bond between students and teachers is established which outlives the confines of an institution.

One Proposal

In the US, there have been all kinds of reports recommencing the revitalization of mathematics curriculum, tightening the admission requirements, enforcing the prerequisites, teacher training for pre-service and in-service, and no less, the early introduction of the computer usage on a large scale. Computers remind me of the encyclopedias which nearly every US home has one or the other kind. The current reading and writing disabilities, and the lack of general knowledge of the students at large alone testify, that the encyclopedias have not been scholastically as helpful as proclaimed. The third world countries have to be very careful and watchful of the pressures of the computer industries about their usage.

In the non-PhD granting institutions, teaching should be recognized at par with research. Without any publication, one cannot be promoted to the associate rank; forget the rank of full professorship. It is common to see a person with his/her name on a few publications, but no good teaching record, is seen getting all personnel rewards.

Three years ago, the Mathematical Association of America (MAA) made a modest effort in broadening the definition of research activity in mathematics at the collegiate level, particularly after the publication of the presidential commission report, ***The Nation at Risk*** (1983), and the David Report, ***Renewing US Mathematics*** (US National Academy of Sciences, 1984).

The MAA recommended that publications in research journals alone should not be the sole criterion for personnel recommendations. Development of innovative courses to meet the demands of special interest groups in the community and high schools; designing college curricula and offering new courses; writing review, expository articles, class notes, and grant proposals; consultation, attending professional development courses; leadership and presenting papers in professional organizations, are worthy of all personnel considerations.

Round up
However, there has not been any follow-up efforts in getting them implemented. As president of the MAA, Steen pushed it for a while. However, MS 2000 project has included the broadening the research activity in its recommendations as given in the preliminary report [2]. Full report is expected in 1990. It is a project of the National Research Council, the principal operating agency of the National Academy of Science & the National Academy of Engineers. The Board on Mathematical Sciences & Mathematical Science Education Board have sponsored it.

Furthermore, ICME is an excellent forum to push such recommendations to the other countries as well. There is an element of universality about them.

REFERENCES

1. Ballew and Sterrett, *FOCUS*, Sept 88, p11.

2. Madison, Bernard L, Mathematical Sciences in the year 2000: Assessment for Renewal in US Colleges and Universities (some highlights presented at the ICME-6).

3. Rollins, Alferd, *VCU Teaching,* Ed. Armour & Fuhrmann, Spring, 1988.

4. Steen, Lynn A, Crisis and Renewal in College Mathematics, point of view, *Chronicles of Higher Education*, July, 85.

5. ...., Renewing Undergraduate Mathematics. *The Notices*, August, 85, pp 459-466.

6. ...., Restoring Scholarship to Collegiate mathematics, *FOCUS*, 6 (1), Jan 86.

Sep 1988/Sep 2015

2. MRI OF EDUCATION ENTERPRISE

[**Note: 09/2015**. I was delighted to unearth this forgotten article in a folder. Its variation was published in the first volume of the *Sahi Buniyad*, the first educational magazine of Punjab. It was launched in Jan 2000 by the Teachers Home, Bathinda. Jagmohan Kaushal continues to be the founding Chairman of the Teachers Home and Chief Editor of the Sahi Buniyad. We have known each other since our high school days. In order to preserve some sense of history, the changes are made only to enhance the clarity of ideas. The format of the article is unchanged. Its ideas still have freshness, and they remain relevant to the present times.]

Abstract
A strong and common criticism of present system of education in India is that it has been reduced to a mean of generating personal wealth and prestige alone. Relatively, it is of less service to the needy persons and sections of the society. Furthermore, it falls short in creating new knowledge through fundamental researches. For years, the curricula in schools and colleges remained stagnant even after independence. Largely, the changes are made in response to educational trends in western countries. This paper attempts to give an overview of general education from a bit of global perspective in order to understand problems at local levels. It raises some fundamental questions while offering a few solutions.

Personal Statement
I feel honored to have been invited to put my ideas on the state of education system as prevalent in India. College/University teaching has been my only profession for the last nearly forty years. Frequent overseas travels, professional writings and working in different cultures and institutions provide a perspective that I have tried to capture in this paper. It is a comprehensive essay on education – without any technical jargon. It is viewed as its MRI (Magnetic Resonance Imaging, a reliable diagnostic test for every part of human body).

Approach to Education
- How does one really approach an issue as broad as education?
- Does one have access and freedom in a society to pursue or/and provide education at individual or collective levels?

- One may even raise a more fundamental question: what is education, and what is its purpose?

Answers to all these pertinent questions are more intertwined together than to be put down in a sequential manner. Thus, they are interspersed in the body of the article.

Brief Historical Background

For the last 300 hundred years of worldwide colonial expansion and domination by West European culture, Three **Rs** (**R**eading, W**R**iting and A**R**ithmetic) have become a hallmark of universal literacy and a benchmark for the foundation of an educated individual or society. It is literally assumed that anyone not well versed in three Rs is uncouth and uncivilized. It was the emergence of demonstrative science in the renaissance period in Europe when this concept was born. Collective thinking is its midwife. Later on, with impetus from early industrialization, it was firmly crystallized in Western Europe.

On the other hand, in most Asian and African countries vast populations continue to live in small and isolated villages. In every village, there was at least one knowledgeable person, like a Brahmin in India or the wise/medicine man in Africa. The Hindu caste system and Muslim Madarsa system have been catalytic in the transfer of knowledge from one generation to the other. For socio-economic and cultural factors, the joint family system has flourished in India. The unit survival was also anchored on the wisdom of a few elders in family hierarchy. The majority of population may not have received all three Rs but they were steeped in moral and ethical values that go a long way in the making of a wholesome person. The diminishing presence of this dimension in modern system of education, in the name of secular education, is turning out educated ones who are efficient like robotics, but morally bankrupt and dry.

There are ample opportunities for the commoners to pick pieces of worldly wisdom from discussions and dialogues in village *chopals*, a place usually situated at the center of the village. Also, people gathered to listen to regular religious discourses in temples. In fact, these forums are not very different from the open dialogues the ancient Greek scholars had adopted in the *gymnasiums* of Athens. One can routinely come across numerous persons particularly in India who are not versed in all three Rs, yet lead an inspiring way of life. The freedom history of India is a testimony to this fact. Parents of most freedom fighters had little knowledge of three R's, yet with the knowledge derived from the folklore of oral traditions, they raised and inspired their children to great heights of personal sacrifices for the liberation of the nation. This raises a few interesting points worth pondering:

1. Are three Rs oversold in modern times?
2. What, alternatives, if any, are there to three Rs; akin to alternative medical systems and alternative life styles gaining growing popularity in USA?

Counter Scenario of Education

In the US, there are growing instances of high school pass students who cannot read and write after **twelve** years of high school education! They are called functionally illiterate. And on the top of that, they and their guardians in some cases have sued the school districts for the 'damages'. In other words, for this ignorance they are holding the school system responsible! There is a degree of truth on both sides of the shared responsibility. The US courts and justice systems admit such a litigation.

In colleges and universities, the number of remedial courses in mathematics and English have been increasing for the last 20 years. The material that students are supposed to have learnt in high schools is being covered in colleges. Of course, remedial course work is not counted towards college degrees. But it does point out to the wasted resources in public school system.

Government Investment in Education

Soon after independence in 1947, India undertook monumental efforts, perhaps unprecedented in history, by opening government schools (called public schools in the US) in every village and area - urban and rural alike. Investigative reports in several states have brought out that many schools existed only on papers or had no classroom facilities. Salary funds withdrawn from the treasury would go into the pockets of corrupt axis of elephantine education bureaucracy and politicians. It is the large-scale failure of government education system that has resulted in the resurgence of the private schools of all kinds on the Indian landscape in the last 20 years.

In the US, only 10% schools are private (called public in India); in India it is close to 80% in urban areas. In fact, academically superior students of all social strata (in India) prefer to attend private educational institutions despite significantly higher fees. In general, only the poor kids end up attending the government. institutions. In the US, K-12 education is mainly funded by formulas based upon the local property taxes collected. Those who send their kids to private schools are still paying for the public/govt. education through their taxes. For various reasons, there is a growing resentment against public education amongst people who are increasingly supporting private education.

During a period of 1960s through 1980s, a large number of universities were started all over the country with govt. money channeled through the University Grants Commission (UGC). The number of PhD granting institutions in India is close to 200 that may be close to what the US has! However, in contrast to private high schools, the number of private universities in India is negligible. Interestingly enough, the government pays 90% of the faculty salary in private colleges too, though the management is in the hands of private body. The general public is not actively involved in higher education in India as one notices it in the USA.

Present Mania for Education in India
Before and after independence, education alone provided windows of opportunity in terms of status in society and financial gains. Though not high in making choices, it was nearly impossible to get into any business or agriculture unless one was born in such a family. There was no production industry and service industry. The country was steeped in utter poverty, from which education was the only exit door.

Like in the US, one could not think of making a decent living by playing an instrument, acting, singing, dancing, painting, creating art, or playing any sports etc. It literally shocks an Indian to observe how in western countries young people make a name and fortune even after dropping out of schools. Indian children are still pressured to study and study, and zero time to play. Academic and athletics are two sides of the same coin - they form and reflect a personality. In the entire west, an ideal student is a combination of scholarship and sports. In India and many other Asian countries, focus is on all academics and little on sports.

My Thesis

I believe education, in general, is an exposure to organized information and accumulated knowledge at various stages of studentship - so that an individual can actualize one's potential for his/her growth for the benefit of the society. Its goal are to provide skills for livelihood, promote art and science of problem solving, and finally providing an intellectual environment for new knowledge through basic researches.

With such dynamic parameters, any specific values imposed on a wide scale in imparting education may stifle it at the same time. There are big dangers and pit falls in it. History has demonstrated how politicians in countries, in the developing ones in particular, try to implement educational policies to suit narrow ideologies. But it has proved counter productive to education in the long run. **An educated mind is a free mind**.

A Hard Look

For centuries, nearly 80% of the Hindu population was excluded from receiving any education due to its strong caste system. It was totally forbidden to some caste members and unnecessary for some beyond a certain level. **That truly has resulted in a tremendous national waste of human resources**! It is no wonder that the Hindu in India have been subjected under so many foreign subjugations.

The greater a role an individual or a group wants to play in life, the greater is the need for formal education. Free and compulsory education for every child at every stage may make a catchy slogan in democratic politics, but I doubt if it guarantee the making of a great nation

One thing is then sure that any aspect of education in a diverse and democratic nation like India must be tackled on a small scale and at a local level. Any national or even state policy is going to create more education managers than educators or educated ones.

In the early economy of India, there was hardly any private capital for investment in education. In a short period after independence and through the pursuit of knowledge for its own sake amongst the Hindus, in particular, there has been tremendous surge of private colleges of all kinds.

There is a new economic dimension to public life in India. Since the 1980s, personal wealth has been steadily increasing. Whether it is properly distributed across the spectrum remains a moot point. But there is no denying that the educational infrastructure of vast number of engineering colleges, medical institutes, national labs and heavy industries are now the new engines of economy.

Proverbial Poverty of India

In the 18th century a great social thinker, Rousseau had called poverty a disease, and in 20th century, the apostle of non-violence, Gandhi called it worst form of violence. From the travelogues of Rudyard Kipling and Mark Twain to the present accounts of western tourists, open-sewage like stark poverty remains the most unforgettable image of India. In my travels and readings, I have not come across a country where there is such a spectrum of abject poverty as commonly seen in India. It can freeze any one's heart and mind. Yet one does not really get a perspective on poverty until one is out of India. Most people living in India are hardened with or towards poverty that they go about ignoring or accepting it.

So, when I see today doctors in India minting money in medical practices, I understand it! Or, engineers taking kickback money on contracts, or judges accepting huge bribes, or professors not teaching in colleges but running tuition sessions in their homes, I understand it. They are only trying to wash the century old stains of poverty from their attires and also of their ancestors! One need not be bothered too much for it. This will slow down within a span of a generation or two.

However, this observation does not condone their greed. It is timely to take the approach that Gandhi adopted towards the rich. Let us not blame the system of education for it and talk of overhauling it! Education is a single tree in a forest. It is a great challenge in itself to find reasons for the perpetual poverty of India. No one denies an ultimate affluence of a few families that exists in India too.

Indian Education System as viewed from Abroad

To justify above remarks, I would like to point out how every year foreign universities and multinationals recruit graduates of Indian Institutes of Technologies (IIT) and All India Institutes of Medical Sciences (AIIMS). It has been reported that nearly 90% of graduates from these premier institutions leave the shores of India within three years. The US consulates are known to issue visas to these graduates without any hitch.

Indian professional students are brilliantly educated by any international standards. Most of them are absorbed in professional careers as soon as they land in US, or go for higher degrees. It is a loss to Indian taxpayers. But most of these graduates find their skills wasted in India for lack of proper working conditions. For instance, a medical graduate cannot practice in a rural area, where there is no continuous power supply required for running medical instruments and refrigeration of medicines.

Ironically, these institutions are no different from factories set up by the multinationals to take advantage of lower taxes and other industry concessions given by India and developing countries. It is cheaper to produce in India whether it is any good, an engineer, or a doctor! Therefore, there is nothing inherently wrong with the education system in India at any level. It has to be made more meaningful to India.

A Few Recommendations

1. It is time to decentralize educational management at every state and national level. Ministries of Education should be the first to loosen their grips on the financial strings and on policies imposed from top to bottom. In the US there is no one elected person or IAS type administrative official, who is in charge of education at state or federal level. Of course, public accountability in US is built at every step.

    In India, the UGC has become too monolithic. Its initial historic charge of setting up universities is already over. Universities, in particular regions, may evolve their own apex bodies for mutual collaboration and improvement. Indian bureaucracy has been known to suffocate initiatives. Radical reforms in education should follow similar liberal financial reforms initiated for the industry and economy in 1991.

2. Let colleges and universities develop their own curriculum according to their local conditions and history. Most ills and evils of the current examination system will disappear. After a few years, initial confusion will transform into innovation at

every level. With fifty years of independence behind, people are now ready to take their responsibilities in their own hands. MaCauley's curriculum was molded into all academics after independence, as if every Indian child has to go for higher studies after high school. Ideally, curriculum in various levels rests on a right proportion of academics, athletics and service. The approach has to be integrated.

3. At present there is no competition between institutions for excellence. There is a conformity of mediocrity. The present education system does not even reflect the rich diversity of India. In the US every academic and athletic program is nationally ranked on an annual basis. It pushes institution to strive for better all the time.

4. The curricula from elementary to colleges should promote independent thinking and research. Presently, it is all a rote system. The US system has gone to the other extreme. However, there is a golden mean of the two. What one remembers and what one can recall measure one's identity.

5. The present 4-5 track system of undergraduate education in India has to be opened up. Let students create their own degree programs around a core of subjects. The concept is futuristic. It is like a buffet where one samples on essentials of fruit, salads and desserts. If you like a major dish, then go for its second serving.

A story of my brother is worth adding here. After moving to the US, he often felt embarrassed to realize that in four years of college in India (1957-61), he only learnt English, Sanskrit, Hindi, economics and philosophy in the arts track - no exposure to any science, mathematics, fine arts, or engineering. In the US, my daughter took 42 courses in 15 different areas for her BA degree. A bottom line is that high school education lays a foundation of a house and the undergraduate education provides its walls and roofs.

6. Indian schools, colleges and universities do not raise funds that are constantly required; say to extend a building, replace

obsolete lab equipment, computers, start new scholarships, special collections of books and journals. **Govt. money is never enough**. In the US, in contrast, millions of dollars pour through bequests and alumni solicitations in the established colleges and universities. For instance, Harvard University Foundation is richer than more than two-thirds of all countries in the world. No wonder great ideas are born there.

On a personal note, for the last two years my family has been trying to institute a few memorial scholarships in schools and colleges of Bathinda, Ambala and Chandigarh with little success. Indian educational institutions must have simple mechanism to accept private money. In the US, small businesses and corporations vie with each other to sponsor all kinds of academic, athletic and internship programs in local schools and colleges. The marriage of industry and universities is one of its greatest hallmarks.

7. It is time to harness the population of retirees as volunteers in schools, colleges and universities. In the US, one finds young mothers volunteering their time as teacher/library aids in elementary schools and elderlies helping in college labs and libraries. Those having a zest for teaching tutor students at no or nominal charges. Math and science subjects are universally difficult. In the US, there is no private tuition industry that is thriving in India. Indian scriptures mention that ideally a child of eight learns from a teacher of sixty. It is called the **aphorism of** *athe* **(eight) and** *sathe* **(sixty) based on a natural bonding.**

Acknowledgements

Thanks are due to my friend, Professor Bhushan L. Wadhawa of Cleveland State University (deceased 2004); son, Avnish Bhatnagar of NASA (now with Google) in San Francisco and daughter, Anubha Bhatnagar of EF Foundation in Boston (now teaching in a Abu Dhabi university) for their suggestions in bringing sharpness and clarity of ideas and expression.

Jan 18, 2000/Sep, 2015

[**PS 02/2016**. Since the 1990s when gradual privatization started almost in every aspect of education, I forsee drastic changes in India's education landscape to the extent that most of the seven recommendations are being adopted in parts. However, the basic curriculum in every degree program is very narrow - no where close to the US buffet variety. In India, the programs are driven by vocations of any kind - not at all by seminal research and innovation.]

PERSONAL REMARKS

3. AFTER ALL, WHAT IS A SCHOOL?

All over India, it is no longer a national debate, as to what by and large ought to be a curriculum at each school level - from elementary to middle, to high school. The boundaries are now clearly set. Subjects like mathematics, English, history and science have been there since pre-independence days. There is no denying a fact that since then, the contents have significantly changed. For example, topics in history no longer have the emphasis on history of Britain, or of British India. In 10+2 high school/CBSE system, there are significant changes in the contents of math and science too despite the fact these subjects are quite structured, as compared with social studies. The changes are now dynamic, continuous, and are observable from the first grade/class through higher up.

A question that needs to be debated is - where a line is to be drawn on the **definition of a school**. In fact, a fundamental twin question is: **What is a school curriculum**? I illustrate my point by drawing some examples. In the US schools (colleges and universities excluded), there is a great emphasis on sports, fine arts, music and communication. Some activities are a part of matriculation (called graduation in US) requirements, and others are encouraged in some 30-club activities in the school itself. It is not possible for a country like India to include all such activities in one-school curricula. The reasons, besides financial, are stronger forces of tradition and culture.

In Asian countries, schools are meant to teach only the traditional subjects like science, math, languages and social studies. I remember growing up in India when parents would often badger children: *parhoge likhoge banoge nawaab, kheloge kudoge hoge kharaab*. (It means, if you study, then you would be well placed in life; but if you spend time in playing, then you would end up as a good-for-nothing fellow). In present India, as far as sports and games are concerned in schools, the situation has gone worst. All the playtime has been taken by additional studies through tuition work. Till the 1960s, only kids deficient in a subject or two used to go for tuition, but now just about everyone is paying for extra coaching. Smart ones are paying so that they can score higher in competitive exams for getting into good medical and engineering colleges.

In the US, not more than 50% students go for higher education right after high schools despite the fact nearly everyone can afford to attend at least a state supported community/junior college. In India, most universities are state funded, though a lot many medical and engineering colleges are going into private hands. Private colleges in India, relatively speaking, receive a lot of government subsidies than private universities receive in the US.

The main point is that in the US, with just high school education, people make a decent living in zillion different trades and occupations. For instance, look at the number of music bands in USA - members are all not even high school graduates. Furthermore, there are several trades in construction and engineering etc., where workers make decent wages. Factories, running on the concept of assembly line of production, hire even illiterates (means who have not even gone to a school), who can do small technical jobs, as most big jobs can be broken down into smallest labor intensive units.

It is obvious that the present system of education in India has been discriminating against children who are either not good at present school curricula, or their parents are not wealthy enough to pay for their education. Imagine the vast wastage of talents that has been going on for the last 53 years on the top of exclusions because of India's perennial Hindu caste system. Indian educators never stop denouncing the ghost of Macaulay for any ill of education system even after independence. They have not thought that the problem is deeper. Real thinking is the hardest thing to do.

India has limited variety of schools for only a limited training of mind and body. Whereas, human potential and capabilities are infinite. It is too myopic to classify human beings into some 6-7 categories of school subjects. New kinds of schools are needed. Time is fertile for the new schools to be opened and supported by pubic and private investments for entirely new curricula where none of the traditional subjects are emphasized. I detail four examples to make this point:

I still remember a small private school in Bhatinda that used to train mostly young *bania* (a trading community) boys in fast mental arithmetic calculations. I don't know whether it was to ridicule that learning, or some meaning of the word *landey*; it was called *landey* school. Bathinda, before independence, was country's second largest *satta* market. *satta* is a kind of unregulated stock and commodity market. Besides, Bhatinda has always been known as one of the biggest grain and other retail/ wholesale market. Every such business requires a manpower that could do bookkeeping and fast arithmetic calculations on their feet. I remember once talking with a student who told me how they memorized hundreds of multiplication tables and their many number patterns. These persons were like modern walking calculators. That training was usually over in 4-5 years, followed by 4-6 years of apprenticeship before landing on a regular job by the age of 16-17 years. It was long before the advent of any calculators, which ran those schools out of business. It has added false sense of prestige for the present system. I am not advocating for their revival either. However, I am for recognizing such special need-based schools. New needs come in new forms.

2. The Muslim *madarsas* are highly functional schools, as testified by their rapid growth all over the world. Some of their graduates in Afghanistan are the Talibans controlling most of the country. The main curriculum of these schools is to memorize Quoran with open heart and mind. Along the way, they also receive training in the use of firearms and a little bit knowledge of the country where they are going to go as crusaders/professional fighters, particularly when a call for *jihad* is raised from any Islamic country. Look what has been happening. They want to conquer the world. Kashmir valley has been ethnically cleansed of the Hindus. The most important thing is that the young ones are gainfully employed in worldwide operations. The Sunday schools in churches are nurseries that blossom outside into Bible schools and colleges. They are an integral part of life in Christian world and have a far-reaching impact.

3. Amongst the *nihang* Sikhs, a school tradition has been prevalent. My understanding of the *nihangs* is that they make the in-house security force of the gurdwaras all over. Their youth is spent in a nomadic life style. Their abode/dera is called *chavani*. Both young boys and girls lead a very austere life from birth –like, their parents, they memorize Sikh scriptures. They also receive training in martial arts, music and *gurbani* hymn singers. Look at the results; with thousands of Gurudwaras opening up worldwide, the supply of gurdwara–related jobs like – *sewadars (security guards), granthis (priests), pathis (reciters)* and *ragis (singers),*

cannot be filled up. Rarely, one encounters a destitute Sikh youth. In the mainstream life, most of them eventually become the leaders of social and political parties, with titles like *gianis, jathedars* etc.

4. The Hindus alone do not have any such socio-religious institution with political overtones. In a dozen of Hindu *gurukuls* (schools of ancient India) that are surviving today, the students called, *brahamcharis,* simply memorize Hindu scriptures including the *VEDAS*. But their life for themselves and for the society, at large, just stopped there unless they join the mainstream studies. At another extreme, Indian youths are often shown in the media doing shoe polish, pulling rickshaws, or working as peons after doing BAs and MAs. I never undermine these so-called lowly paid professions. What I am pointing out is that these 'over-educated' or educationally constipated young people could have saved their precious time and *lacs* of rupees of their parents since they could start at such vocations at a young age of 10 years. The best they can do now is to discourage their youngers from following suit.

The whole idea is to refine and extend these models on a national scale. It makes little sense to have the same school curricula in rural areas, isolated areas, and economically depressed areas, as in affluent urban areas. It cannot work with equal effectiveness. The only remedy to solve some ills of the present system is to break its monopoly. The current system is flourishing without any challenge. Nearly 60% of students, while going through high schools and colleges, spend several years and hundreds and thousands of rupees. Very often, there is nothing in the name of inner fulfillment, job prospect, or future security. Certainly, nothing should guarantee any job, as it deprives an individual of right decisions and being accountable for one's decisions. It is an environment of varied possibilities that is the call for the future.

The present school system is highly discriminatory. It does not favour the youth that want to play any musical instrument. It is against those who want to participate in one of the hundred Olympic-sporting events. It is against the poor. It is against those who live in remote areas. It is against those who live in rural areas. It is against those who wish to be all kinds of artists. It is against those who want to be dancers and singers. It is even against those who have strong and beautiful bodies. If one uses one's brain, then he/she is called a genius. However, if he/she mainly uses one's body talents then he/she may be labeled as a prostitute!

Furthermore, the present system is against those who want to be comedians, speakers and theatrical artists. There is no need to go through 15 years of school and college to become start-up cooks, waiters and bartenders, or any hospitality worker. There are so many other avenues in which the young ones from the age of 8-10 can be directed, that in a few years they can become confident and productive citizens of a society. I am not totally against the present system. I am advocating for the alternatives. For the record, the present system is turning out excellent software engineers and doctors that super industrialized countries, like USA, Japan and Germany, are vying for their services.

Therefore, it is time to start schools, for example, where nothing but all martial arts, firearms, or bodybuilding are emphasized. Just look at the need for private security forces and bodyguards in present India where abduction is becoming a big time industry. At present, the USA has the world's best private academies mostly run by retired army and marine officers. Many so-called 'terrorists' from India, Pakistan and other countries have come to the USA to get this training. They have a culture of their own. The US movies, like RAMBO, symbolize it. While in India, I only knew the dictionary meaning of the word mercenaries, but I had absolutely no idea of the scope of their profession. They are no different from software engineers that India is exporting to the world. Like wise, some countries are exporting highly skilled professional soldiers of fortune to the world. It is worth adding that in 18th century, all the soldiers of East India Company were European mercenaries. Sometimes, they were also hired by India's princely states. It is high time that educators and financiers recognize it as a bonanza – like, they see so far only in medical and engineering colleges.

School is an environment that promotes continuity of a culture, acquisition of newer skills, crafts, and knowledge in measurable manners. Curriculum is any set of skills that involves body, mind and soul in part or whole for the immediate benefit of the individual and society at large. Such alternative schools will alone put brakes on the gallops of the present school system. With fewer students opting for generic schools, it will then divert public funds to specialty schools.

The axis of students and teachers engaged in today's competition mills would lose its power. I foresee number of students yearning for medical and engineering colleges shrinking against the existing seats, that the colleges would start wooing the best students – like, it happens in the USA. This comprehensive and yet a modular systems of schools is no way close to any European model or US. Some outcomes may turn out to be the same. It may be the beginning of a quiet intellectual revolution in a democratic India in contrast to the Cultural Revolution engineered by Mao in Red China during the 1950s.

Oct 07, 2000/Sep, 2015

PS: Sep 2015

This article was solicited for inclusion in an issue of the ***Sahi Buniyad*** (means the Right Foundations), exclusively - the only educational magazine in Punjabi mainly.

4. UNLV READY TO GO INTERNATIONAL

[**Note: Oct, 2015**. During the summer of 2001, the Harter administration invited open suggestions from the campus community in order to bolster UNLV by recognizing its strengths. There was some award for the best idea. This note is a modified version of my entry, which, of course, was not the winning one. But, the award winning entry is out of my mind, but mine does merit its inclusion.]

Last month, on being contacted by the Ohio State University (OSU), I learnt how OSU had a deal with the Zayed University that started three years ago in Dubai. It is worth more than five millions US dollars. All the eleven universities in the Big Ten have formed a consortium, called MUCIA, Inc., which is constantly marketing their degree programs all over the world. Generally, people only understand the economic value of traditional export goods and services to foreign countries.

Exporting higher education is the biggest export. If a foreign country is sold to the US higher education, then it is likely to buy American. What the church missionaries did for the colonial expansion of the European countries during 17th to 20th century, it is now being achieved by the US economic expansion through its models of education. The foreign students, getting the US education whether in the US or in their own countries, are going to be sold to the US models of institutions in education, business, or government. Foreign students are potential leaders in their countries. So, when they come in positions of power, they are likely to favor the US brands. Recently, I read it in the *Times* - how the Berkeley Mafia ran Indonesia in the 1990s.

Harter administration is ready to move UNLV in Phase II. The first phase, though considered cosmetic by some, showed a will to make changes in the infrastructure. It is time to fine tune the infrastructure and bring UNLV in line with large urban universities in the country. Las Vegas is a destination resort for the entire world! Is UNLV keeping pace with cosmopolitan image of Las Vegas? It is dismally behind. It is time to put all the offices that deal with foreign students and faculty coming to UNLV and UNLV students and faculty going to foreign countries along with the staff in Human Resources that deals with the INS matters etc., under one upgraded office of the Dean of International Affairs.

To a certain extent, that is what recently has been done for research in order to push UNLV in a Carnegie category of higher education. It needs to be done for the international component too. The financial return is far more promising in a long term. While at UNLV since 1974, I have spent six years overseas -including three years in the international programs run by Indiana University and IUPUI. During annual overseas travels, I notice an increasing demand and interest in the US education. Strangely enough, all Canadian universities, UK universities (with the exception of Oxford and Cambridge) and Australian ones aggressively market their programs and recruit students in all Asian countries, but relatively fewer US universities are in this field. Besides MUCIA, a few universities of Texas, NY and Maryland are active.

To give an idea of the financial impact of a program in which I taught (1992-94) in a MUCIA/Indiana University in Malaysia, close to 50 US faculty were there at one time. All salaries and benefits of Indiana University faculty were applied. After a three-year instruction of IU curriculum, students (About 100) were usually admitted in the top 20 universities in the US for the next two years for the completion of their undergraduate degrees. In the 1990s, the Malaysian Government was spending $36,000 per student per year. Imagine if ten such students are admitted at UNLV - that would bring $360,000 in the local/UNLV economy per year!

Compare it with a $360,000 NSF research grant. I am not discounting one over the other. I am simply pointing out to one pot of bonanza lying untapped. Actually talking with an MUCIA official, he confided that it is good for MUCIA not getting a competition from US institutions.

Besides EPSCOR and some minority-based programs funding, big time research grants in core experimental disciplines are scarcer and very competitive. UNLV has many academic programs, for instance, in the Hotel College, Fine Arts, Health Sciences, Architecture (in near future), Honors College which can be marketed in several packages. Innovative cooperative programs with foreign colleges and universities can be started, as MUCIA does. That shall provide UNLV faculty a chance to teach overseas.

Who has not experienced a change after one week of vacation in a foreign country? Think when a faculty member is gone overseas for a semester. He/She brings back in the classroom a newness from a cultural experience of having lived and worked there that is markedly different from a tourist point of view. Corresponding to a term Yellow Journalism, I have coined a term, Yellow Teaching, which is imparted from the yellowed notes that some professors use year after year while teaching the same courses.

Above all, UNLV will be on an international map on its own merit. Presently, when abroad, I tell that I am from UNLV, then often I have to expand that it is in Las Vegas. Certainly, a faculty working in a country for a year would enhance the image of UNLV. UNLV should join a consortium of hyperactive universities that would market its programs.

In the meanwhile, the faculty participating in any overseas programs should be rewarded, as it translates into a substantial salary savings for the institution. For example, a senior professor at $80,000 salary may cost the university nearly $100,000 with all benefits added. While on leave of absence, replacement visiting professor may be paid up to $40,000, which nets at least $60,000 in saving.

My suggestion is that whenever such a faculty member returns to UNLV after a year or two, 10% salary savings be given back to that faculty in some form or the other. It is a formula similar to the one applied to promote research at UNLV.

July 8, 2001

5. EDUCATION AND RELIGION

The dominant religion of a land has a great impact on every facet of education - from primary to high school, to tertiary, to the higher one. This article is based on author's long experience with Islamic countries particularly with United Arab Emirates, west of India, and with Malaysia, east of India.

It is not out of place to point out that Hinduism was the only religion of India until the Islamic and Christian forces came upon its horizon in the 11th century. It is a combination of tolerance, receptivity to new ideas, and ultimate individual freedom to inquire into any thought that stand out in Hinduism.

In Islamic countries of Dubai and Malaysia, the educational institutions are guided by a different ideology. The format of the paper is non-traditional - in the form of pertinent questions and observations. A few educational concepts have been parts of author's two articles published in the early issues of the *SAHI BUNIAAD,* the only exclusive educational magazine of Punjab.

1. What is the Purpose of Education?
The question is pertinent from an individual to the societal perspective. The main purpose of education is the amelioration of the general lot of the people. There is no merit in institutional education for the sake of education. To provide and receive education is a function of many factors - from national priorities to mental capabilities, to social and historical environments. Here, religion plays a very important role. Islam considers early Quranic education paramount in the development of a person.

In fact, the Talibans, the 'rulers' in Afghanistan since 1995, have gone to an extreme in implementing it at every level. Their entire mission is to turn out young men into perfect fighting machines. And, they are successful. That is what they believe in the making of a great society. Naturally, these fighters are sought after in every Islamic movement and insurgency around the world today. In contrast, the secular India is number one in the world in turning out 80% of world software engineers. This difference is only explainable by the dominant religions of the two lands!

2. Resource allocations

In India, education, being politicized, has become a rallying point at every level. Relatively, there is very little investment from private and government sources in Islamic countries. In the UAE, the oldest university is only ten years old. There is in no medical or engineering college in the UAE. In comparison, India, because of Hinduism alone, has the finest institutions of higher education in the world. Incidentally, the literacy rate amongst the Muslims in India is the highest amongst the Muslims from all other countries. The reason is obvious. Another scenario: Punjab University, Lahore, the premier university of Asia, went to Pakistan when India was partitioned. The Indian counterpart, Panjab University, Chandigarh, which came into existence in 1947, has now gone far ahead in its academic programs and international ranking.

3. What are the Current Trends in Education?

In present India, the outlay in college education in science and technology is all time high. Amongst students, the first choice is a branch of science leading to the making of an engineer or a medical doctor. Lately, commerce and business areas have also gained popularity. Unfortunately, humanities, fine arts and social studies/sciences have lagged behind. The irony of the science education is that its graduates from top medical and engineering institutions have been leaving the shores of India for the last thirty years. From the investment point of view, Indian taxpayers do not get any return for their heavy investments in higher education.

An economist observed that the institutions of higher education in India are brain factories set up for the West. The human products of Indian educational institutions are greatly in demand and are exported all over the world. The major consumers are USA, UK and Middle East countries where multinationals are running gigantic global industrial projects. India has seen an unprecedented growth in colleges and universities – starting in the 1960s, and finally exploding in the new millennium. This growth is only to be matched by the USA after the Sputnik era. The propelling latent force behind it is Hinduism, not any national capital as compared with the US. No Islamic country can boast such an allocation of outlay on higher education.

4. Evolution of Education in India

Since the 1980s educational curricula is significantly diversified. Overall, it remains more imitative of the West than creative and responsive to its cultural and social needs. It is terminal in a way that it furthers very little fundamental researches in India in any field. Ironically, the difference between the Macauley education system introduced in India in the 1860s and the current one is very little. One was designed to help the British rule over India and other British colonies. The present system is helping the super industrialized countries in their economic expansion. Paradoxically, India does not have a local market for its own products.

5. Education in United Arab Emirates

UAE is a federation of **seven** emirates or sheikdoms around the Arabian Gulf, formed only 30 years ago. The well-known emirates are Abu Dhabi, Ajman, Dubai, Fujariah and Sharjah. In nutshell, the UAE constitution allows a lot of freedom for each member state, yet having common issues – like, defense and education. In 1998, two universities were started for women only with campuses in Dubai and Abu Dhabi. The MUCIA, a consortium of Big Ten US universities has been assisting the UAE in setting up these universities and other academic programs.

The underlying philosophy of US educational enterprise is that once a US model of education is adopted by a foreign country, then eventually any other US product or institution can be pushed there. The US mainly markets 'how to think American'. Indian Education system is not 'export oriented' in the sense that its institutions are deemed for local consumption.

6. Is there a Correlation between Education and Prosperity in UAE?

Prosperity of a nation is not directly proportional to its educated elite. The UAE is a perfect example. It is strikingly prosperous despite the fact it has little indigenous educational bases. The UAE imports labor for its construction projects, domestic servants for household, and professionals in every field – including, accountancy, engineering and medicine. This import of labor and professional is done selectively from the countries of the world.

Literally, in Dubai, there is no building which is more than 30 years old. Imagine the wealth pouring in! The infrastructure of the highways, power, and water through de-salination plants (turning seawater into drinking one) has made the UAE an attractive destination for various investments by the multinationals. People have been getting uninterrupted supply of water and power for the last 20 years. There is no comparison with India. Indians make a larger percentage of expatriates in the UAE and are happier working there than in India.

7. Why such a difference?

In the ultimate analysis, it is the dominant religion that sets India apart from the UAE and Malaysia. The government-funded mosques are seen nearly in every square mile of the developed land in both the UAE and Malaysia. These mosques provide the traditional Islamic education in the *MADARSAS* housed in the mosques. For years, the UAE citizens were either sent abroad to receive any higher education, or it was just was not considered important.

Education does not generate wealth; it drains it. Mind it, the goal of these nations is the generation of wealth first. The per capita income of 500,000 Dubai citizens out of a population of 2 million (2,000,000) is more than US $50,000! Only 30 years ago, they were living in thatched dwellings. India's poverty is still perennial and proverbial in the world.

The sheikhs command a far greater respect than any political leader at the state or central level in India. The display of full size pictures of the ruling sheikhs in the offices and business houses is legally mandated in order to show loyalty. With a general sense of loyalty comes unity at national level for the good of public. Hinduism tolerating diversities means it promotes divisions inherently. Consequently, amongst the Hindus tolerance and timidity have become synonymous.

8. What are the Upshots on Education?

Education in India is being oversold. In urban areas, one encounters educationally constipated young men and women. Too much is expected in life out of the degrees and diplomas. Ironically, it is overwhelmingly discriminatory toward those who are not educationally inclined, or do not have opportunities to get education. However, earning power is not directly proportional to the number of years of education.

In economics, there is a **Principle of Diminishing Return**, which essentially drives this point. With government resources in education reaching a saturation point, it is time to let the private organizations take care of primary and college education. Government resources should be largely allocated to fundamental interdisciplinary and applied research, which are far beyond the traditional doctoral degrees. For instance, India is 'light' years behind in research of the caliber to bring Nobel Prizes in sciences.

July 31, 2001/Sep, 2015

6. A PERSPECTIVE ON TUITION BUSINESS

Background

For the last three weeks, I have been reading off and on in the **Tribune** (an English daily newspaper) the views for and against the tuition enterprise, as run by college professors, in particular. Incidentally, I myself started college teaching in 1961 from Government Rajindra College, Bathinda. After a year, I moved to Shimla, and then on to Kurukshetra and finally to Patiala. In 1968, I left India for the US. I had been resisting my urges to jump into this academic foray while on a short visit to India. However, this morning a particular incident has prompted me to sit before a PC and write this article.

The scenario is of a girl, who last year earned a master's degree in mathematics from Punjabi University, Patiala with high second division. Having known her father, last year I sent her application material for admission and financial assistance for doing an MS in mathematics from University of Nevada Las Vegas (UNLV), where I have been a mathematics professor since 1974. In fact, there is a big shortge of graduate students (for doing MS & PhD) in physics and mathematics in most US universities.

Despite my assurances, her parents did not encourage her to apply. The main reason being of sending an unmarried girl all the way to US was too much for them emotionally. On inquiring today as to what was she has been doing these days, I was surprised to learn that she has not been successful in getting any job. The parents are also choosy about their daughters only working in nearby places, though financially speaking, she comes from a hand-to-mouth family.

Inadvertently, I said that it was good that she did not get into a job, as in today's flourishing math tuition work, she can eventually provide jobs to others. However, I was shocked to learn that she was not doing any tuition work either, as it was against a 'phony' principle. In academic market, she is positioned to have a decent life with tuition income, but a skew idealism has become a hindrance.

To give a social perspective of her life, her father is an office superintendent, and her uncle is no other than Jagmohan Kaushal, a leading social and educational thinker of Punjab, and currently the Chief

Editor of **SAHI BUNIAAD**, a unique bimonthly educational journal in Punjabi! I just could not stomach it, that such a rare mathematical talent of a qualified girl is being wasted or sacrificed over a principle of '**never to do a tuition work**'. This story lies at the heart of this article.

A Brief History of Tuition Work

How this 'ethical' principle happened to grip the minds of some intellectuals and masses alike, is worth investigating. One can easily draw a line at 1947. There was hardly any educational activity in the entire India before independence. Through the 1960s, tuition work was limited to high schools only. In colleges, it was confined amongst a fewer academically weaker students in math, sciences and English only.

The medical and engineering colleges were not attracting every bright students. Indian Administrative Services (IAS) were the biggest draw for the brightest. There was no private capital in the country or banking loans in order to support the high expenses of professional college. I myself declined to attend Thappar Engineering. College, Patiala in 1957, against the wishes of my father. A classmate, admitted in Punjab Engineering College, Chandigarh, left it to join MA in mathematics with me!

Such instances are perhaps unthinkable by today's race and craze for admission into professional colleges. It is interesting to point out that in premier private colleges run by national educational organizations - like DAV and SD in particular, top 5-6 students from each examining class were hand picked and coached by the professors during extra hours and even on Sundays. Above all, it was at no cost to these bright students.

Economics of Wealth and Poverty

The 1970s witnessed a paradigm shift in social values in India, especially amongst the people of Punjab and Haryana. In the 1960s, the city of Ludhiana with private entrepreneurship was already known as the Manchester of India for its flourishing cottage industry in hosiery. **For the first time in India, in 200 years, wealth was being created. Erstwhile, wealth was considered finite, and the problem was of its equitable distribution**. What a collective foolishness perpetuated for 100 years!

The success of small-scale businesses opened the eyes of the people. The male children, in particular, of the *ahratiyas* (middle brokers) in small towns and peasants in villages declined to follow the footsteps of their fathers. In the absence of any government plan or private investments, education was the only door open to step out of poverty, and a ladder for upward mobility. Acquiring wealth was no longer the sole propriety of the *banias* (trading community) and a few hereditary aristocrats. Money, proverbially characterized just a dirt of one's palms, started turning into grease for prestige and power.

Due to small-scale industrialization, it was also the beginning of a break down of some caste barriers. The perennial image of a poor elementary school teacher and a show-off college professor was losing its hold. If more money could be earned by additional work, then why not to go for it. I am aware of the archaic guidelines of the University Grants Commission against some tuition work. I was very much in India then. In its formulation, there was never a feedback taken from teachers. Simply put, they are as non-binding and ineffective as the anti-dowry laws passed by Indian Parliament. Tuition work is a local institutional issue.

Changing Scenario
Indians today have no qualms in accepting an actor earning one crore rupees a year and a singer Rs.10 lacs for an evening performance. Likewise, the judges, IAS officers are living in pomp and power, and some MBAs in large business houses earning Rs. 1 lac PM. The question is under what grounds the college professors are being stopped from earning more money? There is no earning limit for a medical doctor and an attorney. Those who believe that professors should teach free are not being realistic and fair. **Nothing is really free in life - not even clean air, earth, fire, sky and water!** In an enterprising world, consumers always go to the best physician, best attorneys, beat CPAs, they can afford. Students go to the best professors who not only know the subject but can communicate it too. It should be left to all professionals if they give out any free professional expertise, as some lawyers and physician do pro bono work. Accountability is the key to their duties in colleges.

I also recall how university professors were envious of college professors, though they were paid more. But for the tuition work, they did not have an aptitude, or access to the right students. In a nutshell, the decade of the 1980s was a turning point in India, when in the developing and developed world economies, any number of doctors and engineers were eventually absorbed. It has started a new market for tuition work for the bright students too. Now top students want to make sure that they are admitted in the best professional colleges.

The admission cutoff percentage apart from some inflation in evaluation has gone up from 50% in the 1950s to upper 90%, as running today! Recently, the parents in Patiala approached university authorities not to penalize their wards for not attending college classes, as they would rather have them study in the coaching centers! Parents have plenty of money and heart to spend on education.

It is actually viewed as an investment. College time is considered a 'wasted' time. Wake up people! The schools and colleges of the 21st century are not going to be 'detention' centers for students good in academics, sports and fine arts. The youth cannot be forced to acquire knowledge unrelated with life around them.

Is there any periscopic view on tuition work?
Having mentioned my present base in the US, let me describe the tuition work there in passing, though the conditions in the US are very different from that of India. But one thing is universal. Mathematics and mathematical disciplines are not easy for students anywhere in the world.

The UNLV's Student Development Center organizes many study groups of 5-6 students at the beginning of each semester. Tutors are handsomely paid. I have known students willingly paying up to $50/hour near exam days! In the next few years, students in India shall not be running to colleges in this large number. Already, lucrative opportunities in marketing and sales are weaning away energetic male students from colleges, where percentage of girls has been on rise. Once national aesthetics are also developed then, humanities, liberal arts and fine arts shall take a fair share of this market.

In conclusion, it is out of place to centrally legislate or regulate tuition work in the colleges. Professors provide a service through tuition work too. It is time to streamline and recognize its reality.

Aug 14, 2001/Sep 2015 (Bathinda)

7. RETURN OF THE OLD FASHIONED SCHOOLS

It is amazing how a phenomenon - from two vastly different countries - like India and US, can have an identical appearance. Way back 50 years ago, my father put me in a one-man and one-room school during summer months to keep me out of teen troubles. I was 13 and used to walk to school at 7 AM, and return home by noon before the sandy desert heat of Bathinda would beat anyone down. The teacher would take turns to individually help and explain different subjects. Most of the time, we basically memorized and studied on our own. Sometimes, we would be helping each other. I remember stop going there after a month. But this one-man school concept has stuck with me, as it does have merits.

Today, I read an announcement on the September-2003 opening of a new high school in Las Vegas. A Charter school is partly supported by public money. What attracted my attention was that in this school all students from the sixth to the ninth grades would study together in one classroom. The school is called, **Explore Knowledge Academy Charter School.** It is modeled after a charter school in the state of Minneapolis.

Before independence, most schools in rural India were only one or two-room schools. The country had no resources, but the Hindus, in particular, always put a high premium on education. There used to be either one or two teachers covering all the classes from grade one to ten. Yes, until the 1960s, high schools in India meant ten years of schooling before four years of college – not even a day less. Ironically, the situation in rural India has not improved. Most teachers just don't show up in government-run schools - they take turn to go to schools! It is a sign of total failure of mass educational system in India at a great public expense.

In the US, the public education system has grown monolithic. Its infrastructure of bus transportation, lunch programs, drug and violence, school security, state and federal regulations in the name of diversity and equal opportunities have completely smothered the classroom instruction - the real mission of a school. However, in contrast with India, the overall US education system allows new educational experiments - like home schools and charter schools.

The Charter schools follow the same curriculum as in public schools, but their approach is non-traditional. In regular schools, there are different teachers for different subjects who assign different home works. In this charter school, instruction is going to be project based in which students will be working on a real life problem. It is along the way that the students will learn, math, science, English and social studies. For example, while analyzing Gandhi's of non-violent approach, students may explore the social conditions, causes of poverty in India, little scientific tradition, and a variety of Indian languages.

The size of this school is relatively small - capping the admission to only 280 - from grade 1 to 12, as compared with some local Las Vegas high schools (9-12) having more than 3000 students! The funding of such schools is not at par with public schools. Charter schools have to come up with their own start up funds.

There is a striking resemblance with most private high schools in India. While walking along a city street in India, one would pass by three to four high schools within half a mile. There are no play areas, forget playgrounds. There is no room for fine art activities. It is essentially all science and mathematics – besides, English, accounting, or aspects of computers. Emphasis is primarily on intellectual development through hard-core subjects rather on physical development and leadership through team sports. Just like in India, the parents would contribute in many ways. This Charter school mandates the participation of parents in school activities.

During my last December-2002 visit to India, I was astonished at the growth of institutions of higher education in the past ten years, as witnessed in just one state of Maharashtra. It is no exaggeration to conclude that education fuels the engine of Indian economy. There is a sheer explosion in anything associated with education. Once the public realized that the government run schools and colleges cannot deliver quality and specific education, the entrepreneurs in education have jumped into the foray. I was told how one person literally owns nearly 60 educational institutions!

However, most schools are very narrow in their mission. Its advantage lies in their ability to meet very specific needs. But the disadvantage is obvious; the curriculum being narrow, its graduates will have to retrain in future.

April 18, 2003/Oct, 2015

PERSONAL REMARKS

8. SCIENCE CURRICULA IN SCHOOLS

Interaction with the Clark County School District (CCSD) is one of my charges as the Associate Dean of the College of Sciences. The meetings with different groups are held 5-6 times a year. The one held last Friday went on for two hours. The members included were the following: two from the Science Curriculum Department of the District; three science education professors from UNLV's College of Education, one professor from the College of Sciences, and one from a professional development institute.

One agenda item was to review the science curricula in K-12, done in a seven-year cycle. The State Board of Education spells out the general topics. However, its implementation in a school district varies with its location and community needs. The review process begins within each district. It includes open town meetings in which parents are also invited to give feed back. That really impressed me. I said to myself that that is where the societies in India differ from the ones in the US. The entire process takes a few months. The recommendations from each district are pooled and processed for adoption by School Board of eleven elected members from the entire state.

This was quite an experience. There is an involvement of science teachers, science coordinators, parents, administrators, but publicly elected representatives sitting on the top. It does not mean that things still can never go wrong. But the system is such that mistakes can be corrected in the next round.

Back in India, I recall some science and math textbooks and syllabi not changing for **fifty** years! The condition of the laboratories is worse. A year ago, while trying to help my grandson in his science homework, I was totally surprised to find the latest in science. Some of the basic nomenclature, that I learnt 50 years ago, had completely disappeared! In the US, a reviewing of any aspect of life is a continuous process. That ensures progress and innovation.

While participating in the discussion, a question that cropped up in my mind was as to how it can be beneficial to science students of my home town, Bathinda (BTI) in India. In the US, 90 % schools are public, called government schools in India. In a city like BTI, it is just the opposite. On inquiring about the science curriculum in private schools in Las Vegas, I was informed that they are all independent to do their things. The difference in science education is more qualitative than quantitative.

In India, both private and public schools are driven by the same Board of Education for the sake of common curriculum and final comprehensive examinations. In the USA, science is an integral part of instruction from K-12, but it is very different in India. During the formative years, the teaching of science with laboratory experiments lays the foundation of scientific thinking.

I am sure readers of the **Sahi Buniyad** may find it interesting to learn about the **Science Content Strands** for the State of Nevada. Of course, they vary from states to state. In all there are 12 strands under four different **Unifying Concepts**.

A. **Physical Science**: 1. Structure and Properties of Matter 2. Structure and Properties of Energy 3. Forces and Motion.

B. **Life Sciences**: 4. Structure and Function of Cells and Organisms 5. Heredity 6. Relationships among Organisms and their Physical Environment 7. Biological Evolution and Diversity of Life.

C. **Earth/Space Sciences**: 8. Atmospheric Process and Water Cycle 9. The Solar System and the Universe 10. Earth Composition and Structure.

D. **Nature of Science**: 11. Science Inquiry 12. Science, Technology and Society.

Let me clarify that these threads are taught from K-12 with varying depth and breadth. In elementary schools, K-5, there being usually only one teacher to cover every subject, the time and exposure to topics may be limited. The thrust is on the planting of scientific ideas during the receptive years. The kids are encouraged to visit science museums and watch science programs on TV. Thus, the essence and applications of science are reinforced, though they may be studied briefly in the classes. The bottom line is that science is taught in every grade from K-12. Of course, the smart students take advance classes. But, that is true in every subject.

What specifically can be done in BTI schools was a central thought? The *Teachers Home BTI* can take a lead by inviting spirited science professors from local colleges or university for public lectures. To begin with, let there be two lectures a year in the evening, or during a week end. The focus should remain on popular topics of science that are accessible to the general public, teachers and students. That will also challenge the speaker in preparation.

Despite the rigid examination system in Punjab, periodic lectures in schools by local college professors can be stimulating. It would bridge a gap between schools and colleges. **Knowledge is a seamless fabric**. In today's competitive world, the speakers must be paid a decent honorarium. Therefore, it is time to raise money from the local community, business, philanthropists and grants. Media publicity on lectures, awards and recognition shall have an all-round salubrious effect. **I am sure, BTI can lead the rest of the country in this regard.**

The laying down of the early foundation of scientific thinking can go a long way in changing Indian society that is still steeped in myths and superstitions. That is a lesson of modern history.

Sep 13, 2004/Nov, 2015

9. SCIENCE IS BEYOND THE POOR

"Research is expensive," used to say my deceased friend, Bhushan L. Wadhwa of Cleveland State University. It means researchers, teaching less than those not engaged in research, cost more to the taxpayers. Creative thinking in abstract disciplines requires sustained periods of concentration of mind. The 19th century 'prince' of mathematicians, Gauss called teaching a nuisance for doing research. The movie, *The Beautiful Mind* based on the life of the Nobel Laureate mathematical economist, John Nash (1928-2015), captures this scenario - when Nash abruptly walks out of his office to teach, he leaves his mind behind on his research!

Last Tuesday, I gave a three-hour lecture in an interdisciplinary Honors seminar. Nearly three fourths of the students had taken 2-3 general courses in science and math. Therefore, it was essential to devote an hour on the organized nature of these disciplines. Both science and math have pyramidical structures, but the research methodologies are very different. Math, by and large, is a lone intellectual sport. But, science being experimental, it involves a team of at least a few graduate students and laboratory.

In order to put different disciplines in perspective for the students, I asked, "How much salary a new PhD in history gets at UNLV?" Quite a few guessed it around $40,000. When the same question was raised for the sciences, they were still around 40 K! I had to remind them that they were not living in a socialist country. In the US, the free market of supply and demand determine the price. A starting salary in a science area for a raw PhD is around $60,000.

As UNLV has been heading towards research, a new dimension of start-up fund is added for the new hires. It is the money that is given to the new faculty for setting up their research labs. The average tab is $250,000/new hire. Until I became the Associate Dean, I had no idea of this expense. That is one instance how research in science is relatively expensive. Small underdeveloped countries will remain light years behind in fundamental researches.

Nevertheless, a pertinent question remains: Is science relatively more useful for the society? The university administrators, regents and lawmakers tackle it periodically. The year 2005 is the centennial of **Einstein's Miracle Year,** when he published four research papers that have impacted mankind. Talking of the impact, there is hardly a day when a play of Shakespeare is not enacted in some part of the world. In contrast, there are no public celebrations of Einstein's work! The technical nature of science and math makes any great discovery rapidly diminish with time.

With the start-up funds, the faculty members come under pressure to go after external research grants. If the start-up money is 'recovered' in 5-6 years, then it was well 'invested'. However, it is time to encourage research in nodal areas so that some professors do their research in the same lab. Otherwise, on retirement or resignation of a faculty, his/her entire lab may have 'junk' value to other researchers. This reminds me of a famous quote of the 1960s: The American economy thrives on waste! The recycling was unheard then.

Sep. 08, 2005/Nov, 2015

COMMENTS

Dear Satish: This is a very well written article. **C.S.**

Hi uncle, this was a very in depth look at the changing face of research in USA. I totally agree with you that the third world is years away from this kind of research. But, I also feel that a lot of funds are wasted in USA, for lack of ideas & intellect. IIT in India still does amazing quality & quantity of research, if you take into consideration the amount of money they get as grants for research. Interestingly, most of this money is donated by the alumni of the same college, and it's their own hard-earned money. **Raghav**

Einstein and other scientists are celebrated every day with the new technology you use. The return is when one buys that technology. So if you compare the return is much more than that of Shakespeare. Thinking with a *Bania's* viewpoint research is a big investment with bigger returns. The failures of experiments are glitches, which every business has. I think: The very nature of science and math makes any great discovery a good foundation for next discovery. **Rahul**

Satish: Just thought of an idea for your reflections. The year 2005 is declared as the World Year of Physics. This is due to Einstein. His contributions have played an important role in our history. He was a charismatic figure. However, he was not the only one who is connected to 2005. Hamilton was born in this year. His major contribution is in quarternions, which are the basis for scalars and vectors. Without him, we would not know much about vectors, its connections with complex variables, etc. His work played an equally important role in mathematics and physics. His contributions to quantum mechanics are valuable too. The foremost is the Hamiltonian that is commonly used in quantum mechanics. Hamilton was a shy person and suffered from depression. Therefore, despite his enormous contributions, we do not talk much about him. It takes a lot more than just physics to become famous. I would love to read your reflections on him. Best wishes, **Alok Kumar**

10. FREEDOM TO BELIEVE AND STUDY

There is an interesting paradox between the current practices of Hinduism as a major religion and the present curricula in the US higher education. The more I pondered, bewildered I was at the similarity between them that it became a subject of this *Reflection*. Again, at the outset, this comparison may seem odd, but there is merit in it.

The US public (called government schools in India) school education (KG-12) being free (including books and transportation, and lunch for some), compulsory and mandatory runs on a different social philosophy. However, the private schools often set higher and different standards of education. By and large, the US public schools cater more to the students at the bottom and middle of the ladder rather than to the top 5-10 %. The college education is a different ball game. It essentially runs like a business and has to be paid.

The US college education is characterized by its diversity in courses and flexibility in the schedule – whether, it comes to pursuing a bachelor's, master's, or doctorate. Let me state that this *Reflection* is not meant to compare the breadth versus depth in academic curriculum. A broad check-up is that education meets an individual's growth and potential - so that he/she can contribute to the welfare of the society.

The same principle applies to the beliefs in Hinduism. The freedom to inquire and question the belief systems is a hallmark of the present state of Hinduism. It amazes people to see Hindus worshipping multitude of gods and goddesses, certain trees and rivers, mountain tops, lakes, animals and birds for propitiation, health and happiness. I vividly remember in my hometown, Bathinda (BTI), women folks walking with bags of powdered beans and offerings and spreading them at the ant hills for good luck.

In order to place education in a parallel perspective with religion, some personal instances are imperative. At UNLV, one is required to finish at least 124 semester credits (one credit equals 750 minutes of instruction) for earning a bachelor's degree. A course generally carries 3-4 semester credits. Thus, a student ends up taking nearly 40 different courses for a bachelor's degree. A variety of academic courses is like going to a buffet serving 200 food items - in soups, salads, desserts and main entrees. One can sample as many items as possible and go for the second servings for the ones liked first.

The philosophy of liberal arts education in USA compels everyone to take courses in different disciplines for the wholesome development of the mind. On a personal note, I am always delighted to see students of history, English, music and philosophy taking my calculus courses. They want to extend their educational horizons. It is a way of seeking blessings!

In the US, the range of courses is simply incredible. It includes courses on physical activities, vocal instrumental music, various arts, dance and sports. The one-credit course, *Physical Conditioning for Men* that I took at Indiana University in Fall-1971, remains the most unforgettable experience for its organization, structure and long-term benefits. Such courses usually do not count for degree programs. Several European educators -including intellectual like, Bertrand Russell, have ridiculed American universities for offering courses like basket weaving. **However, in the pursuit of perfection, any activity becomes educational**. That is why the US higher education is the hottest commodity in the world.

During my college days (after 10 years of schooling) in India, I mainly studied mathematics and English during four years besides some physics and chemistry for the first two years. The study of Hindi language was on the fringe. The present 3-year non-professional bachelor's degrees in India, done after 12 years of high school, provide a narrower spectrum of knowledge. Blasphemy, a tool of terrorizing the non-believers in several organized religions, has no place in Hinduism.

The universality of Hinduism encompassing and respecting every mode of life has tolerance inherently built into it. India, no wonder, is a living museum and kaleidoscope of life styles. One is free to interpret any scripture. There is no one scripture; instead, there are scores of them - all emanating from the four holy Vedas. One can question the authority of any guru, or the power of any god or goddess.

The dilemma in my mind is that how come this system of education is not an offshoot of Hinduism? Not going too far from the question, one can say that the Protestants forming 80% of the Christians in the US have been historically more open and receptive to new ideas than the Catholics. Yet, even the Protestants are nowhere close to the Hindus when it comes to the openness of mind and its ultimate inquiry.

The stagnancy of Hinduism, brought in by the loss of political freedom in India, has mired its people. It is the Hindus' reverence for every aspect of nature, which the modern environmentalists have been championing for the last 30 years. It was never meant to blindly worship any object. This societal behavior witnessed today is the abyss in which the Hindu society fell due to centuries of foreign subjugation.

Since the 1990s, India has exploded with private institutions of higher educations. In one metropolitan city of Banglore, there are more engineering and medical colleges than are found in half the states of USA! But they are clones. In the US, no two colleges and universities have identical missions and curricula.

Nearly 20 years ago, I met Professor Yash Pal, the then Chairman of the University Grants Commission (UGC) of India, an apex body that controls all the universities in India. He told me how the UGC wanted to free itself from the affairs of the colleges, but the college managing committees did not want the US type autonomy! The archaic affiliation of colleges with one or two universities in a state, has suffocated curricular and programmatic innovations. It is the despotism of the edu-crates in India.

An instance of a typical rigidity of education system is that a student in India cannot finish a three-year degree, say, in two years, no matter how good the student is. At UNLV, the average number of years for finishing a bachelor's degree is eight! At the other end, the UNLV record of finishing a bachelor's degree is two years.

It is time to introduce new format changes. Here is my simple model. No matter what track is chosen for a bachelor's degree, a student must take four subjects during the first year. In the second year, three new subjects must replace the old ones, advancing only one from the first year. In the final year of a three-year degree program, 2-3 old subjects must be replaced with the new ones and continuing with only one for the third year. In this model, the education will have a desired breadth of

8-9 subjects and depth in one. A subject studied for three years may be defined as student's major and one(s) studied for two years, as a minor(s). Of course, there are many variations.

Once a few entrepreneurs have liberated the education from its present shackles, it will dawn a new intellectual revolution in India. Again, I can't help wondering what has been stopping and holding them back. The only reason that I can come up is that the vitality of Hinduism has not fully blossomed. Its believers are not proud of its rich structure and heritage. Nevertheless, I would continue to contemplate on it, and hence this dilemma.

Oct 15, 2005/Oct, 2015

COMMENTS

I think this is an excellent insight in to the US educational system. But it would be inappropriate for me accept your analogy with the state of mind called Hinduism. They are different things. Like, they say in the US, when you compare, compare horses to horses, and goats to goats. Furthermore, US educational system may be the most desirable in the world; it cannot be compared to a religion, or a state of mind.

Also, there are many pitfalls in this great educational system. First and foremost, it's driven by money, business, and shareholders. No one can put a price to the education. Education should be available to the interested & the deserving, like *eklavya*, and not only to the offsprings of powerful/ rich men/kings like **Pandavas**. In that sense, India has done a great job in providing education on the basis of educational competency & intelligence.

I know of eight excellent colleges in India, which have free education for all its students. I went to two of them; one of them is ranked as second best military school in the world. There has been a downfall in this pattern in India, with zeal to Americanize everything. The advent of private college education in India has led to decrease in the standards of higher education, and that has affected high schools as well.

I agree with you that US schools are amazing. But you can get the same results with many different approaches. And, I feel Indian education is still the best in the world. The results are in front of you. You must have met so many people who had their education in India & USA. I am sure you found professionals trained in India better educated than a professional trained in US.....but then this is my personal opinion.... and probably a transient one. It's liable to change with time & experience. Regards. **Raghav**

Thanks for the comments. You propose interesting observations. Unfortunately, colleges in India have become more of a business than primary learning centers. Students are admitted based on how much they can contribute to the college rather than how much ready they are for the higher education. It is a sorry picture yet true. I hope people like you may bring some reform to the system. **Gopal Das**

I enjoyed your well-written article. **Subhash Sood**

11. ACADEMICS IN ATHLETICS & VICE VERSA

Background

Writing on academics and athletics has been on my mind for many years. My unique understanding of the two subjects has reached a point that it is time to put it in black and white. After reading Boyd Earl's article on this subject in the *Caps and Gowns* (newsletter of **Nevada Faculty Alliance**), I called him about it. He invited me to write for the next issue. The foci of the article are UNLV and my personal experiences - both local and global.

Having lived in the US for 40 years, I must say that the Americans, not having foreign exposure, do not fully appreciate their institutions and the significant roles they play globally. At the other extreme, if I have to give out a few reasons for the general societal weakness that led to the 1000-year long subjugation of India, then one I would single out is that athletics were divorced from academics. Growing up in India during the 1950s and 60s, a popular saying in our family circles was: ***prhoge likhoge banoge nawab, kheloge kudonge hoge khrab*** (means that the education will get you in high positions, but sports will waste your life).

Sports and Identity

The spirit of academics lies in the intellectual development of the individuals in various areas of knowledge. The quintessence of athletics is on the physical development, and pushing the intellect to a competitive edge with discipline, teamwork and leadership. Being a history buff, a cursory survey tells that every great civilization is defined by its unique sport. For example, cricket defines the British civilization; bull fighting, Spanish; gladiators, Romans, and wrestling, Greeks. The football captures the heart of American civilization. Sports are integral in every phase of life of an individual and nation.

Any local or national controversy of academics vs. athletics is only of personalities for spotlight, turf fight and revenue sharing. During the 1970s, it was the basketball that put UNLV on the academic map of USA. The academic progress during the last 30+ years of my tenure has taken quantum leaps. I was one of the few faculty senators in 1990-93 that cautioned, "It is easy to dismantle a good program, but very difficult to rebuild it." In the context of post 9/11 wars, the rebuilding of basketball program to its old glory may be like the rebuilding of Iraq!

Academic Performance of Athletes

The biggest myth is that athletes are not good in studies and professors are 'pressured' to help student athletes out of their way. Never ever, have I gotten a call from anyone in the athletics department to favor any athlete? Nor, any colleague told me of having received such a call either.

I have had students from every sport. No athlete has ever failed my course. **The reason is simple; they bring discipline and winning attitude from their playfields into the classrooms.** Tracy Chong (UNLV tennis) was the nearly the best student in *Discrete Mathematics* course (MATH 251) two years ago. Jessica Fields (Swimming) was the top student last fall! They used to come to the classes after three hours of practice in their sports. They are not isolated cases. Based on my 30+ years of data, performance of any athlete has never been at the bottom of the class. On a personal note, the Olympics medalist Gary Hall, the teammate of 7-gold medalist Mark Spitz, and I were in the same programming course at Indiana University in the fall 1972!

Where does It come from?

Sometimes I think that the academicians cannot accept the money the coaches earn, and the influence they wield in the community. Four years ago, I asked a candidate for deanship as to why he was leaving his present position. He answered "The priority of my university are so twisted that instead of spending a few thousand $$ on the academic needs, it has agreed to spend 100 millions on a new basketball arena in order to lure a famed coach." This logic was convoluted. Incidentally, the new coach turned the same team around from an 11-19 record to 19-11 in the very first year! The arena that used to be half-empty now is already sold out. To make it short, the money invested in the arena is generating money for other sports.

Typical Yarn

Why is it a problem, if athletes do not complete their bachelors in four years, whereas, the average graduation period at UNLV is 8+ years? Equating the college degrees with high school diplomas trivializes the higher education. The higher education is watered down on one hand and being oversold at the other end.

Why is that a problem, if a high school athlete jumps to pro? Every once in a while, a kid graduates from a high school at the age of 14 and then gets PhD from a university like Harvard before 20. It is OK both for athletics and for academics. Institutional policies must not suffocate any talent. An academic department is generally measured by the placement by its undergraduates in jobs or going to elite schools for graduate studies. It is perfectly fine for the athletes to keep their pro goals in front. After all, one can study for a college degree even at the age of 80 while barely walking to the classes.

Academic disciplines do not generate money, as most athletic programs do. Each ballgame has a turnover of a few million$$. Why is that a problem for the faculty? College athletics is a rock solid reality of a student as academics. I was impressed when, on assuming the office some 10 years ago, the Stanford University President declared that Stanford athletic programs are going to be as eminent as the academic ones.

Symphony in Community

The boosters generously give money to the winning programs. Winning athletic programs also help the university foundations to raise money for academics. **What thrills me is the power of the sports to turn a community into a symphony by bringing them together**. In high school games, it is on a small scale, but the college games bring the whole citizenry together. This was a revelation to me when I came from India to Indiana in 1968. And, it continues to boggle my mind.

Conclusion

Academic and athletics are two sides of the same coin for the total development of leaders in a society. Rhodes scholarship for the students is equivalent to the Nobel Prize in later life. Its criteria lay equal emphasis on academics, athletics and community service. At the time it was instituted in the 19th century by Cecil Rhodes, a fourth criterion was the willingness to serve the British Empire. I think the fourth requirement is a corollary, if the first three are satisfied. It is evident in the USA today how the leaders in every walk of life are either sportsmen, sport fans, or sports minded.

Even after nearly 60 years of independence of India, Indians have hardly changed their basic attitudes toward sports. Nearly 90% of the schools in urban areas have no playgrounds. However, India has world-class academic institutions, like IIT and IIM. But there are no little leagues or major leagues sports at any level. It is no wonder a billion Indians have not won a single Olympic gold medal for years. That is reflected in the quality of leadership in India's politics, business and other walks of life.

By and large, the issue of academic vs. athletics in the US is of ego and perception. During my overseas travels, it is affirmed every year that the US higher education system is the best in the world. It attracts quality students both in its academic and athletic programs from all over the world. Whereas, there is always a room to improve, but it makes little sense to fix that is not broke.

The sports in the US have come to such a pinnacle that they really drive an engine of national economy. Fundamental researches in several medical fields, electronics, media, nutrition, apparels are directly connected with sports. Who does not remember how Michael Jordon's announcement of his coming out of retirement affected the stock market for one day – by 300 points?

Nov 15, 2005/Sep, 2015

12. AMERICAN *SARVODAYA*

Last weekend, three events took place on the UNLV campus. They cross-culturally registered on my mind. One was the annual Science Bowl/ the National Regional science and mathematics competition amongst 200 selected students selected from nearly 100 high schools of four neighboring states. The second was the 28th Dance Festival and Showcase of Clark County School District (the fifth largest in the country). Twenty schools participated in it. The third event was a contest between the cheerleading squads drawn from local high schools.

I have now lived in the US for nearly 40 years; yet, some of its traditions and institutions continue to amaze me. From the point of educational institutions, education is seamless from high schools to colleges/ universities. The buildings and administration are different, their budget processes are different, and their philosophy and missions are different. However, the two systems recognize individual excellence and promote it. This is the time of the year when university recruiters go after brilliant high school students in both academics and athletics.

After all, the purpose of education boils down to one basic question: What is a developed nation or a society? Gandhi elaborated it his concept of *sarvodaya* (means uplift of everyone in the society) Vinoba and Jai Prakash Narayan took it to the people. Consequently, various state and central governments have tried to implement it during the last 50 years. Gandhi, living in a different era, focused on an even playfield for different social strata. It has been bogged down since it became politicized.

The American education, being pragmatic and fundamental, is truly *sarvodaya*. At the grass root level, it lets a child be what he/she wants to be. During visits local schools as motivational speaker, I can't help wondering at the dreams of the students at 12-15 years of age, when it comes to choosing their career paths in life. Of course, their dreams and visions are not in isolation. It is their parents, and the social environment that shape them.

While watching the young dancers perform on the stage, my mind went beyond their dance movements. The dresses of the dancers were not bought from a store. They were individually designed to fit the mood and lyrics of the song. The recording industry and fashion designers are actively involved. Incidentally, Las Vegas is the largest magnet of the accomplished dancers in the world. There are thousands of dance companies where the employment opportunities are as good as for those who pursue the traditional areas of accounting, computer science, engineering and medicine.

The cheer leading is a typical American institution. During a high school game, college game, or professional game a squad of 6-10 beautiful girls and a couple of well-built boys (sometimes) entertain the fans during the timeouts on the playfields. Their skimpy outfits, curvaceous swings and gymnastic acts during 30-60 second breaks take the breath away. Of course, their looks and personality play an important part in a grueling selection process.

To be a high school cheerleader is the Number One dream or envy of every girl. Dating a cheerleader is the Number One dream or envy of every boy! The competitions are held at school, regional and national levels. They are honored by their TV appearances, and the national champions are invited to perform at the White House.

Science and mathematics are most important to the technological power that the USA projects today. However, there has been a declining interest in these disciplines during the last couple of years. Consequently, many corporations – like, Intel and federal agencies like NASA, have increased their support to science projects in schools. A developed society enhances every talent, and hence, the talent searches are held in every field.

The most important aspect of these events is that they are held on a university campus. For example, UNLV opens its facilities; science labs, fine arts studios and sport arenas to high schools. During the Science Bowl, professors volunteer to give small talks and act as experts. In the dance competition, two items were choreographed by the chairman of UNLV's Dance Department and performed by college students. Athletic Department is involved with the cheer leading contest. Thus, there is an active interaction between the institutions, students and teachers.

In India, the walls still exist between high schools and colleges; students and teachers. It seems that the Hindu social caste system is transferred to educational institutions as well. In hierarchal scenario, the universities sit at the top and elementary schools at the bottom! For the genius to flourish, the walls have to be dismantled.

I could not attend all the events this year. My wife and I attended the dance performances after an evening dinner. Last year, I had addressed the opening of the Science Bowl. Also, a participation in diverse functions dilutes their individual impact.

Feb. 13, 2006/Nov, 2015

13. THE *LEAP* IS A LEAP

It has been exactly one week (July 11-15, 2006), when I attended a leadership program organized by the *LEAP* (acronym for *Leadership Education for Asian Pacifics*, Inc.) for the Asian or Pacific Islanders (API) in higher education. The K-12 education is excluded at this time. The API is one of the six federal classifications of races in the US. I informed my Dean that it was the best organized workshop, seminar, or mini conference on motivation and leadership that I have ever attended.

Normally, I capture such an experience within 24 hours as a *Reflection*. But the program being so overwhelming, it continued to escape me. For three days, from 7:30 AM breakfast to 7:30 PM dinner, it was a total immersion into the API issues and networking. I told my wife, that lately I started giving credits to a book, movie, or a person that can engage my mind for an hour or two. This program will remain unforgettable for not only what went on over there, but also how it brought changes within the individuals. There was a consensus for it being a transformational experience.

The website **www.leap.org** has detailed information on *LEAP*'s mission and various programs offered throughout the year. Initially, I was a bit skeptical. However, with recent turbulent experiences as the Associate Dean (Academics) of UNLV's College of Sciences, I felt the need for some motivation and leadership training in higher education. The information about the program was incidental, but it came at a very right time!

Higher education is a strange enterprise where most managers/ administrators rise from the ranks of faculty, who are trained for research first, teaching second, and administration - distant third. A paradox is that despite this state of affairs, the American higher education is a model in the world! During my overseas trips, I see it every year.

The program involved faculty, staff and mid-level administrators. The group of 50 participants represented 19 different Asian nationalities - including 18 Chinese and 5 Asian Indians. During the first day of introduction, it was amusing to hear some individuals, describing their ethnic profile, as one of the several combinations of six ethnicities. There was a Caucasian white female whose husband was Chinese-Irish! In fact, more than 60% registrants were females!

In the program, the institutional dominance (50%) was of the colleges and universities in California. I noted that like most sport coaches - starting from high schools/small colleges and moving up to the big universities, the college administrators can also follow the same path in higher education. A message was that - It is better to become president of a 2-year college than stay as one of the several directors/deans in a university. It never crossed my mind before, and now it may be too late!

Another revealing aspect was that there are several trails leading to the top of a mountain, the presidency of an institution. One API president of a university, describing some challenges and perks of his job, concluded that it as the best job in the world! In no other position can one make a greater impact on higher education. He definitely stirred the imagination of a few individuals.

A highlight of the program was the voluntary participation of six API presidents (out of over 4000 nationwide!) and a dozen provosts and vice presidents. Yes, they came on their own time and money. They are the real pioneers of a new stream of API in higher education. Their presence was inspiring during such materialist times. It was gratifying to see one Indian out of the six. This also speaks of the importance of role models in institutions that lack diversity – amongst students, faculty, staff, or administrators.

Also, I had no idea that a significant number of top administrators are now coming from the development and student services segments of the university. Presidents, like George Kemney (mathematician) of Dartmouth of the 1960s, are now extinct like dinosaurs. Faculty from hard-core sciences have relatively less people-skills by the very nature of their disciplines - living in labs and with numbers. In life, every aspect is nearly cyclic.

By the end of the second day, I noticed some thing remarkable in the program. Most key organizers and founders were of Japanese ancestry. Currently, the least number of people immigrating to the US are from Japan as compared with other Asians countries. How did they become leaders? **The reason is their persecution, and the losses suffered in 1942 WW II internment in 18 concentration camps in the USA! They have turned this ugly episode around.**

The Jews have paid the heaviest human toll. And, that is what took them to finally organize into a strong nation of Israel. After persecution, a community is easily organized for its greater good. It happened to the Sikhs in Canada and USA, as during late 19th century and early 20th century. They lost their agricultural lands and US citizenship. Today, the Sikhs are dominant in the public life of both Canada and California.

My personal goal of attending the program was to level off my administrative ambitions with a boundary condition of not leaving Las Vegas and mentor the API faculty and staff. I got more than I expected. Now I intend on staying proactive on campus issues, and not simply known as a member of a 'nice hidden' minority.

The API students and faculty dominate in quality and quantity in every major university. Berkeley, the crucible of intellectual movements since the 1960s, had put admission cap on the bright API students 25 years ago! A speaker relived that saga. However, the absence of the API in higher administration is due to lack of strong community groups.

The scene at the conclusion of the program was just incredible. Quite a few men and women were so much touched to their core that they broke down while saying a few words on their experience. It was beyond any body's expectations as to what was heard in key addresses, learnt in mock interviews, mentoring, and networking. On the top, the entire program was meticulously organized.

July 22, 2006/Nov, 2015

COMMENTS

Now and then, I think of some of my friends who might find your article of interest. Is it o.k. with you to share it with them? If that would create a problem, I won't do so. Regards. **RAJA, IU**

I enjoyed reading your reflection as much as I did our chats during LEAP! Let's stay in touch - would like all your mentoring I can get! Will stop by someday just to see you or have a drink! **Philip/Yu Xu, UNLV**

Wow! I have to send you my admiration for such a comprehensive analysis of the conference. Please stay in touch with what you do in UNLV so we get inspired! **Sui Cheung** IIT, Cal Poly Pomona

I would love to know more about your experiences at the conference. At this stage, it is more like an ad for the program. Please share some specific information. I am curious. **Alok Kumar**, Oswego, NY

Thank you for sharing your reflections. They are wonderful – detailed, principled, educational and politically astute. I hope you share them with Audrey and Henry. They will both appreciate and learn from them. **Patrick Hayashi,** Retired Associate President, University of California System.

Thank you for sharing your remarkable thoughts, insights and information. There is so much to your statement--probably enough for an entire seminar of its own! Best wishes to you. I hope our paths cross again someday. Aloha, **Doris Ching**, Emeritus VP for Student Affairs Univ. of Hawaii System

Thanks so much for forwarding the attached comments. Your piece is beautiful. Several alumni and mentors who couldn't make the program this year have asked about it, and if I can, I'd like to share this piece with them! Sorry I was unable to return your phone call. Please let me know if there is anything, I can do to help and/or if you still need to speak with me directly. Hope all is well. Thanks again for your most insightful and inspirational thoughts! **Audrey/VP Student Services, Mountain View College, CA.**

Thanks Dr. Bhatnagar. I appreciate your sharing LEAP experience with me. It is definitely something to look into. Regards. **Alok Pandey**, Faculty Senate Chair, College of Southern Nevada

14. WEB OF INFORMATION
(Reflective Note to UNLV President)

Information also flows like water in a river. The power of water is harnessed by constructing strategic dams. Information too can be of greater service, if its flow is rightly channeled. University is unique in terms of relations between students, staff, faculty and administrators. One, high up in the administration one day, may be back into the trenches of faculty rank in no time.

These days, one rarely retires into the position of a dean, provost, or president due to constant accountability to various constituencies. Communication is crucial in a growing university like UNLV. I recall Presidents Maxson and Harter making key changes in the University Information Office as soon as they took over the rein of UNLV's presidency. Harter had a media officer closely associated with the President's Office.

This *Reflection* comes out like a domino effect. Currently, UNLV has numerous publications in contrast to one 2-3 page flyer circulated 30 years ago. For the last couple of years ago, individual colleges have been outreaching the community and alumni with glossier publications. Perhaps, some individual departments may have them too. I get yearly newsletter from my Alma Mater, Indiana University Mathematics Department. The objective of each publication is to highlight the achievements. It is not easy to balance the individual players.

This objective is pious, but objectivity is bound to become subjective to the person sitting at the top in a unit. History has taught this lesson. I consider Joseph Goebbels, the father of modern publicity, or propaganda. The world followed him - under despots, behind the iron/bamboo curtain of communist countries, and even in certain democracies. In open societies like the US, deluge of information has desensitized the masses.

The buzzword is to keep the lines of communication open. Clogging the plumbing pipes with sludge is bad as the acidic stuff damages the pipes. From a faculty vintage point, you have not turned an apple cart by letting any senior administrator go. I am sure having your own information/

media officer must be at the back of you mind, particularly when the Chancellor is a media savvy baron.

By and large, institutional information and communications should go a long way in strengthening the units rather than some individuals. In other words, let it not become a place of building up some individuals or dis-building others. Information must be accurate. In the world of mathematics, the test of accuracy is not statistical. It is 100%, or none. In a popular parlance, a woman is either pregnant, or not.

I like to call these writings as *Associate Dean Reflections*. That is how my perspectives are gaining depth and breadth on issues of higher education both in the US and India.

Oct. 20, 2006/Nov, 2015

PS: Nov, 2015: In 2008 spring, a new format of electronic communication was introduced campus wide. However, a year later, the President was unceremoniously fired within three years into the job. Since he had negotiated his tenure at the time of his hiring as president, he stepped down into the faculty ranks. That is a good feature of US higher education. Incompetent administrators cannot hang onto a top job, nor are they on the streets when removed from the administrative positions.

15. A SLICE OF DIVERSITY & EQUITY

Diversity is the story of my life - whether it comes to travels (20 countries), living in different cultures (six) and knowing languages (seven) etc. It comes about in the making of my intellect with classic interests in arts, sciences and humanities since college days. As a doctoral student at Indiana University (IU), I took graduate courses far beyond the requirements. At UNLV, I have taught more listed courses (**52**) than perhaps any one! Also, I may have another record in designing and offering innovative courses and Honors Seminars (**16**). My scholarly publications are equally varied, and no less diverse is my service record.

Diversity is a buzzword these days at every level - from a university unit to the nation. With roots in India and living in USA since 1968, I would say from the top of a roof that as a nation, the US has come a long way in blending and accepting diversity. The 2006 *March of a Million Illegals* on the streets of USA speaks of some diversity issues, perhaps, going too far. I recall early days of my family fearing the INS agents sweeping on illegal workers around our apartment - despite us having legal status all the time!

My view of diversity is closer to the history of black players, coaches and owners in professional sport organizations like NFL and NBA. At UNLV, the doors have to be opened for the 'charter' students, faculty and administrators. With mentoring and developmental support, they can be catalytic agents for the diversity in future. No one questions that the starters on the 2007 BCS championship football teams of Ohio State and Florida were all Afro-American! Ultimately, the talent prevails with diversity. Diversity and equity are not to create a quota system, but to provide a jump-start and eventually a level play field.

Like in a famous line; **One investment at a time**, I have touched the lives of scores of African-American and Hispanic students by paying a little special attention to them in my classes. If any one is found struggling in a course, I guide them to seek individual tutoring through various campus venues, and encourage them to see me during office hours. On behalf of struggling engineering students in math courses, I often contact the Director of the **Minority Engineering Program** and figure ways out to help them.

Three years ago, I paid tuition fees for a Hispanic student who was the top student in my precalculus course. She had no plans to study the next course of calculus, as she helped her parents in cleaning the apartments. I sought the skills of the Hispanic fiancé (now my son-in-law) of my daughter. He went to her home and convinced the parents. Eventually, she was admitted in the Honors Program with scholarship, and has plans to graduate with two degrees next year! Two years ago, I encouraged an African-American to go for PhD in biochemistry rather than going for high school teaching after the bachelors. He had no clue what PhD meant!

As Associate Dean, I have interacted with the office of minority student recruitment/retention and the consultants hired for UNLV's Office of Enrollment Management. I am aware of the institutional history of 'Diversity' going back to the 1970s and the hiring of the first Affirmative Action Officer, Jim Kitchen (African American). The second one John Lujan (Hispanic), who left after President Maxson. Since 1994, this office has been re-organized and run under various administrative umbrellas and by persons of questionable experiences. In a nutshell, the present 'office' has no teeth.

About four years ago, I gave one-half day workshop on diversity to the staff of Student Services pertaining to the cultural traditions and life styles in India, as students from India constitute the third largest group of foreign students at UNLV.

Talking of foreign students, I too was one of them. My experience in global diversity may not be easily unmatched. I have been a visiting professor of Indiana University (1992-94, 1998) during its long-term educational programs in Malaysia.

Through the **PAYBAC** (acronym for Professionals And Youth Building A Commitment) Program of CCSD, I often motivate kids in junior high and in two adult schools to finish high schools. Most of the students are African-American and Hispanic. Being a toastmaster for several years, it is a joy to sense the moments of making a difference in the lives of the youth and adults at risk and disadvantaged.

Last week, I presented a paper on *Diversity Perspective* at the annual Joint Meetings of the American Mathematical Society and Mathematical

Association of America during its session on '***Building Diversity in Advanced Mathematics***'. My thesis was that for any plan for diversity to be effective, it has to have commitment and blessings from the top. It is the top to bottom approach in consonant with bottom only approach that goes a long way in diversity and equity.

Last July, attending 4-day workshop organized by **leap.org** was a transformational experience. The focus was on Asian Pacific Islanders in higher education. It has brought some issues at fore that I feel more confident than ever before about my abilities to contribute in higher administration.

The colleges of Engineering and Sciences are planning to organize a national conference on the recruitment and retention of women and minority students. It is proposed to be held during Fall-2008. I have been contacted to be a member of its Strategic Committee. The national exposure to UNLV is likely to have a long-term impact on institutional diversity and equity.

Jan 14, 2007

16. DIVERSITY VISION STATEMENT

My diversity vision for UNLV is based upon my personal experiences for 32 years as a faculty member and 3 years as Associate Dean (Academics). It also comes from being a naturally informed citizen - whether living in the USA, India, Malaysia, Dubai, or visiting any place. My eyes and ears are receptive to the issues swirling around me.

Having a woman in UNLV presidency for 11 years has significantly improved the gender equity amongst students, faculty, and all tiers of administration. However, the story is dismal, when it specifically comes to the Afro-Americans, Hispanic and Asian Pacific Islanders (API). For instance, in the College of Sciences, there is not even a single African American on tenured track position. Furthermore, in 30+ years, not even a single student, whether, Afro-American or Hispanic has majored in mathematics!

Fifty years is a long time in the life of an institution for not being able to meet some minimum goals of diversity. My vision from the top is to recruit minority students with scholarships and hire minority faculty and administrators with equal thrust. Mentors are very crucial. A minority student does not feel integrated, if he/she does not notice any minority faculty or administrator around the campus. Like wise, a minority faculty member is psychologically encouraged by the presence of top tier minority administrators, as deans and vice presidents.

On a personal note, during the peak of oil crisis in 1974, I was hired as a visiting assistant professor. Chairman Verma was also of India origin. I was solidly qualified for the position, as the erstwhile Dean told me in 1975, when I was offered a tenured track position.

In the hiring, I shall have the hiring practices changed so that minority applicants are identified as soon as their applications are received. In the current practice, minority applications do not get any consideration during screening, as they are not even identified! It reminds me of the **Rooney Rule** in NFL of interviewing of at least one minority candidate for a head coach vacancy.

If hiring is not followed by right mentoring and professional development, then the minority staff and faculty may be pushed out by lateral transfers from one unit to the other, or by the tenure and promotion process. I am aware of several prematurely failed cases of classified, professional staff and faculty. As an API member, I never met any discrimination as a graduate student at Indiana University, but certainly felt it during job searches. As Associate Dean, I experienced more of it. That is how I understand the bottlenecks.

My vision mainly includes bringing changes in the heart and head of the campus community by periodic meetings and unit visits. It is not easy to effect changes in academic culture of self-governance. First, a transformation has to take place in the heart of the deans, chairs and various directors by gentle persuasion. At the same time, the head has to execute the right policies. I give myself two years in this position whether I succeed or not in bringing significant changes. I still enjoy being a full time faculty. But, I also owe an obligation to make UNLV a better place in its diversity, just and inclusive climate.

Jan 14, 2007/Nov, 2015

PS Nov, 2015: This was a part of the application for the position of Associate Vice-president of Diversity and Inclusion. It was never filled up.

17. STARTING A NEW TRADITION
(A Reflective Note to the President)

Spring semester is a season of retirement of the aged-out faculty, and fall semester of welcoming the young and new hires. It is a poetic paradox to the meanings of spring, when the new tree leaves sprout out that finally drop away in fall. You may have noted some individuals announcing their retirement through e-mails to the campus community, but a few go out quietly into the sunset years and leaving their legacy behind. Last week, I received a small e-note on the retirement of Boyd Earl, chemistry Professor of 31 years. The farewell party is set in a west side bar. Boyd being a multi-term senator, I broached it with the Senate Chair for some Senate recognition. **Recognition comes in recognizing the deserving.**

Five years ago, a friend, retired from Indiana University, described a gala function for the entire retiring faculty in one place. It was organized with all the fanfare of videos, spouses, friends, and of course, with fine wine, food and music. Besides institutional gifts, each retiree received a video of professional highlights - memories of lifetime.

Since then, this suggestion has been on my mind. Of the new faculty, only 10-20 % retire from the institutions they first join. For instance, UNLV is my sixth stop, perhaps the last one. Anyway, the contributions of the retiring faculty are obviously far greater. And, they are likely to continue one way or the other, if they retire to live in Las Vegas. Hence, it is pertinent that they go out with the best institutional memories. **This is one time when the last impression can be the lasting impression!**

Let me share with you a sample of retirement parties that I have recently witnessed. At a dean's party, only the dean and I were standing amidst the cake, snacks and drinks. A few minutes later, a secretary from the President's office walked in with a gift. The party was set up in staircase foyer of the building. It was embarrassing! A party is defined by its location, friends and dignitaries. Last year, there was a grand party for the outgoing Provost, but nothing for the VP Research! At some parties, proclamations are issued from the Governor's Office, or citations read from the US Senators and House of Representatives from the State of Nevada.

The entire show of the farewell parties depends upon the retiring faculty's relations with the Chair and the Dean. It needs to be taken out of the equation. UNLV has grown in size and stature, that it must embrace new traditions. Once, on complimenting a chair for a well-organized party, I was told that it was all due to the management skills of an office secretary! I told my Chair to invite her for tipping our secretaries.

This is the time of farewell parties on the campus. Let the faculty have the last hurrahs! By the way, UNLV has a longevity recognition luncheon for the faculty and professional staff, who have completed 25 years. The former Provost Ferraro had liked my suggestion on a 25-year Club. Once you have invested as much time and emotion as I have done at UNLV, it is natural to think of such ideas for making it a better place. It would counter UNLV's image in the shadows of Strip casinos. That is all where I stand!

March 24, 2007

18. MY CLOSURE ON VP-DENCY

I was naturally curious to see the finalists for the position of the Vice President of Diversity and Inclusion since my application did not make it this far. The process started a year ago, when I applied for the position of Associate Vice Provost of Diversity and Inclusion. The search was canceled due to change of guards at the presidency. The new President upgraded it to the full rank of Vice President, and it was re-advertised. I explicitly added in my application that tough decisions are needed to correct the diversity imbalance at UNLV, and hence, I won't stay in this position for more than two years.

Yesterday was the fourth and the last open session scheduled for the candidates visiting UNLV for meetings with various campus and off campus groups. Talking of the Las Vegas communities, the Jews are the most powerful; they flexed their muscle during presidential search. The Afro-Americans, through local chapter of NAACP, often exert political pressure. Hispanics are vocal through the Latin Chamber of Commerce since they make up at least 35% of the county population. The APIs (Asians or Pacific Islanders) are not organized under one umbrella, though they number well over 100,000 in Las Vegas valley.

The diversity amongst the finalists is represented by two Afro-Americans, one Caucasian woman, and one Hispanic. They came from Maryland, Nebraska, Ohio, and Okalahoma. Nearly 50 persons applied for this VP position - well worth for over $220,000 plus power to change the landscape. In two years, the retirement fund of the VP will grow to a level that took my first 12 years at UNLV! The ethnic distribution of all the applicants is not yet available. It would be interesting to find out, if I was the only API applicant.

Open sessions attended by 9-10 persons were quite informative. Interestingly, more women were present for the woman candidate, Blacks for two Blacks, and Hispanics for the Hispanic. I was the only common denominator! For the last 20 years, the administration of American school districts and institutions of higher education is dominated by people with EdD/PhD in education. Some of its sub-disciplines are so soft that they make a mockery of the college degrees. People get education doctorates in 2-3 years while working full time and raising families. A few years ago, a person told me that she was not challenged enough in her entire education PhD program as by a single math course in *Linear Algebra*! In fairness, the educationists are skillful communicators.

Three finalists with education doctorates hardly worked as full time faculty members. The fourth one had JD, a law degree. However, any VP without academic experience is likely to have hard time dealing with the academic deans and VPs. A degree in law trains the mind to speak, argue, and respond to questions with passion. **He scored high points from me**. Later on, he suddenly withdrew his application! The number of diversity positions has exploded nationwide. It is time for the APIs faculty and staff to explore, gear up, and train in this newly emerging administrative field that was non-existent 30 years ago.

April 19, 2007

COMMENTS

Thank you so much for sharing your observation and reflection. Will keep your advice in mind as I develop my career. Your friend, **Philip**

Satish, Thank you for your comments. **David (Ashley)**

Thank you much for your reflection that I have received just now. Since I am still a candidate for the provost position, as I have shared with you in the past, and will definitely be on the short list of candidates, I am curious to know more about the process. Please let me know the main questions these candidates faced. What are the main expectations from the administration and faculty? It will help me prepare for my own interview that will come soon. Please answer this part in details, if possible.

Sixty percent of the Afro-Americans in academia are with education degree. According to the last week's Chronicle of Higher Education, these degrees are not helping much to make the field leveled for the African

Americans in academia. It is the science that will change the playing field. Best wishes, **Alok Kumar**

I wrote: You have a right to know the Committee members. And, once you know them, then it is perfectly all right to call them for information, so that you are prepared for the interview. Stay relaxed, as it will be nothing like we know of interviews in India. You will do great!

Dear Satish: Thank you much for your supporting words. I have been interviewed only 3 times in my whole career. Most jobs I have taken were given to me without any interview. This includes my job in California. I was in India twice and once in Germany when I was offered the job in California. As you may know, I resigned from that job three times. My job in Germany was also offered to me without any interview. It is only in my job in Oswego that I was interviewed for. I attended three interviews at that time and was offered two jobs. I picked up Oswego.

I was thinking about the Jewish community in Las Vegas. How can a candidate satisfy them? They already have enough representation in academia and do well academically as well as socially. What can be their concerns that a candidate has to be think about? I am becoming more and more determined to enter in the administration. I have not applied out of Oswego as yet. However, I am quite seriously thinking about it. My target is to deal with multicultural issues. I need to think about the whole plan of attack in the job before I'll send my first application. Best wishes, **Alok Kumar**

19. REINCARNATION OF EDUCATION

Education is a universal subject on which everyone has an 'expert' opinion. In the US, education is a perennial issue in every election cycle - from local to the presidential. A reason is that education covers the entire spectrum from nursery to higher. In India, education is seldom an election issue. Nearly 99% of all schools and colleges, being state supported, neither the budget allocations are open, nor the public is concerned. The difference is also due to the presidential and parliamentary forms of government.

An educational aspect common between the US and India is that men and women with degrees in higher education have the authority over curriculum, instruction and administration of every level of education. That is flawed. At one point in time, I used to think that with PhD, 40+ years of teaching in the universities and extensive international travels, I understand the issues of education. Both of my daughters being elementary and middle school teachers, I think the role of visionary teachers is the most crucial factor in this enterprise.

After requests from the chairman of an education conference in Bathinda, I decided to perch high on an observational spot and look for the formative shades of education in India. Broadly speaking, the following seven points touch upon the salient areas of education

1. The implosion and tsunami waves of online deliveries of courses will divide the Indian society on one hand, but would also propel it further. If education diplomas, and not the experience, continued to gain weight in hiring and employment, then social inequity is likely to brew up.

2. During elementary and middle education, responsible parents are to be encouraged for home schooling. The kids' academic progress will be evaluated at the testing centers once in three months. Before India's independence in 1947 and a few years afterwards, the children in rural areas did not have access to education. Ironically, it is getting to be the same in urban areas today. With both parents working full time at their jobs, urban crime increasing and traffic congesting, home and online teaching have the keys for urban malaise. Incidentally, the

pre-independence education system permitted a few years of informal private tutoring before formal admission in high schools.

3. Religion is the foundation of every action of the masses and latent amongst the intellectuals. The secular practices of the last 60 years in India, the birth place and shelter of every major religion of the world, have failed. In the US, the famous and private universities are all based on religions. Parents will continue to encourage their kids where opportunities are brighter. However, in India, the diversity of Hindu religion and competitive environment will not let any body cover the entire landscape.

4. The mega companies – like, Reliance and Tata, will have twining programs with top foreign engineering, medical and management colleges – thus, turning graduates in shorter periods after 10+2 instruction. They would only like to see specific skills taught as needed in their industries. With the powerful resources at hand, they will have political clout to muscle in their agenda.

5. Neither India nor any other Asian or African country, with the exception of Japan, has created an environment for fundamental research in science and industry of the caliber of Nobel Prizes. India alone has a hope due to its dominant Hindu religion, stable political system and network of basic educational institutions. The collaboration of government, industry and philanthropy of the individuals at the grassroots level can ignite the research flame. The seminal research challenge is akin to winning an Olympic medal for a billion Indians!

6. It is possible to reverse the trend of the educated youth leaving India. The education received from the engineering, medical and management institutions was designed by 'conspiracy' to suit the West. It is frightening to think that many countries of Africa, Asia and South America will continue to lag behind in science and technology. Education was the only door out of poverty when I was growing up in Bathinda, and so does it remain today in the entire country. On the top, it is becoming highly competitive.

7. Finally, world wide, education is at a cusp due to the present war between the West spearheaded by the US and fundamental Islamic forces

symbolized by Al Qaeda and Talibans. If the West loses this war, then it will be due to the failure of its education. On the other hand, if the Islamic forces win, then it will be victory of the *Madrassa* education over the western scientific education.

It has already happened in India. Highly educated Hindu Kashmiris have been ethnically cleansed by Madrassa indoctrinated Mujahiddins (freedom fighters in the name of Islam). It started 1000 years ago when hundreds of great Hindu universities like Nalanda and Taxila were run over and closed. Mind it; Changez Khan established the largest empire in history without any educational infrastructure! In Europe, the barbarians battled the civilized Romans and won.

The **9/11 Attack on America** is of epic proportions culminating after several events 10-15 years prior to it. The US liberal education has weakened its pillars of border, language and culture. Presently, the US is heading in the direction that India took 1100 years ago. If present India does not wake up, then it may lose the freedom again that it won 60 years ago after 40 years of struggle. **Education has the power to liberate the people or shackle them!**

Aug 17, 2007

20. 'INAUGURAL' BUDGET CRISES
(Note to UNLV President)

The seismic waves of budget crises have been bouncing back and forth. It is cyclic, though its period is not constant. The previous crisis was during 1994-95, when Kenny Guinn, the Acting President discovered grave 'book keeping' problems. During the Maxson era, UNLV faculty salaries took hits (Not UNR!). Nevertheless, no VP or director has ever lost his/her job over it. Clearly, there is one office in charge; say of enrollment projections on remedial courses, who have wrongly projected.

Last year, in the inaugural address, the President proclaimed that UNLV won't be the same after a year. The stream of memos from the Provost to the deans, to the chairs, and to the faculty, is proving it right. Math chair wants everyone except the new hires to teach three courses. However, no one was rolling during 'surplus' days. Three years ago, a UNLV task force did develop faculty workload document.

A perception is growing that teaching is punitive while funded research is rewarding. Las Vegas is a capital of retired professionals with PhDs. Hiring them as PTIs is the best bargain. But it is shocking to find that the PTI budget cuts mean forcing the regular faculties to teach more. Recently, a visiting full professor of math taught four courses each semester, and a star researcher in civil engineering was let go in January, 2007.

Research is very expensive. It is time to nurture only 2-3 research zones in each department. Currently, a new hire, freshly out of the graduate school, while working with doctoral students in a lab, gets around $250,000 for setting up his/her lab. Moreover, these amounts are not budgeted! Three years ago, during an EC meeting, I raised this question as to what happens to the lab equipment etc., if the faculty leaves UNLV for any reason. "It (250K) is junked," was a casual response from the Dean and some chairs! As a math professor, having no lab, I was stunned at a potential wastage.

UNLV is young, when it comes to research. Hiring the faculty to strengthen the existing and promising research programs would save millions in start-up money in the colleges of sciences and engineering alone. Moreover, the odds of quality research and funded grants are enhanced when 2-3 faculty members are engaged in collaborative research in the same lab, and submit grant proposals.

On a general note, it is time to have the university and college awards looked into. As associate dean, the college award guidelines that I developed (approved by the EC) were thrown out after a year. It has made a mockery of the awards given out last spring. Also, it is possible to win 2-3 awards for the same record; a kind of double and triple dipping!

My 'final' refrain is that the 'middy' administrative positions of acting/ assistant/associate dean/directors/provost/VP should be filled openly. They are not meant to go to the yes-persons. Of course, the deans and VPs must have their final says, but the selection process should not be handpicked. Finally, you have paid advisors besides recommendations from the cabinet members. Everyone wants a piece of president's ear. My *Reflections* face a stiff competition!

Aug 20, 2007/Dec, 2015

21. ON HIRING COMMITTEES
(A Reflective Note to the Provost)

Two streams of thoughts on hiring committees converged within the last couple of days. Having been at UNLV since 1974, I have experienced every facet of hiring - both controversial (often) and non-controversial (rare). Searches have been canceled and aborted. Sometimes, the then Affirmative Office canceled a search to the extent that it compelled the Department to form different search committees for different concentrations, instead of one for all. Also, I have seen the actions of search committees going to appeals, and a few ended up even in legal courts.

Yesterday, when I came to know that your office has approved the formation of a search/hiring committee in the Department, that I decided to share some thoughts with you. This is a hiring season for faculty, pro-staff and administrators. Being on Faculty Development Leave in the fall semester, I am not updated on many Department issues including the current hiring.

A new faculty in the College of Sciences costs at least one quarter million on the average in terms of start-up funds. During the first year, the new hires teach only one course/semester. Last fall in Math Dept., everyone except the new hires, taught three courses! Therefore, it adds up to the cost of new faculty. The idea of release time is that the new faculty get the research/labs set up, research grants written and funded, and research collaboration with colleague(s) gets going.

The 5-member hiring committee in Math department has two new hires, the 2007-faculty members. Your approval really surprised me. Let me add, that if a department is new or small (4-6 faculty), then including a new hire may be unavoidable. But if a dept that has at least 15 faculty members, then it goes against the purpose of release time for the new hires.

Any argument, like, the new faculty has to do some service, does not hold, as there are some quiet and less time consuming and uncontroversial service roles in every department. In my experience, serving on a certain Dept/College/Senate committee is like teaching one course. Involvement of new hires in search/hiring committees gives an impression that the

Teaching is of the lowest priority at UNLV. Yes, I have known faculty getting (full) professor ranks, deanships and other administrative plums by building good portfolios of service and networking. Just look around you! It is time to stem and change this state of working.

The other stream of thought was when I called an acquaintance in the College of Southern Nevada. There is a math vacancy too. I learnt that the non-tenured faculty members do not serve on the search committees. That is ideal. After all, the new faculty has to take time to know various programs, courses, academic interests of other faculty members (including their names!).

You can relate this scenario with your experience, as to how much you knew the institution in the very first year and the decisions based on it. Now, in the first year, you are hit by one of the worst budgetary crises at UNLV. I owe it to my Department, College and University to be able to share my experiences on such occasions.

Feb 21, 2008

COMMENTS

Thanks for the comments....I should point out that I do not get involved with departmental procedures and policies, other than to make sure that departments carry out the tasks they have and are accountable for the decisions they make........**Neal Smatresk, Provost**

22. PLANTING CO-HORTS VS. MAKING TEAM
(A Reflective Note to the Provost and President)

Yesterday's exchange of e-mails between Ron Yasbin and Ron Smith stirred some of my dormant thoughts. In the US, it is very common for a new President, CEO and Head Coach to form his/her own team. His/her success, at the helm of affairs, depends upon the quality of the key persons that surround him. By the inverse token, pink slips are given to the fired presidents, CEOs and Head Coaches at 5 PM. They are immediately escorted out of the premises by the security staff. It is not good for the health of an institution to keep a lame duck person at the top of a pile for a year – too long. Ron Yasbin should have been cut loose last year – like, the Dean of the Liberal Arts was shown the exit door.

Ron's e-mail on Lambis rubbed salt into my 'wounds'. It is not the first time! For over two years (2004-2006), I was the Acting Director of the College's Graduate Program, Master of Arts in Sciences (MAS). Yasbin placed it into my lap after the death of Roberta Williams, in April 2004. I was already the Associate Dean (AD), and for this additional charge, no compensation in time and money was ever given! Was I a 'sleepy' Acting Director? No!

Let me add a touch of history to the MAS Program, which was started in 1990. I am one of its founding members! However, under the directorship of Roberta Williams, a non-PhD, but tenured assistant professor in Biology, this interdisciplinary program was reduced to a diluted master's program in biology. That made biology faculty very unhappy, while other departments were essentially excluded. The MAS Program was reviewed, but the recommendations have not been acted upon. However, I brought significant curricular changes. While Yasbin refusing to give me one more year as AD, he told me that, the MAS Program won't admit new students. His not appreciating my work for the MAS Program bothered me then and now! It sounds like discrimination.

On the other hand, Yasbin added a second associate dean position. The third associate dean position was 'changed' to college planning/development officer. He hired his former doctoral student in Pre-professional counseling. After easing me out of the AD position, he wanted John Farley/Physics to get it. On not succeeding with Farley during 2006-07, he brought Carl Reiber into it a year later. Reiber was out of Biology chairmanship, and was positioned for new openings in higher administration.

Until 2006, three committees of the past winners headed the College awards in Teaching, Service and Research. After my leaving the ADship, they were compressed into one committee and chaired by AD Reiber! A good selection process brings out good people and a bad ….. The point is to examine the award selection processes in the colleges. Also, some guidelines are needed for naming an award after a person.

Hey, this note is not intended for a litany of old gripes. Not once, in three years, Yasbin showed any dissatisfaction with my job performance. While parting away, I challenged him to compare my any one-year service record with that of my two predecessors. He did not like the Council recommendations on Teaching and the FIR hiring that I chaired. But he did not get better recommendations from the other committee! I told him, that had he heeded my advice on Math Department Receivership and Faculty Senate, he would have been a provost somewhere!

June 05, 2008/Dec, 2015

23. BUDGET TRILOGY: CUTS/SAVES (I)
(A Note to the President)

The campus community appreciates your holding two town hall meetings on the looming budget crisis. Chancellor Rogers and Governor Gibbons have already taken their positions on it. Being out of town, I missed both of these meetings. Still, I may give you some ideas that may not have surfaced up. Do think about extending the town hall meetings to the e-meetings for getting electronic feedback and ideas from the community, at large.

Hey, add a salsa to this public exercise by recognizing the best cost saving idea(s). The big corporations like IBM have done it for years. The Google, that my son (1989 UNLV graduate) joined four months ago (after 12 years with NASA), tells stories as to how the young Google founders openly encourage innovation and productivity.

My idea is to generate salary savings by encouraging the faculty to go on leave without pay (LWOP) from one semester to 2-3 years. It is real savings without drawing any blood of firing or lay-offs due to program termination etc. Currently, the faculty is being pushed to bring in grant money since the institution gets overhead up to 54% of the funded amount. The investigator boosts his/her earnings through summer salary and indirect perks. A faculty member going on LWOP effects saving in solid salary money as compared with soft grant money. However, during budget crises, it is irrelevant to differentiate between soft or hard moneys.

This idea gathered a little steam in my mind two weeks ago, when I was phone interviewed by the Dean of a Middle Eastern university for the fall semester. It materialized due to the recommendation of a friend, and my long record of having gone overseas on LWOP for nearly five years since 1974.

There is another benefit to UNLV. During LWOP, a faculty member is also a PR person for UNLV's academic programs. For instance, I can be instrumental in developing joint programs with UNLV. Today, the entire US is facing financial crisis whereas, the oil producing countries are being rained with money like confetti. Look at Las Vegas MGM-Mirage; they saved their City Center Complex by selling a part to a Dubai oil Prince/Sheikh. Wynn and Adelson are offsetting their US losses by tremendous overseas earnings.

Historically, it happened in the early 1970s too, when the first oil embargo shook the US economy. In the US, the job searches were so bad that I did not get even single campus interview out of 200 applications! Lot of IU math doctorates went to teach in newly opened universities with petro $$ in Iran, Iraq, Libya, and Nigeria.

Well, I have given you a micro and macro picture. However, let me close it on a personal note and with yet another benefit of LWOP to UNLV. Each time, on returning to UNLV, I brought new ideas and freshness in my classes. Recently, my older daughter (1985 UNLV graduate) brought out the June 12 issue of the ***RJ*** listing the names and salaries of the professors earning over $100,000. She asked me, "Dad, how come, you are not making $100,000 even after 34 years?" I will let you answer her!

June 25, 2008/Dec, 2015

24. BUDGET TRILOGY: CUTS/SAVES (II)

(A Note to the President)

"Research is very expensive," used to say my Late long-time friend and Chair in Cleveland State University (CSU). That was thirty years ago, when UNLV and CSU were master's institutions. UNLV has come a long way! New PhD programs have been pushed since 1984 at the behest of President Maxson in order to bring UNLV at par with UNR in terms of the number of PhD programs. He believed it would guarantee funding equity between two sister institutions. Consequently, several one-night-stand type of PhD programs mushroomed - sucking resources in new faculty, staff and space. However, they were the 'good' times, and UNLV was emerging out of 'bad' fiscal times around 1980-82.

In the US, research defines private universities more than the state ones. Private universities have deeper pockets for esoteric researches. During the heydays, there is no distinction between good or bad research, or concern for its accountability. Scores of research papers have been published and millions of dollars in grant money drained on the mountains that did not exist, viruses never detected and theorems proved in empty sets, and so on! The 'fraudulent' and 'pure' researches can never be eliminated, but they can be quarantined during fiscal crises.

UNLV has three prominent red flags on research. **First**; the average start-up fund is at the tune of $250,000/faculty in sciences or engineering. In other disciplines, an amount of $15,000 is not peanuts either! **Second**; the 1-1 teaching load during the first year for the new hires for setting up of labs and procuring grants research programs cost in teaching. **Third** is faculty release time for research and grants, in general.

During my tenure as Associate Dean, I had raised this question in an Executive Meeting on the wasted start-up funds when a faculty member suddenly leaves UNLV. Research, particularly in experimental/applied areas, is collaborative. It is time to prune and consolidate PhD areas in each department. Pruning of trees and bushes is good for growth and ambience. The new hires need to be identified by strong research groups in a department. It would affect tremendous saving in start-up funds alone. Also, the chances of successful grants are enhanced, when a proposal goes out from a group, rather than from a single investigator.

The 1-1 teaching load for the new hires was selectively introduced in the College of Sciences in 1990. There is an ample data for the analysis on this money spent vs. return in productivity. My small sample of math faculty tells me, that the new hires get involved in time-consuming committees and departmental politics; a few served on the Faculty Senate! Naturally, they develop disdain for teaching.

With personal flavor and on UNLV's historical perspective, during my first year (1974-75), I taught eight different graduate and undergraduate courses. A colleague is known to have retired after 35+ years with only six different courses under the belt. "American economy thrives on waste," was the catchy phrase of the economists during the golden era of the 1960s. The term 'Re-cycling' was not even buzzing around! Coming from impoverished India, it was a shocker to me. But the time has come for 'the twain to meet'. Take charge and run with it. You have my support and 'blessings'!

June 28, 2008

COMMENTS

You raised some good points that resonate with me Satish....thanks for your help.... **Neal** (Provost)

25. BUDGET TRILOGY: CUTS/SAVES (III)
(A Note to the President)

During 2000-06, the speculators over-built Las Vegas in terms of housing, shops, and offices. No wonders, Las Vegas also leads the nation in the number of foreclosures! UNLV, nestled in the valley, is over-infrastructured. Hence, it can't remain immune to the financial hard hits. The linear projections of UNLV 'experts' are to be blamed for the ills. UNLV, now a matured institution, must adopt an organic (non-linear) growth model that has highs, lows and plateaus built into it.

As Associate Dean, I got a better overview of UNLV than I ever had it as a faculty member. Still, my radar screen does not cover it all. The higher education is a mammoth and centralized behemoth. However, its three 'ugly' minarets of over-infrastructure stand out in my view. Number One, **University College** (UC), dubbed as the College of the 'Dummies'. Number Two, **Advising Centers** (ACs). Number Three, new layers of **Faculty in Residence** (FIR), particularly in the academic departments.

In Fall-2002 Faculty Senate, I was amongst thin opposition against the creation of the UC. The pace at which the UC went through the Board of Regents is beyond me! As long as the UC stands, it is antithesis to your vision of UNLV. With increasing UNLV's admission standards and UC's diluted degrees, the UC has no justification for its existence. Its scraping will save all the money besides enhancing academics.

In general, the ACs are impediments and its advisors obstructionists. All three of my kids and a niece graduated from UNLV without ever stepping into an AC. But that was during the 'golden days' of no ACs. It is appalling to find the centers having 20-minute advising slots with appointments scheduled weeks in advance! One associate dean told me a story of his students unable to get simple signatures without an appointment for days.

Last February, the ***Bhatnagar Award Committee*** needed the lists of math majors and minors. The AC refused access to the files. It took three weeks for the AC to get the lists from other office! Do I have an alternative to AC? Yes, enforce the core requirements during the first two years and set up advising online! Furthermore, get faculty into advising again for their majors – only at the junior and senior levels. Recognize them for this service. For instance, 30-math faculty advising 30 math majors is no load. Personally, I miss talking with undergraduate math majors. Either the AC advisors are on work-study, or have their bachelors in soft areas. They cannot be expected to advice in 5-9 majors different from theirs. Nevertheless, this is a tip of the iceberg. By the way, if can one get excellent online advice on legal and medical issues, then how come not in academics?

The FIR is a new beast, brought down from the 7th floor, and roaming the campus. It puzzles me, as the traditional system of tenure track and visiting positions takes care of every thing. Incidentally, the FIR was a sore point between Ron and me! FIR smacks of favoritism and is a back door to the tenure track positions. A dean/chair can hire an FIR without due selection process. A separate track for the FIR promotion is sick.

In Math Dept., a person was given the FIR title, when he could not be in the visiting rank after three years. The faculty had no clues. If you intend to continue tightening the personnel grievance cases and potential lawsuits, then the FIR must be cut to size. The whimsical appointments of professional staff are the corollaries of the FIRs.

June 29, 2008/Dec, 2015

26. A SAGA OF UNLV PRESIDENCY

"It is a sad and dark day for UNLV," I told a colleague last Friday, when I learnt of President Ashley's firing. I was on my way to a class. Being fully 'invested' in UNLV since 1974, varied thoughts have been rolling over this news. Besides, my wife and I are the proud parents of three UNLV alumni, and founders of Bhatnagar Endowment Fund with UNLV Foundation. This week, the open forum with the NSHE Chancellor and Regents Chairman did not draw me into it. After a while, I walked out of the hall. The meeting may have assuaged the sentiments of the university community.

I was on leave of absence for the spring semester, and taught at the University of Nizwa, Oman. Contemplating over this firing, in 52-year history of UNLV presidency, with the exception of one president, all have been fired! It seems an American life style of not being satisfied with the present achievements, regardless how good they are relatively. For instance, at the end of every season, the NFL and NBA coaches are fired for a losing season or not making to the playoff. The university presidency is not immune to the sport and corporate cultures.

From my vintage point of a faculty member, Ashley did not commit any act of moral turpitude or financial embezzlement for which Indian Vice-Chancellors (equivalent to the US presidents) are routinely charged and removed. He did not use his office to promote his image (remained low-profiled) or of his friends and relatives. Students were happy with him despite tuition hikes that he had proposed. Last December, 72% of the faculty and staff had evaluated him favorably. Incidentally, former UNLV President Harter refused to get herself evaluated at a corresponding point in her presidency. The external presidential evaluator, chosen by the Regents, had given high marks to Ashley. Still, he was publicly trashed, and so was the external evaluation!

Strangely, I never heard that Ashley had a wife before going on leave. He was known to be a divorcee, when he joined UNLV in 2006. A month ago, when I returned to UNLV, his wife's name was splashing over the media, as if she was going to be evaluated as UNLV's president! It seemed an orchestrated vilification, and it has hurt the image of UNLV nationally.

Ashley acted like a QB of UNLV. He took decisions as an individual captain and team player, as the situations demanded. At the end of the legislative session, he got a good deal for UNLV for which he was hired. Since the Maxson era, the budget parity battle between UNLV and UNR has been raging, and Ashley may have brought a closure to it in due course of time.

Hey, I am not an Ashley's fan; never met him even once. Since he joined, I have sent him similar **Reflective** notes on the lines of **David Letterman's Top Ten**. He never acknowledged any one, but I am certain some of the administrative decisions were influenced by my suggestions.

Also, I am not criticizing the Regents for firing Ashley, since a regular faculty member has little idea about the job of a president. However, I gained some insights from my administrative experience as Associate Dean of the College of Sciences (2003-06). In 2007, I had applied for the position of VP of Diversity with a two-year stipulation. In 2008, I was an applicant for the Interim Deanships of the University and Honors colleges. My administrative ambitions woke up very late. Additionally, let me also add that thrice I was elected on the Faculty Senate. The point is that the good of UNLV has been at the core of my professional life.

Do I have anything to suggest for the new captain of UNLV? Yes, only one thing. Let the incoming president do the job; leave him/her alone for the interim period. The open meeting largely turned into campaigns for Provost Smatresk, the fired President Harter, and the Emeritus Law School Dean Morgan. My only hope is that the Regents don't appoint James Rogers as the president. He has been enough. I do commend Rogers for his many acts of philanthropy for higher education in the US. But for his UNLV legacy, Rogers earns a grade, not higher than D+.

In my opinion, the man of the hour, if available, is Kenny Guinn for presidency. He needs no introduction, no campaigning. He may also repair the national image of UNLV tarnished by frequent firing of her presidents.

Any discussion about the attributes of the next president, is futile, to say the least. Once a president is appointed the Regents and Chancellor must give him/her a breathing space. It is ridiculous to publicly criticize/

fire a president for not returning a Regent's phone call, attending the first commencement of UNLV's Singapore campus, living 30 miles from the Campus, or not stopping his newly wedded wife from excessive communication with the UNLV employees!

The height of presidential politics was seen in the following instance. One of the reasons that Harter fired was for her not doing enough for black diversity, as demanded by the NAACP. However, two Afro-American deans and one VP were hired on Ashley's watch, but the NAACP was nowhere seen/heard standing by him!

The 'sheeple' vote of 11-0 (two abstentions) on Ashley's removal speaks of no independent thinking amongst the Regents. Ashley was given C+ grade. But the Regents get C- (Minus) for handling the UNLV presidency. It was hilarious to read a Regent's comment that 'while the university just lost a great man in the presidency, but it gained a great professor in the engineering department'.

The era is long gone when professors in sciences and engineering were appointed as university presidents. A long period of 10-15 years in higher administration would turn any faculty member into a deadwood in science and engineering researches. That is why the administrators, sent back to 'barracks' i.e. demoted to the faculty ranks, are not evaluated on research for five years. However, Ashley would be hired by another institution as president, like, Maxson was hired.

Finally, the Regents must take back their powers from the Chancellor on the hiring and firing of the presidents. It should never have been abdicated, in the first place.

July 20, 2009

COMMENTS

Satish, Thank you for sharing. Your comments are most thoughtful and appropriate. And by the way, I did read and enjoy your earlier reflections. *I can assure you they did influence my thinking and actions*. Best, **David (Ashley**, Ex-President UNLV)

Thank you for your thoughtful note. If you will contact me next week I would be happy to schedule time for is to speak in person. **James Dean Leavitt**, Chairman, NSHE Board of Regents

Thank you for your input Professor Bhatnagar. **Dan Klaich**, NSHE Chancellor

Satish. Good to hear from you my friend. Too bad it is at such a time as this. I appreciate your note especially the understanding support for my difficult position.

I have forwarded your excellent analysis and recommendation on to Chair of the BoR James Dean Leavitt and to Chancellor Dan Klaich.

John Filler, Ph.D. Professor, Department of Special Education; Chair, UNLV Faculty Senate and Chair, NSHE Council of Faculty Senate Chairs

27. TIME FOR RAMAYANA SCHOOLING!
(A Reflective Note to BhuDev Sharma, renowned educator and organizer)

"....Building a school in my home village. Just now, this has classes from Nursery to VIII.. .. .." Reading this part of your e-mail abruptly stopped me in order to share some thoughts with you. Your village is a place to start a Hindu *madrasa* too! Yes, the term *madrasa* for a faith based early education of children, is taken from Islam. Close to 100,000 *madrasas* are operating in the state of UP alone. The Pakistani madrasas are the Harvards in turning out the fiercest young men willing to sacrifice their lives (*Kurbaan*) in the name of Islam. The youth have been attending them from all over the world. The *madrasas* have been integral to Islam since its very inception in the seventh century.

However, since the 1970s, the Islamic fundamental movement, started by Ayatollah Khomeini of Iran, has gone worldwide by the Al Qaeda and such other organizations. However, historically speaking, the *madrasas* are not truly Islamic in origin. The *gurukuls*, during the time Ramayana, were the replicas of Islamic *madrasas*. I will go a step further in saying that Rishi Vishwamitra was Osama bin Laden of his era. If it feels good, then say it conversely – it is equally true!

The concepts of Islamic madrasas and the **Hindu *gurukuls* of ancient India** rest on the principles of *Shaastra* (scriptural knowledge), *Shastra* (art and science of weaponry) *and Shatru* (state enemies within and without*). The education must include these fundamentals – from the early to adult education. For the follies - like that of Emperor Ashok, the Hindus eventually ignored two out of three components of life. They are only superficially aware of *Shaastra*. The Hindus were the first to stop carrying their arms. On the contrary, the Sikh men and women always refused to surrender their arms before the Muslims and British rulers. Consequently, the Hindus have been overrun and ruled by over 300 different invaders from all over Middle East and Europe. Reason; the Hindus literally stopped fighting against any injustice or cruelty inflicted upon them.

Whenever, there is a talk of India's independence in 1947, I tell that the Christians in India were never slaved, The Muslins in India lost power to the British for at most 80 years, after the fall of Mughal Emperor in 1857.

The Sikhs were ruled for 70 years, after the annexation of Sikh Empire of Maharaja Ranjit Singh. It is the Hindus, who got their political freedom after 1000 years! Even after 60+ years of independence, the Hindus are not the rulers of their only country, because they have yet to taste political power and learn the entire enchilada of governing.

Looking at the demographic map of India politically, there is not even a single political group of Hindus constituting 20% of India's population. The 95% of the communists are Hindus – no Muslims. Why? Furthermore, the Congress Party has at least 70% Hindus, who call themselves as secular Hindus. But for the last 20 years ago, they have been anti-Hindu religion. All other political parties are filled with the Hindus. Hindus absolutely divided! When the British used to say, "*India cannot rule itself*," they meant the Hindus! It may take 100 years before the Hindus would start realizing it.

Nevertheless, the seeds of awareness can be planted today. You have a record of organizational skills. But this work needs real heart and courage. You need at least two Hindus to cover each other's back in order to start on these lines. It is not one-man show. Village is not a place to nurse it, but NOIDA is a perfect place. Have you ever been to Deoband, UP without an invitation? Time to close it with my best wishes!

April 15, 2010/Oct, 2015

RESPONSE: Many thanks for your words of appreciation. Yes, your '*madrasa*' model is inspiring. I have put Principal of this middle school a persons who did Ph. D. in Sanskrit. So some ground for developing your concept is made. Do give me constructive ideas. **BhuDev Sharma**

28. UNLV ON THE ROCK!?
(A Reflective Note to Chancellor Daniel J. Klaich)

UNLV's presidency has lived, so far, up to the 'Rebel' billing of the State of Nevada. Battle-born, from the southern extension of the UNR, UNLV continues to have stability issues even after 50 years - a period that still may be of infancy in the long life of a university. After reading your open letter to the university community and a signed response from eight former chairs of the Faculty Senate, I thought it was 'My Turn' to tell you 'Where I Stand'.

Looking way back, had late Don Baepler stayed on as UNLV President (1976-79), and not 'moved up' as system Chancellor, he would have brought stability to UNLV- comparable with what Joe Crowley did it for UNR from 1978-2001. For two years, UNLV was under an acting president, and then came the firing of President Goodall. UNLV was set backed after Baepler. In the meanwhile, Crowley strengthened UNR in special budgetary lines - a sore point for every subsequent UNLV president.

Moving fast forward, I was critical of the manner of President Ashley's firing; nonetheless, the process of filling the interim presidency did impress me. It was open, inclusive and exhaustive. For your information, I had suggested the appointment of the late Kenny Guinn as interim president. Smatresk's job performance during the last 15 months totally justifies your 2009-recommendation to the Board. I am sure your 2010-recommendation will be equally solid. By the way, Ashley's hiring of Smatresk as his Provost does speak high of Ashley's ability in recognizing administrative talent.

On a different gear, gone are the days of pre-WW II, when philosophers and men of literature used to be the university presidents. The post WW II and Cold War era brought scientists and engineers at the helms. As public accountability increased, management and bottom line experts rose to the top. Lately, the university presidency is all about public relation (PR) inside and outside – showcasing the university and trumpeting for resources.

Smatresk has excelled in projecting UNLV. Let me tell you as a former associate dean, that he is the only president who regularly attends Administrative Development Seminars, which are held for the chairs, directors, and associates deans/provosts. My Dept Chair tells that Smatresk brings information and initiates discussions that help in removing the bottlenecks.

An index of his PR profile is to be recently recognized with more than a hello, '*Hi Neal*' from President Obama, in the White House. Smatresk was walking there with a group, not to meet the President. But President Obama, having visited UNLV last summer, had met Smatresk. The point is that unless Smatresk had made some impact on President Obama, he would not have put Smatresk's name and face together - he could have just waived from a distance. Obama has the largest network of supporters at the edge of his memory - no wonder, Smatresk became 'somebody' from 'nobody' to the US president in just four years and four months.

On a similar note, two weeks ago, while walking on a busy West Academic Mall with afternoon sun falling on my face, I was stopped by a voice coming from a golf cart. Here was Smatresk saying hello to me, while on his way to a meeting in the Lied Library. He chatted on a couple of things and asked me to follow them up. Now, it is up to you to put 2 and 2 together.

I would like to add a word on the bylaws pertaining to filling the presidency. You must have anticipated this letter from faculty chairs. For the sake of stability of UNLV presidency, during this tight budgetary situation for the next biennium, **you may consider extending Smatresk's interim term by two more years**. At this juncture, he is the right person for UNLV. By the way, the average tenure of all UNLV presidents, including that of the acting ones, is 4.9 years! It is a win-win-win situation for Smatresk-Faculty-Regents.

Oct 19, 2010

PS: Dec, 2015: Neal Smatresk was promoted as the President against the wishes of the Faculty Senate. However, after three years, Smatresk resigned to assume the presidency of University of North Texas. It was the first time that a sitting UNLV president was pursued by another university.

COMMENTS

Prof. Bhatnagar- Thank you for taking the time to write such a thoughtful letter. I appreciate your view particularly given your experience at UNLV. **Dan Klaich**, Chancellor NSHE
PS Great recommendation on Kenny.

Nicely said. Thanks for the history lesson and for your service to UNLV. All the best,
Kevin J. Page, Regent/Las Vegas

Thank you for your input on President Smatresk's performance and evaluation. It will be helpful. **WILLIAM G. COBB**, Regent/Reno

Thank you for your note. **James Dean Leavitt, Chair, Board of Regents**

Thanks, Satish. I appreciate the positive comments and you sharing this with me. Regards,
David B. Ashley (UNLV President, 2006-09)

I wrote: Hi Tim Let me first laud you for the open advertisement of the associate dean position. Weirdly, or call it an administrative whim, it was 'flouted' when Carl Reiber was appointed in 2007. Anyway, you know how all administrative positions are crucial and significant - whether it is of an associate chair or university president.

Continued fiscal crisis make administrative appointments controversial. You may like to read what I wrote to the Chancellor. You being new to UNLV, it may give a broad perspective. Feel free to comment.

Thanks Satish, your letter is very reasonable in my opinion. As a new person here, Neal has made my transition very enjoyable. Thanks again,
Tim Porter, Dean, CoS

29. EDUCATION & SALT IN FOOD

[Note: 09/2015. This brief reflection, though written five years ago, has the gist of the gist of my latest thinking on education at large. Once in a while, I do go off without finishing an article or a reflection at hand. With a lapse of five years, I do not recall if this piece was meant to be expanded in any manner. Looking back in time, this conference was a landmark event in Punjab. It did put Bathinda on the education map of the region. Often such events are sponsored by the government with an agenda on education philosophy or implementation of some educational strategies. Its venue was the Bathinda Teachers Home, a center of all kinds of educational activities since 1957. Its septuagenarian chairman, Jagmohan Kaushal was the brain trust behind this conference - from its concept to organization.]

Yesterday, I attended a full day conference on education in a very broad scope. It was non-traditional since we often hear about the conferences of education ministers, education bureaucrats, vice chancellors, professors, teachers and students. Its uniqueness was that it included participants and audience from every stratum of society. It was free - no registration fees, which is in contrast to the US conferences, where everyone pays to attend it.

The slate of distinguished speakers included retired principles of schools and colleges, vice-chancellors and quite a few freelance educationists. They all painted a picture of mess in education - shortage of government funds and unfilled positions at every level. Like many good and bad aspects of life imported from the US and west, I could see the same approaches to tackle these problems too.

Over the years, I am reaching at a conclusion that education, as imparted in schools and colleges, is being oversold. This formal education in life is like salt in food. Saltless food is bland and is associated with the sick persons or ascetics. A person without elementary education may be at social risk in modern high-tech life. On the other hand, in a few food items – like, in the *chaat* (assortment of either fruits or fried edibles), an extra pinch of salt, along with red and black pepper, is always welcomed.

Nevertheless, excess of salt in any food results in a nauseating taste. The bachelor's, master's and doctorates are meant for relatively fewer persons.

They do cause constipation of the intellect. In India, where school and college hardly existed before India's Independence in 1947, people are now going crazy about the college degrees with a twisted vengeance. Moreover, they want it by hook or crook. Literally, every degree is on sale in India!

'Excessive' doses of education – like, alcohol, detaches people from life around them, and it inflates the egos. It also links them with the expectation of making more money and lucrative employment. There is a general belief that more degrees means more money! A proven fact is that the **Principle of Diminishing Returns** applies equally to the pursuits of education.

Dec 29, 2010

30. A FIELDS MEDALIST IN FUTURE!?
(A Reflective Note to the President)

I hope you are still the President, when not too far in future, a Field Medalist shows interest in the Department of Mathematical Sciences. You have repeatedly said it, and I fully agree that it will also boost the image of the entire university. For a quantum leap in the life of a young institution, aspiring to play in major league, a couple of thought-out maverick decisions have to be made. After all, we all live in a universe of manipulable digital images and perceptions than in what the realities are – quantum mechanical - fleeting anyway!

You may be wondering how I base my prediction about it. Well, last year, the Administration pushed the department chairs to include '*sense of the entire faculty towards promotion and tenure in the annual evaluation of untenured, tenure-track faculty members*'. It also requires the chairs to initial and date the following statement: "*I have met with the tenured faculty to discuss this faculty member's progress toward tenure*."

As per the grapevines, the administrative rationale is that recently a faculty member was denied tenure by a faculty vote, whereas, the chair(s) had evaluated his/her annual progress positively. I know the present US culture goes after an isolated case that has potential of becoming a poster case. Here is a parallel scenario to compare it with. In 37 years, I have known only 2-3 cases, when a student failed a written MS exam over the material in which the course grades were As. What do you do with faculty who routinely give nearly all As in graduate courses or 70% As in the undergraduate ones? No new policies were created, the faculty member was not policed, his/her academic freedom was not infringed. The department has moved on. That is an approach, or let there be a significant statistical data for putting a new regulation, otherwise, it becomes strangulation.

A process of faculty input for the chair, in the annual evaluation, has not been incorporated in Math Dept. bylaws consistent with the College (none there) and UNLV bylaws. But two months ago, under directives from the Administration, the Dept. unanimously voted on the following ad-hoc process for the 2011 annual evaluation of the untenured faculty members:

The tenure-track faculty member will make available to the department for their review:

All annual reports including the one for that year.

A current CV.

A copy of the mid-tenure review, if available.

Whatever else the member might want to include, if anything.

The Personnel Committee will summarize the information and provide this to the department.

A meeting of the tenured members of the department will be convened where the progress will be discussed.

The chair is responsible for "a summary of the tenured faculty's comments."

The tenured faculty will also individually and by secret ballot rank the progress as "Excellent," "Commendable," "Satisfactory," "Unsatisfactory," or "No opinion."

Particular note (in the summary by the Personnel Committee) should be made of work in progress (e.g. manuscripts submitted for publication), since the department will rightfully take this into consideration in their evaluation, but negative outcomes (e.g. rejections) might justifiably affect future evaluations.

Just now, I have come out of the tenured faculty meeting. I put myself in the position of a new faculty member, say, of joining in Aug, 2012. In a lighter vein, I told the Hiring Committee to let the candidates know of Math Dept.'s new tenure and promotion process. On the one hand, new hires have all the release time from teaching and service to do research and get grants, but even before they settle down in a new place, the specter of annual evaluation would stare them. Collecting the materials, submitting to the Personnel Committee (PC), (while remaining submissive!) worrying about faculty vote and Chair's evaluation, three months –Dec to Feb are not going to be productive. Good research needs a relaxed mind.

This process is repeated in the second year. But look at what happens in the third year, when besides annual evaluation, the faculty member would be subjected to midterm review after only two months of the annual evaluation! The entire spring semester is academically 'busted'. The fourth year may be like the second year, but not mentally. It is the fifth year when in the fall, tenure will be evaluated internally and externally, and in the spring, facing the beast of annual evaluation! Under such circumstances, any research would be third rate and inflated.

Did anyone think of all the implications of this process and its impact on the family life, professional life – forget physical and mental health of the candidate? Let me tell you an interesting **'Fields Data'**. Out of the 8 (3 women and 5 men) math faculty members hired since 2002, two men resigned from UNLV after putting 4-5 years. Under the new process, this number would increase!

One day, this process may be grievable! At the meeting, I did tell my colleagues that Math Dept. might be putting the toughest tenure process in the country! On the other hand, look at the colossal waste of start-up funds and other resources, when a faculty member 'prematurely' resigns.

As a matter of fact, I am more concerned about the long-term sociological and psychological implications of this process, as it affects collegiality within a dept etc. When you vote too often on personnel matters, more heat of animosity is like to generate. It is a tip of an iceberg.

Here is a caution. Very soon, some fine print reader may extend this administrative directive from tenure and promotion of assistant professors to tenured associate professors! It would be hellish then. Please have it sorted out with your advisors and the Provost. Ultimately, the buck stops at your desk.

Where do I stand on this process? This ad-hoc process shocked me, when I came to know of it only three days ago. I was gone overseas and had missed a portion of the Dec meeting. My suggestion is to keep the Personnel Committee out. Let the entire faculty review yearly annual report, CV, and simply vote Yes/No on 'progress toward tenure' **(Delete promotion)**. Let the chair take it from there. Also new hires should not be submitted to this rigorous process during their first year and midterm review year.

There is both subtle and gross 'tyranny' of the tenured faculty toward the untenured ones. I will conclude it with a personal exploitation (like a rape victim 30 years ago, but not seeking any compensation!). In 1976, a colleague asked me to teach his Math 132 course during summer for 3 weeks out of 5. I did it - no compensation, no appreciation! The chair and some faculty knew of it.

Well, think it over while enjoying the Super bowl!

Feb 03, 2012/Dec, 2015

COMMENTS

Thanks Satish. One factual correction to note is that this didn't come from "Administration". It came from Faculty Senate. **Michael Bowers, Provost**

PERSONAL REMARKS

31. FERTILIZING THE US INNOVATION!

One of the undisputed showpieces of the US excellence is its system of higher education. In bits and pieces, the US university model is being copied and transplanted in every country - including the Islamic states. Yet, there is hardly any country that has a comprehensive university like the ones in the US. There are many reasons for it - including intellectual traditions, political ideologies and religious interface. This observation is prompted by Oct 30 memo - from the Chancellor of Nevada System of Higher Education to the presidents of all the colleges and universities.

The focus of the memo is on the implementation of e-learning/knowledge programs, which means using IT to enhance delivery of education at both local and global scales. It is mainly prompted by shrinking budget outlays. The traditional system of education is getting expensive every year. The state support is reaching its limits, as to how much public can be taxed in a democratic society. Historically, the US relies far more on the innovations by individuals and private entities than on the government bureaucrats.

Personally, this memo hit a home run with me, as similar ideas have been fermenting in my mind for the last six years. Hey, I frankly tell people that I live in IT caves, when it comes to its nuts and bolts. I only know emailing, Microsoft Word and Excel barely enough to manage my courses and books. For every IT problem, I call my Googler son, if working from home, or UNLV's Help Desk, if at the office. Most of the time, the problem is resolved in minutes – call it their expertise or my lack of **IT**!

But I very well understand what IT is doing in higher education and how some universities are reaping and raking its advantages. During annual overseas trips, I see several US universities – from Ivy League to outfits like University of Phoenix, offering individual courses and degree programs all over the world. Then, I ask, why not UNLV? It is simply a global entrepreneurial business in higher education.

For the last six years, I have been involved in the teaching of three special graduate courses, and I see tremendous potential of their being taken by students all over the world. A typical course for the 'captive' UNLV students can also be taken by 'outsiders', who may register in it - mainly on the reputation and integrity of the instructor and courses. Since the course is built by the instructor, an x percentage of the external revenue should go to the instructor and the rest for IT overhead to be ploughed back into the course development. It is a WIN- WIN- WIN scenario.

Above all, this revenue sharing would make teaching attractive and competitive like grant-driven researches, in particular. In the US, the state of university teaching has been hitting new bottoms for the last 30 years - with 'release' times from teaching for engaging in all kinds of researches, committee works, and administrative chores.

An unforgettable 'hate teaching' scenario was witnessed last spring during the hiring negotiations with a candidate. One of his conditions was that until he gets tenure, he would teach the same one course for 12 semesters in a row! I have known faculty members retiring after teaching only 5-6 different courses in their entire professional life. In such a prevalent culture, how can anyone understand that I have taught 52 different catalog courses and designed 15 experimental courses and honors seminars in 38 years at UNLV?

This kind of highlight in an instructor's record would sell courses on the air and internet, provided, the right IT marketing personnel were in place. Two years ago, I had a meeting with 'experts' from the IT office, but the matter did not move any further. With the consultants' report and comments from faculty and staff, a digital era for teaching at UNLV may be ushered in.

Going back to my initial comments, the strength of US higher education comes from good ideas that are openly welcomed from every quarter – students, staff, faculty, administration, and community at large. This one is coming from the top of the pyramid. It does not happen in other societies routinely. I have offered ideas to the vice chancellors (executive heads) of Indian universities, and a chancellor of Middle East university, they are just not receptive and responsive to innovation. Based on my six years of overseas teaching and frequent overseas travels, working in a US university is the best academic job in the world. I have enjoyed communicating with every UNLV president and provost.

At times, it does happen that a unit gets 'internally sick' and is not able to help the students and meet its obligations to the community both on the campus and outside. In that case new leadership is recruited from outside. It is observed at every level - from the hiring of a department chair, college dean, provost, president and chancellor. Outside consultants are hired and their report is implemented. Stalemate is anathema to any aspect of US life. I am optimistic about the e-future of UNLV.

Nov 04, 2012/Dec, 2015

COMMENTS

I see what you mean by universities being unreceptive to new ideas. I've come across this when proposing the Astrobiology course to them. **Francis**

Thank you for this very thoughtful reflection. **Richard Katz**, Educational consultant

Really interesting note Satish, and worth discussing. **Neal Smatresk**, UNLV President

Thank you for your thoughtful comments. **Dan/Daniel J. Klaich**, Chancellor, NSHE

Your thoughtful letter is extremely helpful. We do look forward to your involvement in UNLV's e-learning programs as they move forward. **Jane Nicholas**, Vice- Chancellor, NSHE

Regarding your most recent piece. I realize and acknowledge that distance education, education electronically is probably an inexorable force, the wave of the future--because of the spiking cost of higher education, because of the need to compete for students and funding. It is not necessarily a good way to educate. As a humanist, I have serious doubts. What made a Harvard education great, unique, was the convergence of outstanding faculty, a select student body, a conducive environment, and shared purpose--and more--all reinforcing one another.

How much of that can be replicated over the Internet or NYU-Singapore, or Yale-Shanghai? I wonder. I have my doubts. How much was learned by lingering after class, a couple of students and the professor?????? A lot of this is not measurable. Reproducing form is not the same as replicating the content, the "soul" of the experience. Sure, we can move and fill our heads with insights and information watching and hearing a great Professor give a lecture on our computer monitor. But will it convey the intimacy of that old classroom. I doubt it. Will that TV lecture stimulate the same kind of innovation, thought, the ideas spring in the brain???? **Noel Pugach,** Emeritus Professor of History, UNM

SECTION II
EDUCATION–ADMINISTRATION

The bulk of Reflections in this section were written out of my administrative experience and encounters as the Associate Dean (Academics) of the College of Sciences for three years (2003-06). It was an enriching period both personally and professionally, as everyday, I saw different facets of US higher education. Once I told a colleague that a good administrator lets the faculty stay focused on their teaching and research, as administrators – like department chairperson and dean, take care of many distracting issues relating with students and faculty.

It opens with ***Reflection # 32*** on the autonomy of colleges and universities in India. In this context an interesting connection was made between the pre-independence Congress Party and the University Grants Commission, an Indian government agency, formed in 1950s after independence. In the US, there are no walls between high school and college students – likewise, between school teachers and college professors. As associate dean, I saw how high schools students are periodically invited to the university campuses for a taste of university academic (33, 36, 37, 53). It encourages the students to finish high schools and go for higher studies. Also, education includes developing faculty, courses, and good teaching practices and research areas (33, 35, 40, 41, 44, 56, 59, 63). Research in the US universities has no bar in any area. For example, some UNLV faculty in sociology and psychology are engaged in the studies of pain during sexual intercourse and various aspects of prostitution.

There are quite a few reflections on the administrative side of education. Education is not simply about teaching and research; students and faculty. Administrators at different levels play very important roles. I had no ideas of it until I became as associate dean. While the selection, hiring and removal of the department chairs are clear but the process of hiring and terminating associate deans and several mid-level administrators is arbitrary (39, 43, 45, 52, 54, 57, 60, 67, 68). During 2006-2010, there were many issues at UNLV, which provided me glimpses of various slices of education enterprise. Not being of the type of a silent faculty member, I wrote on sundry issues (46 -51, 55, 58, 61, 62, 64, 65, 69, 72).

Some of these *reflections* were written from Oman when I was a visiting professor at the University of Nizwa during Spring 2009. There is a contrast between the two cultures. The Omani administrators never acknowledged my feedback. It mirrors the dictatorial political system from top to bottom. The US administrators always appreciated my communicating ideas – coming from democratic practices and ideals in public life.

32. EXTRAPOLATION OF A GANDHIAN THOUGHT
(Note to Devendra Kumar, VC, Gandhigram Rural University)

I had left Gandhigram equally impressed with you and the Institution. On return to the US, as you rightly noted in your letter, I got wrapped up in a few things - both wanted and unwanted. Individuality is truly sucked in by the fast US life all around - like a novice swimmer into a vortex of water. Lately, I find myself communicating with India most of the time. Whenever, I am in India, I wonder at the life I live in the USA. Likewise, it happens when I am here in the US. Am I split, or leading a double life - with a wife and a mistress?

I just learnt that Arya Bhushan, a young Gandhian-in-Action, would contact me during his US visit. Two years ago, we talked on phone. This time, I would like him to address a university audience. Last August, I met Subbarao in Olema, California, where he conducted a one-week youth camp. His dedication and single-mindedness in nation building through the character of the youth, has always impressed me. He is indeed a Gandhian-in-Action. There is a glut of theoreticians and armchair Gandhians - both in India and abroad. If suddenly Gandhi comes back to life, then this time he would kill himself on seeing so much being fabricated in his name!

Personally, neither I am a Gandhian in thoughts nor in actions. Besides, his autobiography read twice, I have not read his writings. He is so much quoted in and out of context in India that everyone would eventually pick up bits and pieces of his thoughts. Well, the one I have liked it was his advice on dissolving the Congress Party right before he saw independence coming to India. Over the years, I have pondered and discussed its implications in the reconstruction of free India, and political problems that India faces today.

I find this advice very relevant when extrapolated to the universities in India. Indian universities tend to mimic European/American universities – forgetting them being on the soil of India. We threw out the foreigners, but after independence, started blindly transplanting their intellect in all and sundry places.

A fountainhead of university problems is the University Grants Commission (UGC). Since the 1980s, I have been opposed to it, as Gandhi was to the development of large-scale industry at the expense of village/cottage industry. Today, India is confronting the problems of super industrialized countries before having reaped its advantages. Through powerful and uncreative bureaucracy, the financial strings of the UGC coupled with local and central politics, Indian universities neither reflect India's heritage, nor are in tune with social reality around them.

Last March, I happened to meet Professor Yash Pal (UGC Chairman) and asked him to write an 'obituary' of the UGC before his term expired! That is what I meant a Gandhian advice when applied to the production of intellectuals in India. I believe universities have reached a level of maturity that they have to make a mark on their own.

Nov 03, 1987/Oct, 2015

33. NEW FACULTY ORIENTATION

Last week, there was an orientation for the new faculty and staff. For this event, the Alumni Tam Center was excellent - high ceiling and its polyhedral architecture. I was invited as an Associate Dean. It was nearly a full-day program. It started with continental breakfast, but it was sumptuously Americanized. There was a round of brief remarks and speeches by the President and all the senior members of President's Cabinet. They hardly left out anything guessing about the university, its goals and directions etc.

The new faculty must have left the place fully informed of UNLV's academic life and their contractual obligations. My mind would often drift in and out of the program, as I would go back to my half a dozen occasions of starting on new jobs.

I joined UNLV as a visiting assistant professor in 1974. Neither that year, nor the next year, when I was in a tenured-track position have I recalled any briefings for the new faculty members. UNLV was small then, and city of Las Vegas was smaller. We adjusted to the academic life without any big problems, or fanfare. I do remember going to the Human Resources office, then called the Business office, for the signing of a couple of papers on my retirement benefits etc.

During those good old days, one thing was certain. If I ever needed any information, I was not without it for a long time. The campus community being small, we would be running into each other all the time –thus knew each other. In 30 years, a sea of social and legal changes has taken place. The face-to-face interaction has diminished. Consequently, such ordinations are invaluable.

The luncheon section of the orientation was very well organized. It included the participation of a few last year's faculty, who reminisced and shared their survival tips. After lunch, the new group spread out to several information booths about various offices and programs for them. Success of this orientation speaks for itself, as the next year's orientation is already set in schedule.

Aug 18, 2003

PS: Nov, 2015. In India, I joined four different colleges in 1961-68, but there was not even open introduction. However, in Aug, 1968, at Indian University, Bloomington, there was an unforgettable half-day orientation for the graduate students. Over the years of global experience, I would venture to say that such academic practices set the US institutions of higher education apart from that of other countries. Some US colleges have handbooks of information for the new faculty and staff.

PERSONAL REMARKS

34. CULTIVATING SCIENCE EDUCATION

Monday, November 17, 2003 was declared as the **Science, Engineering and Technology Day** by Kenny Guinn, the Governor of the State of Nevada. Incidentally, this day, set on the third Monday of November was the 17th annual event organized on the campus of UNLV. In the past, my participation has been limited as a faculty member. However, this year being the Associate Dean of College Sciences (includes departments of biological sciences, chemistry, geosciences, physics and mathematical sciences) this whole show was organized under my supervision. The experience is of unique educational value that I thought of sharing it with the readers of the *Sahi Buniyad.*

There are several objectives of this event. The Number One is to showcase the science and engineering facilities including labs, libraries and faculty research activities to the high school seniors (12th graders). Every US university tries to lure the best students and best professors. It is the quality of students, faculty, labs, libraries and administration that define a good university. The second reason is to have a continuous communication with school district in terms of curricula and academic programs for school teachers. The third reason is the outreach activity of the university telling the community that university is not of ivory towers, and professors are not just engaged in esoteric scholarly activities.

The preparation for the Day starts in August each year. In the past colleges of Sciences and Engineering (includes departments of civil, mechanical, electrical, computer engineering, and computer science) have pooled their resources. But this year, I extended the domain to some departments in College of Health Sciences, and anthropology in the College of Liberal Arts. The idea being that whoever is using science be included so that students get to see a picture of science as wide as possible.

A couple of organizational meetings were held in September and October to check out logistics and budgetary matters. In the CCSD (Clark County School District), there is a division of science education and they hold their parallel meetings. Besides regular communication between UNLV and CCSD, one meeting was held between some members from both institutions.

Since the main objective is to match students with science professors, two parallel planning are done. Faculty are encouraged, coaxed and persuaded to open up their labs, office hours for one or two 2-hour session(s) for high school students. At the same time, high schools are contacted about their participation. Once professors have intimated the projects they want the students engaged in, that information is sent to all the interested high schools - some 30 in number. The schools are asked to send the names of 5-6 motivated science students and their order of preference of three projects. Every effort is made to do the best matching. It requires a dedicated staff to meet all deadlines and keep the communication lines open. This year, I made sure that UNLV public information officer covers the event in a campus newspaper and local media.

By 8 AM, the students arrive on the campus with their science teachers. The number of students in each session varies from only one to ten. They register and receive some gifts items and lunch coupons. In a plenary function, lasting one hour, all the students are briefly addressed by the deans of colleges of Sciences, Engineering and Honors, Admission Director and the student body president. They disseminate first-hand information about their programs in order to make an impact on students. Remember, these students being best local science students, UNLV wants to have the first shot at them for recruitment.

As soon as the function is over, professors escort students to their respective labs and lecture rooms for two-hour sessions. This year there were nearly 20 morning sessions, 10- noon and 20 in the afternoon from 2-4 PM. Some students attend two different sessions. Bringing technical research at a common level is a sign of scholarship.

Here are the examples of some laboratory projects: Structure and function of the Nervous System, Acid Rain: Could Las Vegas soils handle it?, Looking at Leukemia: A Perspective on Cancer Research, Magic and Mathematics, Earthquake Effects and Engineering site Investigation, Building a Computer, Electronics in the Gaming Industry, Methods of Assessing Human Performance. High school students who know little beyond basic scientific principles are generally turned on by such topics that affect every one in a day-to-day life.

In between the sessions, students are encouraged to take a tour of the campus. They can take their lunch free at any of the several university eateries. While students are engaged in sessions, their teachers are also free to attend those sessions with students, or spend time in a lounge where they can relax, or do their own work.

Science education is very expensive. Public money being scarce and accountability on the rise, state universities try to reach for private money through grants and donations. Holding such days bring awareness about science education amongst the public at large. But, think of inspiration that a 17-year old may get when a research professor shares the latest in his/her area of expertise.

This is the Part I in which top high school students visit UNLV for a full day to have a taste of high science. In Part II of the next article, I shall describe about the **Science Bowl** to be held in February in which select high students from the states of Nevada, Utah, Arizona, and Eastern California shall be competing in various science contests for one full day.

Nov 18, 2003/Nov, 2015

COMMENTS

Science Education is my subject also. That you are interested in it has raised you very high in my eyes. After all, this is what is needed in India. There is no doubt about it that SENIOR STUDENTS will love to hear about progress of research from the mouths of Professors. SCIENCE FAIR is a FANTASTC IDEA; Science Labs, Science Books. It can really help Indians. I am waiting for your next article. Sincerely, **Subhash Sood**

35. POPULATING GRADUATE COURSES

Yesterday. two diverse situations converged to a point. Enrollment management of the College comes under the charge of the Associate Dean. Before a semester rolls in, the Associate Provost sends out periodic reports on ongoing registration, and constantly points out to the departments to open up new sections of some courses, increase the cap of others, and cancel some sections.

Therefore, it is essential to know the 'popular' (that draw students) courses and 'unpopular' (that do not draw students) courses in each department. That is a lot of work initially, as there are hundreds of courses. The reasons vary with each department. I noticed that 700-level topic courses in some departments were under a flag of monitoring or cancellation.

The Graduate College requires that a description of each **Advanced Topic** course and **Independent Studies** course be kept on the file for record. Ideally, instructors should post and publicize them on bulletin boards. On the same day, an undergraduate student petitioned to the Dean's office for taking a 700-level **Advanced Topic** course.

Giving a hearing to such students is also a charge of the Associate Dean. The student was quite upset despite the fact he was counseled by two faculty members and the Department Head. On examining his transcript, it was discovered that the student had not taken even a single course 'required' for taking this 700-level course. After an hour, a first-year graduate student came over for taking the same 700-level course. On checking his math background, it was found again, that the student had taken no prerequisites whatsoever!

A couple of such cases come up every semester. For various reasons, more faculty members want to teach graduate courses, but the problem of attracting students to math degree programs remains acute. It is not ethical to 'recruit' undergraduate students into graduate courses without a strong background. It sets up the student for failure sooner or later.

The provision of undergraduates taking graduate courses is only for well-prepared and exceptional students. The Department has an excellent array of upper division 400-level courses for the undergraduates to bring breadth and depth in their math background. A 700-level course without any pre-requisite is a 'suspect' graduate course. It is time to exercise a quality control particularly when a mathematics PhD program is on the horizon.

Jan 14, 2004/Nov, 2015

PS: Nov, 2015 - The Board of Regents approved the Mathematics PhD program in June, 2004, but it was implemented from Fall-2005.

COMMENTS

Good job! – **Ron Yasbin,** Dean –College of Sciences

Satish, I like this very much. I hope we will be able to get rid of "700"-level classes that achieve only A's but teach nothing. This way, graduate students will need to go to real 700-level classes. On the other hand, there should be some exceptions for some very smart seniors to attract them as our graduate students. Best regards. **Angel**

36. TENDING THE BUDS OF SCIENCE

In the US, study of science is not merely a subject in schools and colleges, but a way of life. Science is practiced every day. Schools and colleges are nurseries, where kids imbibe the scientific thinking along with extra curricular activities. Apart from availability of world-class popular science magazines, high school students frequently interact with university professors at least 2-3 times a year! By and large, the high school (H/S) students are aware of the cutting edge of every scientific discipline.

I had no idea about the annual **Nevada Regional Science Bowl,** though being held, since 1991 on the UNLV campus. Every February, it starts on a Friday afternoon and runs through all Saturday. I only thought of it as some kind of a big science event as the word **Bowl** suggested. The word 'Bowl' is taken from Super Bowl, the grandest sporting event associated with American Football.

Being the Associate Dean of the College of Sciences and a regular contributor to an educational magazine, the *SAHI BUNIYAD*, I wanted to understand the whole thing. The preparations begin almost a year in advance. The Nevada Regional is sponsored by the Department of Energy (DOE), a US federal agency. Most federal agencies have education wings for encouraging youth into their line of work. Actually, the major organizational work for the Science Bowl is done by the DOE and its Nevada affiliates. They raise the funds and volunteers from nearly 25 sponsors – including, Bechtel, Cox Communications, Southwest Airline, utility companies, and Best Buy – besides, state and federal entities. That shows the corporate support for science at the grass root level. It is an investment in future. Of course, in every flyer, program and publication, the names of all the sponsors are prominently acknowledged.

There has been a declining interest in science at least in Las Vegas high schools for the last 5-7 years, but through such events, the educators are able to target the smartest H/S kids in science. Certainly, the future leaders in research and management of science shall emerge from such a group.

Thirty-two teams of four H/S seniors (12ᵗʰ graders) and juniors (11ᵗʰ graders) and one alternate are chosen on the bases of their class performance. Students who come to the **Nevada Regional Contest** are mainly from Nevada, but a few from the border cities of Arizona, Utah, and California. Accompanied with each team are one or two science teachers. The logistics of their transportation and hotel stay are all taken care by the DOE. Kids are transported to the campus on Friday morning after breakfast. I noticed their groups touring of the campus and taking pictures in front of the new UNLV library.

While they are on campus, UNLV makes every effort to recruit them. The College of Science Advising Center looks after all the on-site arrangements of rooms for various activities, communication and training associated with this event. The planning meetings are held every week as the date approaches. It is a mammoth event involving lots of volunteers behind the scene particularly when 16/17 year-old boys and girls are involved.

On Friday, after registration, students and teachers assembled in a big auditorium for a science symposium. This year's theme being *Race Cars*, all the presentations were geared accordingly. A biology professor spoke on the importance of microbes in cleaning up oil spills; a chemistry professor on a research hurdle in finding a cancer drug; a mechanical engineering professor on the architecture of race cars. A talk on a brand new area of **Entertainment Engineering,** a collaboration of mechanical engineering and arts in the context of lavish Las Vegas shows, was an eye opener. Finally, a mathematics professor spoke on the connections of graphs theory with problems of computer science, engineering, chemistry and physics. The lectures being a Power Point presentation had beautiful graphics. Consequently, they elicited lot of questions from the students on each topic. At times, the quality of questions stumped me. I am convinced that despite declining interest in sciences at large, its future is safe in the hands of such bright kids.

The symposium was followed by a quick dinner of pizza and cookies, favorite of the teens. It was served in the hallways of new physics building so that kids could also glimpse at its facilities. They re-assembled in the auditorium for their welcome and review of the contest rules on Saturday. I delivered the welcome remarks. It was my first opportunity to speak in front of 200 science students and teachers. In summary, I shared with them the story of my love for science that lasted for only two years, as science courses were not offered in my college beyond two years.

For me, the next best alternative was to study mathematics, the language of sciences! I also told them about my visit in Nov 2003 to my alma mater and being honored as a distinguished alumnus of the college. But the state of its labs has hardly changed in nearly 50 years! Reminding the students how lucky they were to study science in the most scientifically advanced country of the world, I exhorted them with the famous line of US Army: *Be what you can be*. Next day, a few students and teachers came up to tell how they liked my remarks. Without the toastmasters training, I would not have done it! The Friday portion of the program ended with a key organizer carefully going through all 50-some rules followed by a mock contest! The day was over by 8 PM.

Saturday morning was about the running of the contest. One room was set up as a **Command Center,** where all kinds of organizational assistance and trouble shooting was done, resolved and sorted. A big bulletin board had a display of all the brackets of contesting teams, their schedule of times and rooms. There was no room for confusion. As soon as a result was known, it was immediately posted. A small crowd of students and their supporters was there all the time checking on winners and losers. During the first round amongst 32 teams, no one except the contestants and organizers were allowed inside the room. Reason: maintaining the secrecy of questions and answers. Timing may have been staggered for limitation of rooms and contest organizers.

I watched two contests. The teams of four are called A and B Teams and hence names of contestants become A1, A2, A3, A4 and like wise B1 thorough B4. Each contestant has a press buzzer to answer when a moderator calls upon an individual, or a team. The format of question is multiple choices W, X, Y, and Z. The **seven** persons running each contest are the following: **Moderator** who asks the questions and runs the contest with humor and authority within the rules. **Time Keeper** controls a high-tech clocking gadget with strobe lights and dials connected with the buzzers of each contestant. **Science Judge** adjudicates a challenge by a contestant on a ruling of the moderator. In case of a complex situation, some UNLV professors are available on their cell phones. **Rules Judge** ensures that the contests rules are adhered in letter and spirits. **Scorer** records the team scores in front of everyone. **Messenger** runs between the contest room and **Command Room** for any problem. Finally, **Room Monitor** watches and checks the observers in the room. No one is allowed to leave or enter once the contest begins that lasts no more than 25 minutes with a two-minute break.

Since I was watching the contests from the perspective of an organizer and a spectator for the first time, I found the pace of question and answer very fast. It amazed me the speed with which students answered. They had 20 seconds to answer with a warning when 5 seconds were left. In all, I was told there are about 25 questions in each contest with bonus questions.

The questions come from astronomy, biology, chemistry, physics, mathematics, earth science and general science. Not all the subjects are taught in every school. On inquiring from the teachers on coaching, I learnt that each student is coached in one area and regarding the rest, they study on their own. That requires quite a motivation. Of course, there is a lot of self-help material available.

While watching the students in the hallways, auditorium and ballroom, I informally tried to assess the demographic distribution of students. Girls were nearly 33%, no Afro-American, though there were 3-4 students from Indian subcontinent, quite a few Chinese, and some Hispanic and/or Pacific islanders. I know if it were an athletic event, the Afro-Americans would have been 90%! It speaks of environment, family priorities, and school programs.

One thing that stands out is the moral support the event gets even from the politicians. Letters of commendations were read from both (Nevada) US Senators. One US House representative sent his aide, and the other was personally present during the luncheon program. For the students, it provides a break from the contest. A popular weatherman of a major network was the master of the ceremonies. The highlight of the luncheon hour was a motivational speaker. This is what defines an American function from that of other nationalities. He inspired students to study science, and effectively related science with his life in auto racing.

Before lunchtime, 16 teams were eliminated and 16 were left. The Championship round was set up at 6 PM in a big auditorium for every one to see. Every contestant got a souvenir bag of goodies. However, ultimate awards come when these students apply for admission to colleges. Such participation goes a long way in getting academic scholarships. The local high school that won the Nevada Regional Championship also got $2500 in prize.

Such regional contests are held in every state, and two in the populated states - California and New York. The winners go to Washington DC in April/May for the seven-day National Finals. It is a glittering show of youth, science talent and sponsors.

All the time, my thought would take me back to my days in India, and what is happening to science at grassroots even today. During my remarks, I also said how I wished to be 17 again! The fundamental difference is the faith in scientific thinking in solving social problems. By and large, the US society heavily invests in science in improving the quality of its life. As a result, there is an explosion of research in new technology in every aspect of life. The developing world simply waits for the technology transfer.

Feb 08, 2004

COMMENTS

Unless a man becomes a ROBOT, it is difficult to live only for a high standard of life or luxury or money. Unless one becomes a ROBOT, it is difficult to have interest only in Science. But I agree that one ought to have interest in SPIRIT and SCIENCE at the same time. You are right that we should take help of Science. **Subhash Sood**

Well said and well written. Agree with what you said but you gave no solutions for India (the country you compared it to). What do you plan to alleviate this? As JFK said, ask what you can do. I ask you the same question. **Rahul**

I wrote: Rahul, I am coming to a reconciliation that the best change is the slowest one in many situations. This article, when read by a large number of teachers and administrators in Punjab, may ignite a desire to try it on similar lines. It would be an imposition if I give any blue print. Also, I believe it is easy to see a change in a lab first. Bathinda is my lab, then Punjab.

Rahul: In this situation, the words need to be backed up with resources. Institute an experiment in your lab by starting something concrete (for example an annual science fair) with incentives. May be being as a dean of major US university you could divert some funds to your lab.

I wrote: Resources do follow of when a good idea is sold to only a **few persons** for execution. Though my life is lived in two worlds, but I can only divide my personal resources. In this Science Bowl, UNLV did not spend even single penny! All the money came from 25 sponsors in cash and kind! Sure persons like my self spent a significant time on it. It is a web, and that means a total societal awareness about science.

37. FANNING SCIENCE IN THE FAIR

Yesterday was a gala award night on the UNLV campus for the winners in the Southern Nevada Regional Science and Engineering Fair. Being the Associate Dean, I gave the welcoming and closing remarks, and distributed six major prizes. It was a very satisfying experience since as a faculty member, I had no clue of such campus activities.

The **Science Fair** is the final outreach activity in which the Colleges of Sciences and Engineering are involved with the Clark County School District (CCSD) and other agencies every year. In the past, my occasional participation has been as one of the judges. However, as the Associate Dean, I oversaw its organization from ground zero. There is one person in the College Advising Center whose main job is the coordination of this event. The past records do help in improving its organization further; still it takes at least 4-5 months of planning.

The schools being divided into elementary, middle and high levels, it adds to varied communication with respective key persons. Also, the projects vary in depth at different school levels. Science being compulsory in middle and high schools, schools have several science teachers in different areas. However, in the case of elementary schools, one teacher generally takes care of all the subjects. Except for one hour, the children stay in one classroom with the same teacher.

What impressed me most was how in the US, a scientific thinking is inculcated at a very young age. The value of simple science projects, experiments and surveys at K-5 level goes far deeper. Three weeks ago, all the top projects from each school in different categories were displayed inside a basketball hall. It was a sight to see, rows of projects about 270 in number, from K though the 8th grade. The distribution of projects by grade levels are: K (15), 1st (20), 2nd (20), 3rd (30), 4th (47), 5th (57), 6th (50), 7th (36), 8th (41). Themes and categories were like Environmental, Scientific Observation, Technology Design/Inventions, Biological/Behavioral Science, Earth and Space Science, Physical and Mechanical Science,

This year, there was no participation from high school students! The setting up the projects in an allotted space and specific layout is the responsibility of the participants. It is done by Friday afternoon. Late in the afternoon, the projects are judged in various categories. UNLV faculty members volunteer their time for judging. On Saturday morning, the projects are open for limited public - including parents, kids and teachers. Again, some professors volunteer their time for any questions that the parents and kids may have about any science course and program at UNLV. I took my grandson along. On seeing some of the projects, he felt enthusiastic about participating in it next year.

I particularly could feel the impact of simple projects like, *The effect of colored water on evaporation, Are people really lucky, Or It is their attitude?, How various kinds of bread develop fungus in different conditions,* etc. The accuracy in measurements and integrity in conclusions are instilled at a formative age. Some engineering projects included the models of bridges assembled with basic squares, or triangles and were tested for their strength. Experiments are perhaps not new, but students performing them are new each year. They need this training of mind, as the reliance on one's experiments is the foundation of scientific progress.

All the time I was thinking of my childhood where the importance of an experiment in science was just not explained and understood. Thus, in my two years of science study in college, I hated to be in the labs. Those of us who did go to the labs would often cheat on measurements, and manipulate it to fit into a conclusion.

In the US, science education is not confined to schools. Parents are equally enthusiastic about their wards' projects, but the teachers are the driving force. On inquiring how so many winners were from one particular school, it was always due to one dedicated science teacher. In all, 45 prizes and certificates were given out - including one called, **Sweepstakes Award,** which a 6th grader won of out of 45 winning projects from K-8. The kid was excited when I handed him the big trophy. I know he would be pursuing science for the rest of his life.

In my opening remarks, I told the audience of nearly 200 students, parents and teachers that excellence in science and mathematics defines the greatness of the USA. Yet, only four days ago, the premier scientific organization, the National Science Foundation issued a press release on the projected shortage of scientists in the country. Two thoughts flashed my mind. One is the continued importance of science in a super industrialized nation. Two is the involving of public, lawmakers and educators for science support as early as possible.

The program, from 5:30 PM - 6:30 PM, was followed by refreshments and select project viewing. UNLV opens it facilities to the public and prepares the ground to attract future bright kids for their college studies. The barriers between schools, colleges and universities are coming down. During my high school days in Bathinda, I used to feel the barrier between school and college, as if a Chinese wall separated them.

The question on my mind is the relevance of Science Fair to the students in Bathinda schools. It has to begin with a change in daily thinking. For example, it appalled me to see an 'educated' Hindu living in the US and crediting **sain vibhuti** (sanctified ashes) for a successful surgery, rather than to the best surgical facilities gotten in the US! Similarly, another person credited the recovery of his wife from an ailment to his 40 uninterrupted visits to a **sain temple**, but did not thank to the best medical treatment that she got in the USA!

I am not dead against visiting temples, Gurus and having strong non-scientific beliefs. However, let there be some open mind and moderation in practice. The situation in India is far more challenging. Organizing public lectures by distinguished speakers on the power of scientific thinking can go a long way. The **Teachers Home Bathinda** is an ideal place for its organization.

During my Nov 2003 visit to my alma mater in Bathinda, I was in a state of disbelief to see the conditions of its science labs. It seemed that the time had stopped since I left it in 1957. Conditions of labs in schools are far more deplorable. However, there is a way out, if the local high schools can pool their lab resources. Let chemistry lab be in one school, physics in the other, and so on. For the optimum usage, the labs must be open from morning till late afternoon hours. The presence of students in science labs for 15-18 hours a week shall bring a change in the science culture of that society.

In the US, money in donations etc., from private sources to the state colleges, universities, has been increasing. At the same time, some state universities are refusing to accept the state money for its bureaucratic regulations. Nearly all big and small companies, federal and state government agencies – like, Navy, Air Force have fund allocations for public education. For instance, in this Fair, four awards were sponsored by the Las Vegas Water District, and five by the Navy. They encourage science education and hire employees with a good science background.

After independence in 1947, the private capital has grown in India too. Before independence, the state treasuries were empty, and so were the pockets of the masses. Through the 1980s, the government opened all the large projects in industry and education. Private money was invested only in small cottage industries, schools and colleges. However, since the 1990s, the private capital has been on rise. There are signs of big educational investments, but a lot more is achievable in an organized effort. What it needs a little steering of collective thinking. The *Sahi Buniyad* can provide a forum of leadership in this direction.

May 08, 2004/Nov 2015

COMMENTS

I 100 per cent agree that TEACHING of SCIENCE can help in saving our superstition-ridden culture. It is regretted that with the improvement of economics conditions in India TEACHING of SCIENCE at SCHOOL level has not improved, but in fact has deteriorated, as have other values. We shall do something about it. **Subhash Sood, MD**

Hello Satish: Many thanks for sharing the write-up. I enjoyed reading it. I agree that such projects or fair cultivate a culture of science in the minds of students. Best wishes,
Alok Kumar, Chairman Physics Dept, SUNY, Oswego

Use the money you have raised for Bhatnagar endowment (in the name of your parents) to fund the labs at your alma mater. You are the solution. You are the private capital. Solutions start at individual level. Be the leader. Let other follow by your example. **Rahul Bhatnagar, MD**

I wrote: Rahul, so far the UNLV Endowment Fund does not have enough money to generate even $900 in awards given out each year. I have absolutely no control over money. It belongs to the University. We can only direct its income in awards as stipulated in the Memorandum of Understanding that was signed up three years ago. Since such an Endowment Fund has not been feasible in India, we do have a Trust Fund in rupees to recognize excellence in six schools and colleges. Eventually that may be pooled for science promotion. Thanks.

Rahul: You have a good start with the Trust Fund. May be it is time to start fundraising -American Style"

Planning Science in the Fair is an educated item for me. Thanks. **Nigam,** Retired Director, Delhi School of Economics

38. PARAMETERS OF TEACHING EVALUATION
(A Report on Teaching Evaluation)

I hope this e-mail brings the 'flying' differences to ε - close! Here is my perspective on the issue of Teaching Evaluation that Ron (Ron Yasbin, Dean of the College of Sciences) has charged the Undergraduate Affairs Council that I chaired as the Associate Dean. It is one of the four Councils the Dean had formed in consultation with the dept. chairs.

The charge was to develop criteria for the evaluation of teaching in addition to the student evaluation **mandated by the Regents**. There is a reference to the College's commitment to the Accreditation Body, but no dept. chair had its documented recollection. Anyway, the Council proceeded with it along with other dynamical charges.

In order to gauge dissatisfaction of the faculty with the current mode of student evaluation, a comprehensive e-mail was sent out to the College faculty on **12/07/04**. **Only 10 out of over 100 faculty members had a modicum of complaints with the current practice.** It was reported back on **02/15/05**. Not even a single chair communicated the faculty displeasure. We all know that only a couple of students make too much noise against an instructor. Today's students are tomorrow's faculty members. Statistically, 10% dis-satisfaction is not that significant!

The Council surveyed the practices in other colleges of UNLV and had TLC Director explain teaching portfolios. The Council members had to and fro feedback with their depts. On 05/21/05 and 08/21/05, the Council submitted the following recommendation to the Dean. They are geologic in nature and mathematically continuous! Include the Faculty GPA (Class Grade), Retention Rates and Contact Hours.

Additionally, the Council recommended that the College Teaching Award winners of the same Dept visit a class of the faculty member each semester provided a prior arrangement has been made between the faculty member and the dept. chair. The tenured faculty was initially excluded from the Peer Review. The Council recommendation was for the College faculty to vote on it.

For a closure, I take your liberty to stretch this memo. The current practice has served the College well for over 20 years. Nevertheless, we should improve it with evolutionary approach. The current practice has no demand on faculty time. In some colleges, faculty publishes papers on student evaluations! Our College faculty can't do it! Last Spring with your cooperation, the Council implemented a set of guidelines for the administration of the student evaluation forms. That has plugged all the holes, and Michael Bowers (Vic Provost) complimented the College for leading other colleges.

Consultants are welcome to improve the system. But if they are going to charge like $25,000 for effectively telling what the Council has recommended, then it is wasteful. Moreover, it may burden the faculty and staff with time-consuming work and cause expensive softwares, when the problem is not even statistically significant in the first place!

With these parameters, my personal suggestion is that an ad hoc faculty committee deal with the Consultants. Some of us know stories of costly decisions with consultants.

May 2005

39. ADMINISTRATIVE DEVELOPMENT
(A Note to the Dean)

If I do not explain my request for attending the annual meeting of the **Council of Academic Administrators**, then you may remain under an impression that perhaps I was not serious about it. The question that I put myself is what you may have thought too: What is the return to the College for the expenses gone into attending it? Let me then go back up to the one-day workshop on fiscal issues that I attended in Washington DC in March 2004.

I brought back the idea of a special fee on the students who repeat/ withdraw from courses. You had raised it in some meetings. Subsequently, Judy Belanger and I met once and exchanged a couple of e-mails on this subject. In the meanwhile, you picked it on the W grades for the integrity of students' transcript. The new 2005 policy on W grades was a spin-off of my attending that workshop. Once Judy stepped down and retired, its financial aspect has not been pursued.

But it is futuristic and will become a reality sooner than we think. I would call it an assessment fee of $10 on the 3rd and 4th time repeaters, and $25 on the fifth timers and onwards, whether to improve a grade or remove a W. In Dawn Newman, we have a person, who will be willing to take it to a next level. It sure will increase the retention rate of the students as well as the graduation rates.

Attending professional meetings at least once a year is an expectation. Annual meeting is full of actions and interactions of all kinds. As a bit of history, at the time of the 2003 annual meeting, I was to visit India and the 2004 meeting clashed with my family plans.

About the expense, I am certain if that were an issue, then the Provost office would pitch in too. The deadline being Sept 30, I hope you would instruct Linda to process the registration fees. Thanks in anticipation.

Aug 15, 2005

PS: Nov, 2015 – He did not respond to this note, but he did attend this meeting himself. Professional development is essential - both on the part of the employee and support from the supervisor. Looking back, there was something amiss, as a year later; he wanted me return to full time faculty position.

PERSONAL REMARKS

40. ON ENROLLMENT INTEGRITY

The enrollment management is one of the major charges of the associate dean of a college. It mainly concerns fall and spring semesters. Summer sessions run differently, as no state money is involved. Actually, summer session is a pseudo business. Nearly, two months before the classes are to begin, the Office of Enrollment Management starts sending out periodic data to the deans and associate deans on the number of students registered in each discipline. My job is to optimize the number of students within the boundary conditions of classroom/lab space and viability of courses.

Associate Dean has nothing to do with the scheduling of the courses or the choice of instructors. Each department does it independently. Understanding each discipline and nature of courses is a learning experience. I regularly monitor the registration in each course from the university SIS software system. My general recommendations to the department chairpersons are to cancel a course, if the enrollment is very low, open another section, or increase the upper limit of class sizes in demand courses.

One may pose a question why can't the chairs do this job? The question is simple, but its answer is complex. It is only five years ago that the associate deans of all the eleven colleges started overseeing their respective college enrollments. University wide, a vice provost monitors various components of total enrollment that is nearing 30,000.

During regular semesters, the faculties like to teach classes with small number of students. Mathematically, that limit is not one, but zero! Yes, in 30 plus years at UNLV, I have known cases when students canvassed to the chairperson for a particular instructor or students were coerced to register in a particular instructor's course in order to make it go. At times, students drop it before the deadline and get their 100% fee refund. That is how an instructor ends up teaching an empty class towards the end of the semester!

This 'unethical' practice is generally seen at the upper division and graduate level courses. Assume a course goes ahead with say, six students. Sometimes, by the end of the 3rd and 5th week, the number dwindles down to one or two. It undermines faculty-teaching load, creates inequity amongst the faculty members, and wastes the room space. Yes, there is an option of teaching 2-3 students under Independent Studies (IS). Usually, 5-6 IS students are equivalent to one course teaching load.

I hear such stories all the time. The chairs need to be cognizant of this problem, as the enrollment integrity begins from the departments. This fall, I will collect data on the low enrollment courses in terms of the number of students on Day #1 and Day # 30, and share it with the chairpersons.

Sometimes, the programmatic needs, acute demand from students and rotation of courses do justify offering low enrollment courses. That is why there are no cut and dry minimums for the courses at various levels.

Aug 17, 2005/Nov, 2015

COMMENTS

Dear Satish: This kind of thing only happened at UNLV. It is unthinkable to have such problem here. I am glad I don't have to deal with such problem here. I started to realize how much power a chair can have and how easily this power can be abused. I must be very careful not to allow myself to abuse such power. On the other hand, I am glad I finally have my own identity and in control of my destiny. When I look back, I felt miserable at UNLV. I have to beg to purchase even little things, not to mentioned computer. After almost a month on my job, I am absolutely sure that our department is peaceful. It is time for me to focus my attention in research grants. **C.S.**

41. EDUCATION IS BUSINESS TOO!

A typical academic year in the US runs from mid August through mid May. It is in the mutual interest of students and faculty that there are different formats of summer sessions. Summer teaching provides faculty some compensation while the students are able to finish their degree programs quicker. However, the summer session is not supported by taxpayer money! Faculty are paid accordingly to the money generated by their classes.

I remember 1975 summer approaching and I inquired a colleague in the Business College of his summer plans. He right away said, "I have been driving trucks coast to coast. It is fun, sight seeing and brings a lot more money than teaching courses." At the other end, a few faculties are able to get some research support for summer.

At UNLV, summer session is big in terms of the number students and the course offerings. In addition to UNLV students, the local students who study out of state take summer courses at UNLV at cheaper rates while staying homes. For the last 25 years, summer school has been a source of income. A percentage of the summer surplus comes back to the departments for faculty travel and development. A challenge before the department chairpersons is to maximize this fund while keeping the faculty satisfied.

Last year, a newly hired department head said, "For summer sessions, I would rather hire part time instructors!" He was frustrated with regular faculty demanding full pay for their under-enrolled courses, and asking for travel support afterwards. His argument is that you get a fair share of what you generate. Students shop for instructors and can easily check their teaching reputation on web. In the US, everything is ranked and rated!

Here is a moot scenario. Let us say that 20 is the minimum number students for a full $1500/credit (varies with rank) payment in a typical 5-week summer session. This number is taken from the last Friday before the first day of classes begin on Monday. The courses are prorated in the sense that an instructor having 15 students is paid $1175, and $75 for only one student. Of course, an instructor can refuse to teach a course.

The students dropping the course by the first Friday of classes get 50% refund. In fact, it is very common for 6-8 students to drop a math course for various reasons. That means whereas the instructor is fully paid at 20, the summer school goes under red for this course.

After witnessing several scenarios over the years, I suggested that the faculty, generating more money at end of the session than they are contracted, must be rewarded with a bonus check after the summer. The idea is simple; if it is a business, then run it like a business!

August 27, 2005

42. AWOL IS HISTORY!

UNLV has adopted a new policy on professors missing classes. The campus publication, the *Rebel Yell* reporting it last week typically quoted a John Doe favoring it and a Jil Dee opposing it. Personally, I welcome the policy, as it is good for the academic image of the university. In order to get some idea on the problem that necessitated this policy, I gave the following brief anonymous survey in my class that has no freshmen:

1. How many instructors have been tardy (**late by at least 2 minutes**) to the classes?

2. How many instructors missed classes, but have them covered by substitute instructors?

3. How many instructors missed their classes without having them covered?

The sample 12 (3 absent) may be small, but being diverse, the data is significant.

   (a) Out of four **sophomores**, four checked on Question 1, two on Question 2, and 4 on Question 3.
   (b) Out of six **juniors**, five checked on Question 1, five on Question 2, and five on Question 3.
   (c) Out of two **seniors**, two checked on Question 1, one on Question 2 and two on Question 3.

That says it all about the state of classroom instruction that has warranted this policy! The number of instructors varied with the class standing. A typical response of a junior is that 5 instructors have been tardy, 6 missed classes with substitutes, and 4 just missed.

Looking back to my academic life for over 40 years, I used to tell my colleagues and friends in India, "In American universities, professors do not submit an application before going on leave. However, the faculty and department chairpersons make sure that the students are not adversely affected in their studies." They marveled at the integrity of the US system.

I have known a colleague for not missing even a single class for nearly 25 years! Personally, I have tried to model my professional life after Prof. Hans Raj Gupta. It was Jan. 1960 and Jawahar Lal Nehru, the first Prime Minster of India was on the campus of Panjab University, Chandigarh. A lunch was arranged in his honor with the department heads and the Vice-Chancellor (equivalent to the president of a US university). There were no other layers of administrators – like, various derivatives of provosts, deans, and VPs between the Vice Chancellor and the department heads at that time. Prof. Gupta missed the luncheon as its timing clashed with his class time. I was in it!

After the survey, the students were talking about some professors leaving the classes in the middle to respond to calls on their cellular phones. Sometimes, they are gone for 20 minutes, not once, but twice in a 75 minutes period! I could not disagree with students' comments, as I have heard such stories myself. The day is not far when another policy on the use of cell phones in classrooms may be adopted.

Nov 17, 2005

43. VOTING BY ASSOCIATE DEAN

A couple of things have happened during the last week that I thought of putting them down for a record. A colleague, knowing that as associate dean, I was not eligible to vote as a regular faculty member, asked me to take care of a job at the same time when the Department faculty was to elect a chairperson.

The upcoming election of the Department chairperson is a bit historic. When I joined the Department in 1974, the biennial elections of the chairperson until 1987 used to go unnoticed, as Sadanand Verma was unanimously re-elected again and again. In fact, he was the chairperson for solid 22 years. In a strange contrast, this 2006 election is being held after nine years!

During the last six years, the Administration placed the Department under receivership twice. It has generated a lot of friction amongst the faculty and administration, and now it has spelled out to the Chancellor and all the way to the Regents. During the meetings, tempers have flared up and emotions have run high. The memories being short, I strongly believe that I, presently as associate dean, should not be sidelined. My future is also at stake! Just think of scenario, if I have to work with a chairperson in future whom I don't support today. Therefore, I must have a vote in this process.

During the summer and fall deliberations of the bylaws, I openly spoke in favor of a full professor to be the Department chairperson. A person must have demonstrated leadership in all three areas - namely, Teaching, Research and Service. The Department has now a PhD program, therefore, its leadership must be in the hands of a complete leader.

However, my point of view, during the bylaws deliberations, was in minority both for the qualification of the chairperson, and for the voting privileges of the associate dean. I accepted it. Nevertheless, let me remind you with my long years at UNLV that lately a disproportionate number of the administrative faculty have used the administrative positions to get their promotion to the full professor rank. I can tell any number of stories.

Adding a little more of institutional history, ten years ago, there were no more than three assistant/associate deans at UNLV, today there are nearly 30. All are experienced faculty members! Also, during 1985-1998, Math Dept. had 8-10 non-PhD lecturers. They did not have the regular voting right. But, the Department took their separate vote as advisory vote on several matters - including curriculum and the elections of the chairperson.

My suggestion is to let me vote separately from the regular faculty, and my vote be communicated to the Dean along with other votes.

Feb. 27, 2006

44. THOUGHTS ON CAREER DAY

What a world of employment opportunities India of the 1950s offered when I was in college in contrast to the one that I witnessed today at the 27th Annual Career Day of UNLV. On this particular day, held during the second semester, the employers and graduating seniors meet for job opportunities. Students may or may not apply for jobs. In fact, most explore their options. They are still in the college and have a few months left for graduation (formally finishing a degree program).

India of the 1950s did not have any industry and private companies! Agriculture was in poor condition. The only jobs (called welfare jobs in the US) were with state and central governments. I remember 10,000 young people applying for a single opening! Things have dramatically changed since then. The real boost in economy and employment came after the government de-regulations and privatization of industry in the 1990s.

In May, nearly 4000 students will graduate. More than 200 employers were at site to talk with the students about their companies and job opportunities. The other day, I was talking with my granddaughter whose air travel was partly paid by the University of Chicago for checking its campus out. Bright students are admitted in several colleges, but they attend the schools (means college or university too) that give them the best scholarship deals in their academic programs.

When I asked her about the advantage of going to the University of Chicago, she told me that some Fortune 500 companies directly recruit the graduates directly from the campus. I have known campus recruitment for many years. As a little historical footnote, UNLV had five employers coming to the campus during its 1st Career Day held in 1980. They only recruited graduates from the Hotel Administration Program, now world famous. This number going from 5 to over 200 indicates the caliber of the graduates as well as the strength of UNLV's academic programs.

In the US, at the undergraduate (bachelors) level, there is a very strong connection between the academic programs and the needs of the society at large. Consequently, the courses and programs are continuously under revision. For instance, at UNLV, every new program is mandated for the first review after five years, and then every ten years. The evaluating process, being extensive and 4-layered, takes at least 12 months. My experience with the University Program Review Committee remains unforgettable. No wonder, the US higher education is a toast of the world today.

For nearly 40 years after independence, the Indian college education had no interface with the society at large. The British did not want to encourage Indians to be scientists and thinkers at large. The education system that they enforced was to help them rule over India with the help of the British trained Indians!

The changes are very slow in India due to the dominant Hindu religion that does not reject any system of thought and practice. The socialistic democracy of India, another reflection of Hinduism, has slowed the pace of progress as compared with that of the Chinese. There is a merit in 'geological' change too. It is long lasting!

For years, I did not understand and appreciate various review processes in a US university. Actually, I remember resenting a department committee reviewing textbooks for a multi-section course when the publishers would announce a new edition of a textbook. It is the American way whether it is re-modeling a kitchen counter, new home, or car etc. The olds do not have to live out their lives except perhaps for human beings.

During my India visits, I am often appalled to see the textbooks and syllabi running unchanged for 50 years! **The principles of science and theorems of mathematics do not change with time, but it is their newer applications that generate and drive new knowledge**. There is another example. At UNLV, this year a new program is introduced to replace one-third office computers every year. The new computers are faster and more efficient. It stimulates innovation, research, and boosts production and employment opportunities. Forty years ago, it was commonly observed by the foreigners that the American economy thrive on waste. Now it is a model to live and develop.

Another important aspect surfaced up during this event. The representatives of most hiring companies were the alumni of UNLV. Here is scenario of the old successful students visiting their university campus after 10-20 years, and networking with a new class of students, faculty and administrators. The alumni play very important roles in the life of their institution. With their financial support and advisory roles, they influence many facets of the university. Literally, the assets of a university are directly proportional to the size of its alumni association!

Most public functions are around food and soft alcoholic drinks – like, wine and beer. This event was set up from 3:30 PM – 5 PM. The atmosphere of the Board Room added an elegant touch to it. The tab of the function was picked by a few sponsoring companies. It was a nice setting to relax and engage in small talks and hellos. There were no boring speeches. However, everyone who worked behind the scenes and front was publicly recognized.

Mar 01, 2006

45. EDUCATIONAL ADMINISTRATION 101
(A Note to the Dean)

Our second meeting on Wednesday brought a new set of following three surprises for me:

(a) A 'weaker' A-contract that you offered me at our first meeting (04/27/06) was 'gone' by the second meeting (05/03/06)! That is why soon after the first meeting, you instructed Rychelle to send me an e-mail on consuming my 5 weeks of annual leave in 8 weeks!! You know, like in 2004 and 2005, I am scheduled to teach in Summer Sessions I and II.

(b) On your talking about 3-year terms of the Associate Dean (AD), I gave you instances at UNLV of the ADs serving from 5-12 years. For instance, Ted Cummings served the Business College for 14 years. Also, I gave you a short history of the ADs in our College. The common practice is that an AD serves as long the annual evaluation by his/her dean is mutually acceptable. You also admitted it. Neither had I told you of my desire to leave, nor did you ever give me any cause for separation.

(c) After listening to your 'revised' offer, I wanted to know the person in your mind who can do a better job as AD than I. Earlier; I had challenged you to compare my College contributions with that of any past AD. The way you inaudibly uttered John Farley's name, your facial expression betrayed you! You know that you are not treating me with the principles of fairness and frankness.

Where do We stand?

1. Let me reiterate the main point from our second meeting. The Upper Administration in the NSHE system is unstable, and more so at UNLV. You may survive as Dean after June 30, 2006, but not after June 30, 2007. By demoting me in rank, you are sending an unjust message to the campus community about my competence. This would hurt me in very near future, when I seek a better opportunity in the Administration.

2. Let me put a closure on your offer. As I told you earlier the 'weaker' A-contract was less attractive, and the revised one is really insulting. You are putting me in charge of a one-credit orientation course (SCI 101) that is un-approved by the departments and is not mandatory for the students. As long as I am your AD, I would give you a right advice; give this charge to Joseph Nick who also knows a brief history of this course.

3. As we departed, I told you of my desire to stay as AD for one more year. That positions me for better shots at the new openings at UNLV and outside. If that does not work out, then it would give me enough time to plan to go back to fulltime faculty status. This is the type of openness that I expect from you.

4. Now, let me add other derivative scenarios. During the past months of Jan and Feb, I was approached by several faculty members including Ho to be nominated as Department Chair! I assured them that I was happy as AD. Last week, during the elections of various department committees, I was not eligible to vote there; let alone serving on a committee.

5. I had Faculty Development Leave approved before I joined as AD in August 2003. However, it was negotiated with the Interim Dean, Bachhuber and Provost, Alden that it would be available after I was no longer AD. I plan to spend some time overseas that requires applying for Fulbright Travel grant and letter of overseas institutional support.

6. I hope you re-consider your reorganization plans of the Dean's office that already has set an all time record! Let us meet again on this subject, if necessary. Nevertheless, I do want to discuss the related matters with President Harter and Provost Alden. Last Friday, I had sought your 'approval' through an e-mail.

Finale
In a nutshell, **it is a question of my image**. My name literally means (in Hindi) integrity and character in the Department, in the College, and on the Campus, at large. It is the result of my 32 years of dedicated service at

UNLV! There is no strong lobby, or a body like NAACP behind me. Last Wednesday, Melvin, one of the three presidential candidates for UNLV remarked, "I want at least one of my advisors a truth teller." That hit a home run for me. Who is a truth teller in your Cabinet, Ron?

May 06, 2006/Nov, 2015

PS: Nov, 2015- I returned to the faculty rank in the fall-2006, but there was no AD for the College during 2006-07. The Dean stepped down a year later and left UNLV soon after.

46. WELCOME TO UNLV
(A reflective Note to President David Ashley)

Honestly, I cannot bring myself around to address you as 'David'! It requires mutual familiarity, if not closeness before saying one day, Hi, David. My Indian American heritage acknowledges appropriate dues to age and status. Age wise, you are younger than I am, but much higher in position. Presidents leave lasting marks on their institutions.

This name enchilada is strangely funny and serious. There is a 'mathematical' touch to it: **Greater the fame, smaller the name**. Who are the famous persons with three names (first, middle and last)? I don't see anyone except Martin Luther King! Yes, Bill Clinton, Tiger Woods and Charlton Heston, which come in 2-name category. But look at the one name category: Jesus, Buddha, Alexander of yore; Newton, Gandhi and Elvis of modern lore.

The meaning of my Hindu name, Satish is the God of Truth; the middle name Chandra simply personifies it. Thus, living up to my name is the *mantra* of my life! In that respect, your name David may remind you of meeting every challenge squarely. One challenge before you is to take UNLV to the next Carnegie level, fully at par with UNR.

I love to ponder over life around and frequently write various pieces, called **Reflections.** Any thing can trigger it. Your letter of July 5 prompted me to write this reflection as soon as I read it. It impressed me to note that you took time to craft it and had it delivered the day you arrived on the campus. That speaks of your engineering mind tuned for precision. What a phase shift in UNLV presidency - from literature to engineering!

I must welcome you on behalf of the class of 1974 faculty, as there are three of us still around. If ever you want to hear early stories of UNLV, I have a long yarn. However, the university presidents have little time for past and present, as their main business is future. Since the first oil crisis of the 1970s, a college president is increasingly for off campus engagements. I predict a new position of an Associate President for campus affairs.

You may not wonder, but I do, as to how come it took me two weeks to write this **Reflection**. Well, July 5 falling near the end of summer session II, I was into the last days of teaching and grading. On July 11, I drove to LA to attend a 4-day leadership program for the Asian Pacific Islanders (API) in higher education. This was the best seminar, workshop, or conference on leadership development that I have ever attended.

Having worked at UCLA, Ohio State and Berkeley, you know the high quality and quantity of the API students. But when it comes to the API in leaderships positions in higher education, one needs a microscope to find one. Next February, when you receive a letter from the LEAP President, please encourage the API faculty to attend this program. UNLV will be shinier. Thanks for this opportunity!

July 19, 2006

PS Nov, 2015. I was the first API member to be appointed to an administrative rank higher than a department chair. A diversity breakthrough came in 2010, when Rama Venkat was appointed as Interim Dean of the College of Engineering, and he became a 'regular' Dean in 2014.

47. STANDARDIZING ASSOCIATE DEANS
(A Reflective Note to UNLV President)

Twenty-five years ago, UNLV did not have even a single associate/assistant dean (AD). Today, there are nearly twenty-five of them. Besides, recent personal experience as associate dean, a couple of campus announcements have also prompted me to apprise you of some side effects.

A focal point is that the AD position should be advertised within the college. The choice of AD, of course, is in the hands of the Dean. If the Dean is new on the campus or/and the applicant pool is large, then he/she may seek advice from a committee or chairpersons. It is a question of fairness and equity amongst the faculty that are sensitive towards this position.

The AD position has significant financial gain; as I found it out two weeks ago, when I re-signed my B-contract after three years as AD. It provides administrative experience for a future leap into a deanship, as often is the case. By advertising the position, faculty with administrative ambitions can re-assess their professional goals.

Let us be honest, no matter how great one is as an instructor or researcher, it becomes less exciting after 2-3 decades. At least that is how I felt after nearly 30 years at UNLV when I applied for the ADship in 2003. The AD position has indeed energized me for higher education, which is a vast enterprise! The AD experience is no less exciting than that of a sabbatical leave that only stimulates one's teaching or/and research.

The Graduate Schools prepare the faculty mainly for research; teaching obstructs research, and any service is incidental. During the last 25 years, the US higher education has been dominated by faculty from education with doctorates in educational administration, leadership and psychology etc. I would venture to add that you might be the only President of a comprehensive university in the US with PhD in a traditional area of engineering!

It is paramount that you take time to examine the key AD positions on the campus. This is the first position that provides interactive experience outside one's department and college. I can vouchsafe of its usefulness and enrichment. It becomes all the more crucial when a dean suddenly resigns and AD has to step in as Acting/Interim dean until a permanent dean is appointed.

Adding a touch of the AD history in the College of Sciences, the first AD position was created in 1998 and was filled in with an internal search, and so it was in 2003, when I was selected. In 2004, another AD position (unadvertised) was added in the College, but it only lasted with the Dean.

Aug 29, 2006/Nov, 2015

48. DE-COUPLING PROMOTION & TENURE
(A Reflective Note to UNLV President)

This is a season of promotions and tenures (P&T) in the universities. The weather and sport seasons last for 3-4 months, but the P&T season goes on for the entire year. During August and September, the P&T clouds hover over the departments, in October, they move over the colleges, and in November onto the University committee. Those who are denied promotion or/and tenure at any stage, a round of 'reconsideration' takes January and February. If 'reconsideration' is turned down, then the regular appeal process may take the rest of the year. If someone decides to seek justice in a court of law, then another year or two is a norm.

I feel compelled to share a couple of P&T thoughts with you. It is time to disconnect tenure with promotion at the assistant professor level. One should not imply the other. The research caliber of faculty is raised by the new hires with strong research records. It would gradually raise the bar for the ones on probationary periods. With a statistical significance of 90 %, I can say that in 70 % of the cases, tenurable were not promotable.

Promoting an applicant and not tenuring may run into technical problems with the System Code and institutional bylaws. But, there is no problem in granting tenure to an assistant professor, but denying promotion to the associate rank. In such a case, the person is not kicked out of the institution. Tenurability implies that research and scholarly work are on a cusp. Mostly likely, he/she may bring a stronger record after 1-3 years. To the best of my knowledge, UNLV has only two tenured assistant professors with PhDs!

The de-coupling of tenure and promotion is a measure of scholarly expectations of an institution. The practice of keeping the two together has been fine for UNLV in its formative years. But it is no longer sound, if you want to take UNLV one notch above and bring it at par with the UNR.

It is time to minimize the institutional time and money on the P&T grievances and litigation. Most of the time it is the evaluation of the cases at the lower level that matters. However, I also know of a recent case strongly supported by the Department and College but denied by the

161

Provost. If the P&T committees at the department and college levels are of the elected faculty, then my experience is that the number of appeals and grievances can be reduced.

Here is a current scenario from my College of Sciences. The Chair makes his/her P&T recommendations. At the College level, the P&T Committee is not of the elected faculty members, but the College Executive Committee of the Chairs acts like the College P&T Committee. The chairs don't have the time to thoroughly examine the 4" thick documents. Also, they have their ongoing agendas. The chairs have a double or even triple dipping in the voting process. This is not right. In P&T matters, the chairs tend to support each other. Often, their written recommendations are different from what they advocate in the meetings, and yet different from their votes.

Here are the two points. It is high time to disconnect P&T and ensure faculty elected P&T committees at the department and college levels. Sooner they are corrected, faster will be UNLV's march to its higher status!

Sep 29, 2006/Nov, 2015

PS Nov, 2015: In CoS, the elected P&T committees did start in 2008.

49. CULTIVATING ADMINISTRATORS
(A Reflective Note to UNLV President)

By now, in three months, you might have seen most of the nuts and bolts of UNLV. In July, when I wrote you my first *Reflective* note, my son (1989, UNLV graduate) said, "Dad, you should have brought out a list of ten topics to President's attention in the style of David Letterman!" Well, here is the following issue, let us call it, **Number Three**.

"He does not have a chance to be selected since he is not a (full) professor," remarked a colleague about a common friend who is upfront about his administrative ambitions. Yesterday, we were discussing a newly advertised position of the Associate Vice Provost for Academic Programs. His remarks stopped my thoughts in the tracks.

With increasing institutional accountability, assessment, accreditation, diversity affairs, and various compliances, there are layers of unbudgeted administrative positions between the department chairs and college deans, between the deans and provost, and between the provost and president. I was critical of these 'middy' administrative positions until I became the Associate Dean of the College of Sciences (2003-06)! Now, I believe that the administrators shield the faculty from several distractions, and thus let them carry on with their researches and teaching peacefully.

Nevertheless, the above remarks point to a genuine problem too, and it begs for a 'solution'. While doing PhD, even in the softest discipline, one does not get any administrative training of any sort, while a new faculty member can get knee deep in service in the first two years. As a matter of fact, the graduate schools until very recently did not even help in the craft of teaching. Graduates are trained to do research! However, university culture has changed during the last 30 years.

I remember the days when UNLV Provost found time to interview candidates for academic positions. I was one of them! Now a faculty member may have to wait for a month to meet with the provost-forget meeting the President. As I noticed that, the dean's time is significantly spent on off-campus affairs. The administrators are needed to quickly respond to any situation and run the campus smoothly! Where is the beef (problem) then?

A problem arises when the 'layered' administrators use their 'influence' to get full professorship, the ultimate crown in academic life, if not already in this rank. During the last 30+ years, I have known department chairs/directors, associate/acting deans pushing themselves for the full ranks. It is legal and within their rights, but, unconscionable.

Administration is a full time job with new questions or problems facing every day! It is absolutely inimical to scholarly activities. That is why the administrators coming back to the trenches as faculty members are given five-year holiday from research. Until then, their merit raises are based upon teaching and service only. In theoretical sciences and mathematics, this period may never be enough to catch on research.

Sept 30, 2006/Nov, 2015

50. A SHADE OF PLAGIARISM
(A Reflective Note to College Dean)

At the outset, I must say that under your deanship the awareness against plagiarism has been raised higher than before. In this context, recently you have been quoted in leading national dailies. Also, the focus is not just on the undergraduates cheating on exams and in labs, but also on graduate students and faculty involved in research and publication.

Yesterday afternoon, campus publication, *Inside UNLV* (Oct) stacked on a counter caught my attention. Glossing it over, I stopped to read the update on the College of Sciences. That turned out to be a shocker and a brazen show of plagiarism. No credit is given to me or to the members of the Undergraduate Council that worked on SCI 101X for six months! What a tryst of destiny, exactly a year ago, I was profiled in this publication, and now openly ignored!

The writer may have thought that plagiarism does not apply to the **Service** category of the profession! Plagiarism in **Research** is universally condemned. In **Teaching,** punishment is severe too. You know how early this year, the president of a major university was chastised for plagiarizing a single passage in an article or speech. Eventually, he stepped down. **Plagiarism in any form comes from the same one mindset.**

I recall your asking the chairs to write the college piece for *Inside UNLV,* in rotation. The article simply does not smell right, as I read it again. During early spring, you and I first talked about the need for such a course for our College. I surveyed all the colleges for similar courses. The senior members, Boyd and Rohan gave valuable suggestions, young Matt brought out the issues, and Nick searched various universities including UT Dallas for models. In May, the Council made a recommendation to you on its number, title, feasibility, description, instruction and scheduling formats. In July/Aug, as a part of final recommendation, I forwarded you the e-mails exchanged with Patty on the subject.

This story reminds me of the Muslim students in Malaysia, where I taught for two years (1992-94) in a program run by Indiana University. Cheating was rampant there. The students used signs and native language, and took advantage of Americans' ignorance of their culture. One day, appealing to their religious sensibilities, I sermonized, "You never steal books, bags and valuables left outside the prayer room, when you go inside, because it is forbidden in Islam. But, stealing the ideas of others is as much a crime or sin as is the stealing of items. Ideas constitute intellectual property!" Well, it had a desired effect.

This publication has been circulated across the campus. The readers of this article will have a wrong picture of SCI 101X. Members of the Undergraduate Council must be disappointed. As a former Chair of the Council, it becomes incumbent upon me to bring it to your attention for immediate correction.

Oct 14, 2006/Nov, 2015

PS Nov, 2015: The Dean never responded. By then, he was on his way out of UNLV.

51. SOULE AND PORN
(A Note to the President and Chairperson of the Faculty Senate)

The Soule episode is a soul-searching experience for everyone on the campus. It has been going on for more than a month now. The **Rebel Yell** and the daily **RJ** have been covering the story with their own twists and spins. But the Administration, Faculty Senate and Nevada Faculty Alliance have all been silent. It is puzzling!

Soule's case raises pertinent questions on the welfare of the students, faculty, staff, and administrators on child porn on the office/home computers. In the UNLV community of over 30,000 students, faculty, staff, and administrators, has Soule been the only one watching child porn? But, Soule alone has been apprehended and is being punished to the fullest extent of the system code, state, and federal laws. He has lost his job, livelihood, and professional recognition. Disgraced at 62, he would live with embarrassment forever.

Ignorance of law is no excuse – however, it comes from a time when the laws were simple and few. Now attorneys hire attorneys when caught by the laws! UNLV Human Resources run workshops on **sexual harassment, cultural sensitivity** and **ethnic diversity** because their infringements are all serious crimes. But never there has been a workshop on watching porn on computers! A paradox is that it is impossible to fire the most incompetent tenured faculty on the bases of his/her incompetence in teaching, research or/and service. But watching child porn on the office computer can **can** anyone in no time.

The scariest aspect of the whole episode is that the IT technicians can watch any one downloading anything on the university computers. Was the department chair or college dean duly informed? As a three-term Senator and 'one-term' Associate Dean, I am disappointed! I have to speak up as a senior faculty member. All my three kids are UNLV alumni, and are concerned too.

On a rather personal note, Soule and I joined UNLV in 1974, and lived in houses across on the Chestnut Street for 12 years. My older daughter, now 41, babysat his two boys several times, is in a state of disbelief. All his three kids attended good schools. He was a good neighbor, Music

Department Chair, Graduate Council Chair, the winner of teaching awards at the College and University levels. He guest lectured in my Honors Seminar, and I sat in his music theory classes. Let me stress that I am not opposed to the law taking its course for whatever laws Soule has knowingly or unknowingly broken.

My concern is that while I am using my office PC, some lower rung IT technician, hired by the college, can watch over my PC at the instance of an unhappy chair, dean, or provost. My office is accessible to many in my absence. Any IT hacker can download child porn images on my PC without my knowledge. It appears from the reports that Soule could not be warned for his porn crime (involving 10-16 year old girls). On the other hand, his PC was monitored for gathering more evidence against him. This process as reported is sinister and stinking. I urge you both to bring all the facets out for the welfare of the campus community. It is high time to legally protect them and serve them well.

Nov 19, 2006/Nov, 2015

PS Nov, 2015: No educational measure on this issue has been taken yet.

52. TIME TO RE-INVENT

"Get PhD in any field; be that in lawn mowing," I told Alok Pandey yesterday. Alok is a promising API (Asian Pacific Islander) instructor in a community college. I have known him for over 15 years. He has been active in Indian community affairs and Nevada Faculty Alliance, a statewide organization of all post secondary faculty. Currently, he is chairing the Faculty Senate of his college. He is in his 40's and holds masters in statistics. He would like to get PhD in statistics, but is not enrolled in the program. With a full time job, statistics is too much with working wife and two kids. Some thing will give in.

Two things struck my mind. One, the APIs lay greater emphasis on the study of science and engineering disciplines. The first generation of the APIs in USA seldom thought of arts, humanities and education - forget areas of sports and entertainment, which in Asian countries are still considered life wasting. Our children in the USA were pushed in the same directions. Test this hypothesis amongst the dominant Chinese and Indians. However, it is time to spread and diversify pursuits for ourselves and our children.

The API faculty without PhDs are missing out opportunities in higher administration that are very lucrative. This needs to be emphasized during the next **LEAP** workshop. The irony is that most APIs continue to believe that unless one does PhD in hard-core science area, it is no good intellectually! This is fallacious. On the other hand, an API can knock out PhD in any area of education, counseling, and psychology in 2-3 years, while holding a fulltime job. The administrative goal is met by right strategies. For many administrative positions, the areas of PhD are open.

This cord struck my mind last week during the campus visit of a candidate for the position of senior vice president and provost of UNLV. Currently, he has been a vice president (VP) in a Missouri university. His administrative experience includes being department chair for two years and faculty Senate chair for one year. During the middle of his one-year administrative fellowship, he got into an interim VP position and then the permanent one six years ago!

He was articulate and smooth talker on the top of having good academic credentials in psychology. Communication skills and lack of confidence can be developed and built up by joining 1-2 toastmaster clubs. In six months, the transformation is unbelievable. It is essential for the APIs to develop communication skills.

The bottom line is that if you are set upon staying in the largest professional field, education including K-12, then get a PhD in the softest discipline as soon as possible. But go for an accredited one. The likes of University of Phoenix may be taken as last resort with 'upper' understanding.

The domination of administrators with educational background is astounding. With due apology, I call it a **revenge of the duds,** as no one paid attention to them in high schools and colleges. They failed to go to professional colleges, become medical doctors, engineers, or accountants etc. **Sometimes, life is fair!**

Feb 04, 2007

COMMENTS

Satish, Your point is well taken. However, I'd like to submit that, in the long run, one has to show stuff. Peace of mind is important, too. **Jing Luo**

Thanks for your thoughts. **Philip**

Satish, You are absolutely correct in your bottom line, i.e., "if you are set upon staying in the largest field of education including K-12, then get a PhD in the softest discipline as soon as possible." In the long term, each of us must answer a call. Some will ignore that call, preferring a parasitic life of comfort and mediocrity within the most egalitarian prosperous society in the history of human existence. A precious few will eschew material wealth and influence to advance knowledge in respected professions. Still others will make their contributions as administrators and organizers--many will call them leaders.

The difficulty with each track--apathy, advancement, administration--is that we're given only a short time to engage and perhaps make a difference. Can the gifted scientist and professor become the great leader of a renowned research university? Yes. We have known them. But most of us lack some of the attributes that allow such achievement in one lifetime. So we must honestly assess our abilities, our values, and our goals. How can we be most effective? Best serve.

I have no advanced degree in the sciences or mathematics. I do have a terminal degree--one earned quickly without acclaim. I have long known that I could not be a great scientist and professor. Instead, I've labored to become skilled as an administrator, taking every opportunity to deliver success to my institution, organizing and structuring the institution to facilitate the work of those who advance knowledge, and in the process garnering greater responsibility with each passing year. I might be a "dud"--but I am also making a contribution within my abilities. So... each of us must self-assess, commit, and act rather than agonize over what might be. As another colleague has written: "Peace of mind is important". Regards, **THOMAS** D. KLINCAR, Colonel, USAF, Community College.

53. A SMALL WINDOW ON EDUCATION

I always look forward to objective feedback on my courses and lectures. Evaluations, from individual to organizational, are solicited in the USA more often than in any other country. It comes out of the philosophy of life that not matter how perfect you are in any one aspect of life, there is always a room to improve.

Yesterday came the evaluation sheets minus the identities of the evaluators on a motivational speech that I had given to the 8th graders in a junior school. **PAYBAC** (acronym for **P**rofessional **A**nd **Y**outh **B**ringing **A** **C**ommitment) is a wonderful program of the School District under which community leaders including active and retired professionals, university regents, state legislators, and successful business men/women, volunteer their time. They come out to motivate kids to stay in school and do their best.

The underlying ideas behind PAYBAC are very simple. Everyone has stories of success, and we all want to tell it to the world! This program provides a forum, where one can also build and hone skills on pubic speaking, if lacking in the first place.

Out of 2-3 school engagements, I visit Roy Martin Middle School every year. The reason being that my younger daughter and her Hispanic husband met each other while teaching there. Two years later, they got married. The school is situated in an economically poor neighborhood, where only 4 % are Whites in contrast with 75 % Hispanics and 14 % Blacks. This demographic profile of the school must be kept in mind, as data analysis is presented below from the 9-item questionnaire.

The US public schools are measured by the graduation rates and students' national test scores. I think the focus of early public education should rightly be on careers and vocational education since nearly 90 % of them are likely to make the bricks and mortar of the society. Any elitist emphasis on knowledge for the sake of knowledge, as it goes on in Indian public schools (called government there), is misplaced during teen years.

At age 13, the kids think of fun and play most of the time, yet they see their parents trying hard at multiple jobs to make both ends meet. The first three questions of the questionnaire are related with students' career awareness. Number 1: *Before the PAYBAC presentation, have you thought about what job would you like?* 9 out of 25 said **No**. Number 2: *What type of job you like to have? First Choice; Second Choice*: The **First Choice** included Brick Layer, Magazine publicist, Mechanic, Construction, Army (2), Psychiatric, Sports (2), NASA, Doctor (4), Cosmetology (2), Game Designer (3) Police (2), World's greatest fighter (Hispanics are dominant in boxing these days), Banker, Adventurer, Don't know. Despite the US being litigious society, not even a single student chose to be an attorney; only one had it in the Second Choice!

Number 3: *Who helped you in this decision? Parents, Relatives, Neighbors, Teachers, Counselors, Others.* Since some had checked more than one category; 14 had Parents, 9 Others, 5 Relatives, 2 Teachers. Interestingly, only one student had checked *Neighbor* indicating how even in 'poor' neighborhoods people are getting disconnected with their neighbors. It has caught on in urban India.

The most interesting response was that no one checked *Counselors*! I believe that the jobs of the counselors and advisors in the US schools and colleges are far from helping the students; particularly on course matters. Counselors' academic backgrounds generally being narrow and below average, they often create bottlenecks of inefficiency and frustration amongst the students when advising is mandatory. On the other hand, the instructors in schools and colleges have been disconnected from academic advising even at the junior and senior levels. For lack of contact between faculty and students outside the class, the quality particularly of college teaching is becoming clinical.

Number 4 and 5 dealt with the speaker's emphasis on the **importance of education** and **students' future**. Number 6 and 7 are about the merit and evaluation of the PAYBAC Program. Number 6: *Would you like to attend this kind of program next year*? 11 out of 25 said **No**! However, Number 7, on the evaluation of the Program on a scale of 1 (lowest in quality) - 4 (highest); One checked 1, Two, 2; Ten, 3; and Twelve, 4, with an average of 3.33. The class teacher's evaluation separately included was 2.5.

Number 8 *Do you intend to finish high school?* (of 12 years) Twenty out of 25 said yes. Certainly, my presentation may have made a quick impact on the students. Number 9 was descriptive: ***What did you learn from the PAYBAC Speaker?*** All the 23 respondents, out of 25, were positive!

A highlight of the programs was that one of the motivational speakers was a former student of this very school. He recalled the impact PAYBAC program on his life. On a personal note, I still have 55-year old vivid memories of a few engaging guest speakers addressing the students. Motivational speakers provide a healthy interlude in class routines. By and large, the education within the confines of the school or college must be meaningful with life outside it. Any dichotomy is short and temporary.

April 01, 2007

PERSONAL REMARKS

54. THE ADMINISTRATIVE FACULTY

As I pulled out the current issue of the *Alliance*, a quarterly newsletter of the **Nevada Faculty Alliance**, the heading, *'Administrative faculty rights are a worrisome issue at UNR'*, caught my attention. For three years, I was the (academic) Associate Dean (AD) in the College of Sciences.

It was a year ago in May, when my Dean suddenly told me that my term of three years would be over in summer. There was no term mentioned in the appointment letter. I explained that at UNLV some ADs have served for 10-12 years. Generally, an AD remains in the position as long as the Dean is satisfied with the AD's performance. Neither was I given any low annual evaluation, feedback, or a hint before this meeting.

Last year, with the 'firing' of the President and departure of both the academic VPs, UNLV's upper administration was in flux. I was positioning myself for the next administrative shot once the new President takes over. I clearly told the Dean that my chances for the next administrative position would be hurt, if I were taken out. But he declined to give me the 4th year. Consequently, this month, I lost my bids for the two interim dean positions, which were internally advertised. In a small circle, it makes a difference when my application suggests my 'removal' from the AD-ship.

Yes, it is time that the campuses have some guidelines, though a distinction must remain between the traditional and non-traditional administrative faculty positions. The positions of the deans, VPs and presidents are historically well defined and budgeted. The crux is the growing number of acting/interim/assistant/associate/director/dean/provost/vice-president positions. To the best of my understanding, these positions are not budgeted.

A dozen faculty members applied for the two interim dean positions. In another setting, quite a few faculty members were upset when the dean appointed an AD without going through an internal search, as had been a practice in the past. These 'mid-level' administrative positions carry A-contracts (12-month), which boost the salary and benefits by at least by $ 25,000. Besides, it becomes a springboard for a regular position.

Do I have specific suggestions? Once again, my concern is on the intermediary positions in academics, though a larger number of such positions exist in the divisions of outreach, student life and business of any institution. A side bar observation: the teaching load of the AD varies from no course to one/semester. Yet, my dean pressed the department chair to assign two courses to me! The assistant/associate provosts/VPs don't teach at all.

There are many nitty gritty things that collectively may bring out a tangible picture. The most important thing is that if a faculty member has served in a 'mid' administrative position for 2-3 years, then a 'notice' of 3-9 months is called for. At UNLV, when a VP or dean goes back to the trenches of a faculty position, he/she gets five-year holiday on research evaluation and one year of post administrative leave.

May 08, 2007

55. JOB - A JOYOUS JOURNEY
(A Reflective Note to Exec. VP and Provost)

Yesterday, I read through your interview in the *Inside UNLV.* It was candid, however, your phrases, "drinking from the fire hose" and "running to catch up with trains that have left the stations", have me concerned. I hope you are not 'exhausted' like those overheated firefighters and commuters who beat upon the train timings! Being originally from India, which has the largest network of trains in the world, there are literal dangers. The *Law of Large Numbers* eventually catches up.

Americans work hard with their body and mind. Consequently, they get out of touch with their inner core. For balancing the life, both medication and meditation are resorted to in equal measures. As a matter of fact, the American work ethics is America's main export to the world, particularly to the 'sleeping' nations – like, India and China.

Amongst many things that you might have familiarized yourself about the student body, here is my pop quiz for you on *UNLV Orientation 101*. It is related only to the *Elementary Calculus I* (**MATH 181**) course that I just finished teaching during summer session III. Ideally, freshmen take it in the first semester. *Elementary Calculus* **defines an institution** in terms of its student quality, FTE generated, faculty involved, and much more. Also, it has been identified as one of the four courses, one from each department, except geosciences, for special allocation in fall. Here are the questions, just put your answers down across them. Good luck; it's fun time!

1. Ratio of males and females
2. Percentage of 18-year old
3. Age of the oldest
4. Percentage of freshmen
5. Percentage of sophomores
6. Percentage of working (part/full)
7. Percentage of repeaters (including twice or thrice)
8. Percentage of math majors
9. Percentage of physics majors
10. Percentage of bio, chem, comp. science and all engineering combined
11. Retention rate

12. Cumulative class GPA
13. Student Evaluation of my instruction
14. Profile of the Top Student

You are welcome to communicate it with any one. It takes new comers a few years for UNLV perception to gel in. The new faculty members eventually re-orientate themselves, but the administrators move on to other pastures.

Finally, the specific answers are: 1 (55 : 45), 2 (2.5), 3 (47; 3 over 40), 4 (12.5), 5 (20), 6 (60), 7 (50), 8 (00), 9 (00), 10 (58), 11 (80), 12 (2.05), 13 (2.43), 14 (freshmen, in 30's, married, father of 2 kids; 10 & 7; wife in the 3rd year of Touro's DO program!)

Aug 23, 2007/Dec, 2015

56. SCHOLARSHIP OF SEX EDUCATION

During my 4-month sabbatical (Sept- Dec, 2007) in India, the Americana that I often missed were the free cultural programs–like, art exhibitions, musical recitals, public debates, and expert lectures. The scanning of the Sunday newspapers of metropolitan cities would often draw mostly blanks on such activities. In the US, even a small university town has an array of intellectually stimulating events almost every day. It distinguishes the US from the rest of the world.

Yesterday, UNLV's **University Forum Lecture Series** presented "*The Complexities of Supply and Demand: Intimacy, Sexual Labor, and Commerce.*" The speaker, Teela Saunders, is a Senior Lecturer at the University of Leeds, UK, having PhD from world-renowned Oxford University. The lecture, organized by the College of Liberal Arts, was also sponsored by Departments of Sociology, Counselor Education, Hotel Management, and Women's Research Institute of Nevada! It all lends a prestige to sex curriculum and research, as an academic domain. The breadth of disciplines is an inherent strength of an American University.

Sex markets anything, and sex sells everything including sex! However, Saunders' entire power-point presentation did not have any semblance of erotica. She herself looked pretty - wearing Britishy dress skirt, jacket and boots. Her research intersects with that of two women faculty members in UNLV's Sociology Department. It seems easier for women sex researchers to develop rapport with female sex workers and their male seekers. She has authored three books; one based upon a survey of 300 female sex laborers, and the other on 50 johns going after sexual services. Seven doctoral students are currently working with her. Naturally, these new scholars will be hired in institutions where 'prostitution' studies is an academic area.

At the end of the lecture, I asked Saunders about prostitution and its economic impact in Middle Eastern countries. She admitted to having no knowledge. In Islamic countries, prostitution is a corollary of the institutions of harems, sanctioning of four wives to a man, and submissive status of the women. In India, where social laws are not easily enforced, prostitution covertly goes on. For instance, the red light district,

Sonagachi (Golden Tree) in Kolkata has over 10,000 prostitutes. It goes back to the 18th century. Before 1947, prostitution was not illegal in India.

Saunders pointed out that in Nevada, 5500 prostitutes work in 500 legal brothels. Las Vegas has 37 gentlemen clubs. Here comes a staggering figure on the economic impact of gentlemen clubs, where 'raw sex' is not on sale. However, the lap dances alone generate whopping 600 million dollars a year! I missed whether this figure belonged to Nevada alone, or to the entire western society that she focused on. Furthermore, Saunders only investigated male-female sexuality. Homosexuality is another research area in the academe.

The audience was mainly of women, from young to old. Yes, college students are drawn to this commerce expecting big bucks in a short time for fun and pay for their education. In the 1950s, when I heard that the girls of Miranda House, Delhi's premier college for women, were 'supplied' to the bigwigs in Delhi hotels, I disbelieved it! Today, Delhi college girls are entrepreneurs in this business. Saunders' position on controls of sex trade was to let the free market of capitalism take it its own regulatory course with local checks and balances.

Feb 28, 2008/Oct, 2015

COMMENTS

I liked the caption of the presentation...Interesting...I think Muslims allow 4 wives for restricting prostitution...Are men more polygamous than women? **Raju Abraham**

Saunders' position on controls of sex trade was to let the free market of capitalism take it its own regulatory course with local checks and balances. What about forced prostitution and sexual exploitation? **Rahul**

Fascinating.................................It's a giant leap from being in a monogamous state of living to even thoughts of being a prostitute.
Admitting to having many lovers after my legal husband died is uncomfortable, but it's the truth. Each affair was purportedly a love match with ideas of being committed and "forever" together.
But taking cash ??????????? hmmmm? it's a problem for my emotions to accept that idea.
From, **Anonymous**. I'll never admit that I wrote this.

There is much to be said retiring in a university or college town. Which partly explains why we moved here. **Bob Moore**

57. ASSOCIATE DEANS ARE FOR REAL!
(A Reflective note to the Provost)

"---Finally, you also complained that I hired an Associate Dean without any input. I discussed my choice with the Chairs of the Departments and with some of the other senior members of the faculty. But, in all honesty, a recommendation to the President to appoint an associate dean is a decision of the dean. I choose associate deans based on their abilities, their dedication, their commitment and how well we work together. The associate dean position is not a hereditary one. Associate Deans don't morph into Deans if a Dean leaves as you erroneously stated in your article. Please check the past record at UNLV and at most universities concerning this issue. I would also challenge you to check and see what Associate Deans have ever been elected at UNLV??" (From Ron Yasbin's e-mail of **04/17/07** to the NFA President, Paul Aizley, and copied to the entire College faculty)

This is a 'season' of hiring and 'firing' of the deans. That implies some associate dean (AD) becoming an acting dean (AD), and eventually (full) dean here at UNLV, or elsewhere. It is time to throw some light on the status of the ADs in general from my personal experience. The spring of 2006 was a period of turmoil at UNLV due to the hiring and firing of its president and two senior VPs leaving UNLV. The System Chancellor was involved from the top, at the presidency level to the bottom - for example, in the receivership of Math. Dept. It was during such an air of uncertainty, that Ron suddenly told me in May-2006 that I was not going to be his AD from next semester. Prior to that, at no time, during annual evaluation, he gave me any indication. The AD job may be at dean's pleasure, but not at dean's whims.

The history of AD in the College Sciences is only 10 years old. The oldest AD position, in the Hotel/Business College, may go back to 25 years. As a matter of fact, 30 years ago, there was no associate/assistant Provost/VP, at UNLV! With tremendous growth of UNLV and demands for speedy decisions and accountability, these mid-level administrative positions are now a part of a national trend.

The question at the front burner: Is AD a yes-man or a garbage picker after the dean? I have known some ADs from outside hired as deans at UNLV. Likewise, the ADs at UNLV have found deanships at other places. As UNLV celebrating its 50th anniversary, let it become a defining moment for these 'middy' administrative positions. I don't mean to underestimate these positions. For any one of these positions, several faculty members would put away their teaching and research on the shelves. After all, there is a gain of at least $25,000 plus the 'juice', and a lot more. For some, it is a path to (full) professorship. It is staggering, if department chairmanships are also included.

Concluding it on a personal note, I told Ron, "Give me just one more year, otherwise, you are depriving me of a fair shot at new administrative openings." Incidentally, the Administration gave him a year that he denied me! Why am I writing it today? There are rumors, that in case, the new dean is not hired, the AD Carl Reiber may be appointed as Acting Dean. **Then I would be grieved and discriminated.**

It is time to look at a tree as well as its forest. The AD position demands your attention and resolution. Based upon my long experience, all the 'middy' administrative positions of the ADs/AVPs should be internally advertised with contractual obligations.

Apr 24, 2008/Dec, 2015

PS, Dec, 2015: Whatever were the reasons, Reiber was not appointed as the Acting Dean and Yasbin left UNLV. Three years later, Reiber moved up as Vice Provost.

58. MULTIPLE DIPPINGS IN ACADEMIA
(A Reflective Note to the Provost)

After two weeks of reviewing the sabbatical leave applications, I said, it was time to revise the eligibility criteria to the tenured faculty, who have completed five years at UNLV. "Here's a real scenario. Say, an untenured faculty member applies for tenure and sabbatical leave in a fall semester after completing five years. For tenure, he/she must be considered, and he/she is eligible for Sabbatical or Faculty Development leave under present guidelines. Let us assume that by the end of the fall semester, he/she is recommended for leave, but rejected for tenure."

A committee member said, "So what?" The sixth year being the last year, the faculty member denied tenure, is gone for a semester or whole year, and is not coming back. Where are the benefits to UNLV?" A leave clause, that faculty must serve UNLV for the time spent on sabbatical, is contradicted. It was not enough for one member, when he said, "Sabbatical would help him/her in getting a new job." This kind of thinking is a reflection of recent bad real estate loans and risky investments by financial institutions across the country!

This year, out of fifteen applicants for twenty-one sabbatical slots, five are also going for tenure/promotion at the same time. My cursory look at their records tells that not all are tenurable. I don't know when the Administration faced the scenario described above, but it may show up on your watch. The committee does not care, as it is a Provost's problem.

Here is a big picture. You know, how some state universities have abolished or cut down on number of sabbaticals during times of financial exigencies. UNLV is going through one. It is time to save money. By strengthening the eligibility requirements, the Administration sends a message to the community, at large, that the resources are being used efficiently.

There is a corollary. The chairs hate faculty going on leave with pay, as the departments lose money as well as faculty time. For the last one year, almost every department is hit in every respect. A faculty on leave does cause sudden scheduling problems. This financial crisis is not going to be permanent, but as long as it persists, it is very painful.

A person like me knows nooks and corners of academic life that the new administrators may not ever notice. Here is a scenario of quadruple dipping. It means essentially the same application material is submitted for 4-5 personal considerations. For these five persons, it is already two; sabbatical/faculty development and tenure/promotion. Come spring semester, a subset package may be submitted for the College awards in Teaching/Research or/and University/System awards in Teaching/Research!

A cynic may say, "What is wrong with it?" Well, it is your call now! UNLV has been transitioning very rapidly. The sabbatical/faculty leave criteria have not been visited for at least 20 years. The same applies to various college and university awards and recognitions. They are crying for revision too. This buck stops/starts at your desk!

Oct. 15, 2008

COMMENTS

This is so strange as to cause me to forward it to our senior VP, and legal counsel for response....thanks much. **Neal**

59. EDUCATIONAL FRACTALS

America is a land of material stimuli. Las Vegas, my hometown in the US, is the world capital of sensual delights. But when it comes to intellectual stimuli, then the environment of its university is incomparable. Apart from one's scholarly research, readings, and communications, there are several other venues – like, public lectures and traveling exhibits on the cutting edge of information, education, and awareness.

This line of thought was triggered today while participating in a 10-member Sabbatical Leave Committee, drawn from 10 colleges (each college comprising of 4-6 departments) of the university. It just concluded its 3-week deliberations over fifteen applications for sabbatical leaves available for the academic year, 2009-10. Every member went through each package of 100-200 pages, but one person from the applicant's college gave a comprehensive report. It really re-educates the other members.

Here is the joyous part of this committee work. These days, no one has good ideas of the qualitative and quantitative research in other disciplines. Due to decades of over-specialization, for instance, I know little even of many areas of mathematics. Therefore, it is incumbent upon an applicant to bring the technical aspects of his/her intended research project to the level of the non-experts. That is an American way of life in general!

One proposal in sciences deals with life in high temperatures to the order of 200-300 F degrees. If a life model is only associated with that of human beings, then it would shock people. Another researcher from biomechanics studies the flight trajectories of flies, bees and humming birds, hopping from one spot to the other due to dangers, food, or mating. It is a fusion of mathematical modeling, robotics simulation, and high-speed videos.

Mathematicians tend to downgrade research in the so-called 'softer' areas in education, humanities and social studies. A proposal on a paradox and cognitive organization in social work caught my fancy. One word that separates mathematics from behavioral disciplines is 'cognitive', which mathematicians never use it. An expertise of a faculty in architecture is 'passive' solar heating system for buildings under new standards of low carbon emissions. An unheard expertise in multimedia research is **Second life**, virtual reality, a place for the Hindu religious concepts of *Avatars*. But the money it generates is not virtual; it is all green!

Every year, some watchdog groups, monitoring various federal research organizations, release regular reports on the grants awarded in esoteric areas. They essentially tell of research pollution and both shady and shoddy researches. Bigger is the pot of research money, greater is the number of phony researchers and ridiculous topics. Many fraudulent ideas are paddled in the pious names of research, education and information.

Well, the discussion on each applicant brings another round of understating. Since no one on the Committee is an expert on applicants' areas, the points for and against a proposal coalesce in the middle. At times, the comments are amusing, and at others, revealing and clarifying. Nevertheless, new knowledge and information do settle down in the mind.

Over the years, it has remained funny as to how one becomes a scholar by critiquing the works of another scholar. In mathematics, no one gives a damn, if you re-prove, or provide a new proof of a celebrated theorem. Yes, the norms of originality and scholarship are poles apart, and they should be!

One professor plans on writing a manual on the SUVs, and the other a book on the Dragons, as seen in the folklores of Indo-China. When I noted his plans of visiting Kerala, India, it tickled me. There were interesting proposals from engineering, computer science, MIS, management, and psychology. Some claim to do more than feasible, but a few may achieve more. Most of the proposals are interdisciplinary and collaborative in nature.

It is interesting to touch upon the word 'sabbatical' derived from Greek or Hebrew. Sabbath means 'rest on the seventh day'. It has some Biblical meanings too. That is why a faculty member is eligible to go on leave only after completing six years (one applies at the end of five years). The public may think it is extravagant to grant such leaves to professors, when they hardly put the type of hours the store clerks do. Sabbatical leave is never granted for going to the beaches and drink beer. It is granted to finish viable research projects requiring undivided concentration of mind that is not possible during an academic year. Creation of new knowledge is the most difficult of all human endeavors!

However, sabbatical leave does not require that one must travel to other places and foreign countries. It may be essential for making some rare observations in particular spots on earth, or collecting unique data. The modern technology has definitely brought books, journals, and human interaction at the clicks of a mouse.

Twenty-five years ago, when I first served on this Committee, either I was not sensitive to other's research, or too wrapped up in my own tenure and promotions that I have no good recollections. But UNLV is forging ahead into a research university. There are new signs of quality and quantity in research. Finally, the Committee only makes the recommendations; the ultimate decision rests with the Provost. It is a good committee in the sense, there is always a lot to learn and be informed.

Oct 22, 2008/Oct, 2015

COMMENTS

Hi Satish: Greetings! Your reflection on 'sabbatical' is thoughtfully conceived as also the work of the committee that deliberates on diverse applications. The outside world doesn't have an iota of understanding about sabbaticals; frankly, those outside the academic don't have to know or understand. Good luck with your ongoing efforts at bringing to light esoteric topics. **Moorty**

60. A PROFESSIONAL MILESTONE
(A Note to my Colleagues)

Since last week, after reading e-mails from Derrick and David on their seeking the chairmanship of the Department, a few thoughts have run through my mind. First, I must congratulate Ho, not only for successfully completing the first 3-year term instituted in 1997, but also for steering the Department during tumultuous times within and without - in the College and Central Administration. Since he has not informed the Department about not seeking the second term, the door may have been left open.

Both Derrick and David have deservingly faculty support, hopefully, of non-intersecting groups of faculty members. Naturally, it made me wonder that no one has asked me to go for it. May be 'Out of sight means out of mind' has factored into this thinking. Ever since joining the Department, in 1974, I have fully supported every chairman for reasonable lengths of their tenures, and never worked against them.

Do I have an appetite for or experience of administration? In the very beginning of my professional career in India, I was really assumed to become an administrator. The cultural shift from India to the US mainly derailed me from that course for a long time. The younger faculty may not know, and others may have forgotten that I was the first Associate Chair to the 3-year term Chair, started in 1997. Also, I served as Associate Dean (Academics) for 2003-06 and Acting Director of College's Master of Arts in Science Program (2004-06).

The Chair needs to have communication skills, particularly verbal. He/ She has to be a good listener and be able to stand up and down when needed whether in the Department, College, or up to the 7th Floor. Well, you be a better judge on me for these attributes.

The most important consideration is of fairness and its conjugate trait, vindictiveness. In a democratic set up, a person is always elected by majority. But once elected, then he/she is the Chair, or President etc. of everyone in the group. Going after the non-supporters or wholesale favoritism to the supporters are the last acts that I would ever resort to.

There is no question that the department chairmanship is a springboard to higher administration, be that a deanship. Let me clearly state, with due modulo, that I 'intend' to serve for one term only, unless burnt-out sooner, like it happened once.

A question may be asked why one term? Didn't Ho find three years enough? I think the Department is still on an unsteady course. It is not fully out of the woods yet, as the phrase goes. Another Ho-like term will bury the ugly past from the administrative memories.

So here is my bit from overseas, in case, some one has not noticed my absence. This note is not my throwing my hat in the ring – it is just an exploration. It is certainly meant to gauge faculty support. I have not called or e-mailed anyone. Conversely, if no one throws support behind me, then it is over forever! Well, it has turned out to be a *Reflection* on seeking support for chairmanship! Of course, any chairmanship would provide a lot of material for *Reflections*.

If someone prematurely wants to know my position on the contentious issues of hiring or developing graduate areas, then for the doctorate, with two doctorates already awarded in Statistics and Applied Mathematics, these two areas will be pushed for the next three years. However, with growing interest in the Teaching Concentration of the MS Program and its high rate of employability, at least one more faculty in mathematics education needs to be hired.

Thanks.

Feb. 14, 2009 (Nizwa, Oman)

(PS: Nov, 2015. On not hearing from any faculty, I decided not to run for this election.)

61. MATCHING UP UNLV AND UN
(Note to Chancellor Ahmed Alrawahi)

This note is a follow-up to our conversation in the cafeteria about how 50-year old University of Nevada Las Vegas (UNLV) and 5-year old University of Nizwa (UN) can collaborate and enrich their environments. Being at UNLV since 1974 and at the UN for over three months, it uniquely qualifies me for this academic match making!

1. UNLV has one of the most active **Extended Education Programs** in the US offering non-credit and credit courses to meet the specific needs of their clients. During summer months, regular courses are also run through this division. Nearly 10,000 students register in courses offered in flexible formats. Since 50 UN students went to UK last year and 50 are scheduled to go to the US, perhaps in Madison, Wisconsin this year, UNLV is worth exploring for its innovative programs.

2. According to the media reports, the Sultanate of Oman is one of the popular tourist-friendly countries in Middle East. Since I live in a flat of Hotel Al Diyar, I witness hoards of Europeans tourists checking in and out every week. It perfectly matches with world famous **UNLV's College of Hotel Administration**. Any courses, related with marketing, management and multimedia communication of tourism and hospitality can be taken at UNLV. Las Vegas is the tourist Mecca of the world, drawing more than 40 million visitors a year. Of the ten largest hotels in the world, seven are in Las Vegas.

3. UNLV's **Entertainment Engineering program** is one of its kinds the world, where fine arts, high-tech engineering and computer technology confluence. The students of arts and engineering at UN can have non-traditional insights into their disciplines. Modulo 20-degree latitude, the topography of Las Vegas and Nizwa are identical. UNLV's **Hydrology Program** in Geosciences addresses water related issues too.

4. I get an impression that the **Nursing program** at the UN has a rocky start in terms of instruction, training and placement of students. UNLV also went through these birthing crises 30 years ago. Since they are professional programs, I am not fully conversant with the details, but UNLV's nursing program and the top-notch hospitals in Las Vegas area

can find a platform of collaboration. Related with nursing is an area of public health, which has a young graduate program in **Public Health**. I am already impressed with high Omani standards in public health, as enforced in Nizwa municipality.

These four areas of collaboration have many sub areas to meet the needs of traditional and non-traditional students. I would be happy to sit with you or a VC to work out the details. I am also keeping the UNLV Administration including the President David Ashley and VP & Provost, Neil Smatresk informed of these initiatives. With greetings and regards,

April 25, 2009

PS: 09/12/2015
The office of the chancellor of the UN corresponds to that of the president of UNLV.

62. OMANIS READY FOR UNLV!
(Reflective Note to the Provost, Neal Smatresk)

Hi Neal, UNLV does not have to come to Oman, as the Omanis want to come to UNLV! It is time of the year when the Legislature is about to take tough financial decisions. This is the third time that financial crises have hit the State. Despite them, UNLV has made great strides. Here is a good news. Chancellor Alrawahi told me yesterday that he would willing to send the UN students to UNLV, during the summer months, provided out-of-state fee is waived. The main reasons being that the selected students are not from well-off families and are unable to pay this 6K dollars on the top of airfare, board and lodging.

I present this scenario as a part of a big and small picture. The small picture is that UNLV gets new students at a time of falling enrollments. Revenue, coming from overseas, would stimulate the state economy. Also, the Omani students staying in the dorms would alleviate its vacancy problems.

Oman is one of the 22 Gulf Coast Countries (GCC). They have their own political, religious, and economical organizations. Of course, most are oil rich. The point is that the Omani students attending UNLV will do good PR in the GCC. The big picture is what President Obama has spoken in Turkey this month. He assured the Muslims world that the US was not their enemy. UNLV can be more positive by welcoming the Omani Arab students and allow them to take courses at a special 'in-state' rate.

During the last 35 years at UNLV, I have spent 2+1+0.5 academic years in India, 2+0.5 years in Malaysia and now a semester (0.5) in Oman. One observation is that the American education remains the hottest product in the world. The UN is administrative set on a pattern of a University of Wisconsin campus. The textbooks are shipped from the US! It is an interesting story by itself.

There is bigger picture. Being a history buff, I think what the missionaries did for the expansion of European civilizations in the 16th and 17th century, the US educators are doing it for the American Civilization. Educators like me are the foot soldiers and missionaries of the yore. When American universities impart education by setting up programs and institutions overseas, or educate the foreign students in the US, they are really selling American way of thinking. I see it clearly in my own life after coming to Indiana University in 1968, particularly, when compared with my Indian friends who never left India for the USA.

The UN students are only the second-generation college students of Oman. They are potential leaders in every aspect of Omani life. It is a great long-term investment. You have an opportunity to plant Americana in the minds of young Omanis, when they attend UNLV. Let me also add, that Chancellor did his undergraduate work in North Carolina and doctorate from Berkeley. He served as agriculture minister. The point is, if he ever quits UN, UNLV will stand to gain from a different point in Oman. Since I plan on leaving Oman by May end; therefore, any Memorandum Of Understanding should be quickly drafted and negotiated for action.

All the best!

April 28, 2009 (Oman)

PS: 09/12/15
Partly due to Las Vegas culture, UNLV was not chosen for the young UN students.

63. A REWARD OF TEACHING!

"Dear Dr Bhatnagar, I'm not sure if you would remember me. I was one of your students in Shah Alam, Malaysia in 1992. I went to Tucson & did BA in Math from the Univ. of Arizona, graduated in 1994. I came back & taught in Malaysia for a while, and got married, then went to do M.Ed. at the Univ. of Ottawa, graduated in 2003. I'm a PhD candidate at The University of Melbourne. My study is on secondary mathematics teachers' assessment practice in Victoria, Australia. Having met some of the great math teachers here, I reflect back on those math teachers who made a difference in my life, and of them is you. I'm writing to you just let you know that. Enjoy your life, great to know that you r now in LV, & have two grand kids! I am now a mother of four growing sons. Life is full of wonders. Kind regards; Rohani Mohamad IU-93".

It makes my day whenever, such a note or e-mail suddenly crops up. Teaching is different from the point of view of 'customer satisfaction' (short or long term?). One does talk about teaching in an era of public accountability and quality assurance. No matter how hard I try to reach each student by knowing their names, majors and connecting them out individually, there is always at least one student who remains turned off by my style. It took me years to reconcile with this aspect of human nature. It is no different from what generally is observed in life – no one food, movie, or song is equally liked by everyone. In other words, the impact of a book, or effectiveness of a medicine is not uniform. Human individuality can manifest itself in extreme outcomes.

During 1992-94, I was a visiting professor of Indiana University, which ran a 10-year undergraduate program for Malaysia's Ministry of Education. Since this e-mail flashed last night, I have been trying to re-construct Rohani's persona on a premise, if she was impacted by my persona, then its converse must hold to some extent. With all the mental powers harnessed for it, her image that emerged was of a fair complexioned, healthy girl from *kampong*. Physically, she was in contrast with most Malay youths who were darkish and thin.

With the exception of one male student, simply known as M, the good math students were all females. Yes, one girl was admitted to the University of Arizona (Tucson). Also, I vividly remember, her message once conveyed to me through her junior friend, that she had gotten nearly straight A's in the very first semester. It had filled me with joy at her thoughtfulness, and pride at her performance.

When I put myself in the role of a student, then the memorable tidbits that I had about some teachers were not the same, as they had of mine. In schools and colleges, the influence runs on a principle of flux moving from higher potential to lower potential. It is totally one-sided through middle schools, but becomes two-way, if it progressively moves to a doctoral level.

Rohani, thank you for making my day! It is credit worthy that math has stayed with you despite big changes in your marital life. You remind me of Mary Rudin, who as 'housewife' proved great theorems in point-set topology - while doing laundry, watching kids play out, and working in the kitchen. You may Google her name.

June 12, 2009/Oct, 2015

COMMENTS

This is indeed an e-mail to treasure...**Archna**

Congratulations on the respect and regard that you received. The trouble arises when the student thinks he is only a consumer whereas he is truly a product as well. Best regards, **Ajit Iqbal Singh**

Congratulations! Sure, we do as teachers make a great impact on our students. Your 'reflection' hits the nail on the heath, to use a cliché' for a change. Teaching is a fulfilling profession. **Moorty**

64. STAYING CONNECTED WITH THE UN
(A Note to Chancellor Ahmed Al-Rawahi)

Off and on, I have been e-mailing you items of particular interest to the University of Nizwa (UN). Any time, you decide to hire a Special Academic Advisor to the Chancellor (it is needed), it would be my pleasure to work with you and make UN a better institution.

This e-mail is a bit personal too. It is prompted by the acceptance of my paper at the writers' conference being held during Dec 12-15, 2009. The paper was submitted earlier when I was working at the UN, as this conference was then set to be held for April 12-15, 2009.

It so happened, that I have to attend the joint annual meeting of mathematics organizations in San Francisco, during Jan 13-17, 2010. So, I would miss this trip to Nizwa. However, I have requested a good friend, writer and English professor in Nizwa College of Applied Sciences, to present this paper on my behalf. It is a common professional practice, as the communication of ideas is more important.

As a Chief Patron of this Conference, I need your support to defray the registration fees (US$ 100), required, of my proxy. For your information, during Dec 20-23, 2008, I was fully hosted for a *History of Mathematics Conference* held in Manipur University, Imphal, India. As a matter of fact, it is time that the UN hosts a similar conference on the *Contributions of Arab and Islamic Mathematicians*. I would be willing to help in organizing it.

An institutional practice is to pay for the registration fees for the local students and faculty members. Though I left UN five months ago, but my heart is still there! The campus date trees, social lunches in the cafeteria, conversations with staff while waiting for the bus and during rides, fragrance of Frankincense, and mystique of Omani men in *dishdashas* and women in *abayas* - they all haunt me, at times.

Let me also add that my name and that of UNLV in the Conference Program/Proceedings will enhance UN's image. First, someone is interested enough from far-off USA. Secondly, the Creative Writing

Program, housed in the English Department of UNLV, is currently ranked Number 5 in the nation.

Therefore, it is win-win situation. I look forward to your quick response, so that I can start preparing the proxy for my presentation. With regards,

Nov 04, 2009

PS: It is marked to Dr Mohammed Ismail, who still may be the Dean & Vice Chancellor of Academic Affairs.

Sep, 2015: By and large, the Omani administrators keep a distance from the faculty, as they are mostly from foreign countries and hired on two-year contracts. I never got any response. The academic culture of a university in the US is diametrically opposite to the prevailing states in the universities of all Gulf countries.

65. ACADEMIC SACRIFICIAL LAMBS

Last week, the office of the EVP & Provost announced the elimination of some master's degree programs and a center. A Joint Evaluation Team (JET) is reviewing all the programs both academic and non-academic. UNLV is facing the severest budgetary crises; worse than hit during 1991-1993, as I can recall. The Governor's office is projecting tougher financial times ahead. An emergency legislative session may be called in January.

The college reports, as presented to the JET, are understandably written in 'defensive' modes. During the Holiday Party, I had a small talk with Carl Reiber, the Associate Dean. I asked, "Where is the College list of the sacrificial lambs?" It may not be released right way, but it has to be played out like the cards in a Poker game. After the conversation, I posed this question to myself. Having been here for 35 years, I felt incumbent to have a perspective too. Well, here are potential College sacrificial lambs; a starting point for the Executive Committee to work around.

1. Twenty-year old MAS Program. Three years ago, the dean unilaterally stopped new enrollment in the program. I had spent a year (2004-05) in broadening it from a diluted master's program in biology. It does not have a core of courses drawn from each dept. Any way, it is Number 1 on the chopping block, if it would save any money – at least it is symbolic.

2. Math, Science and Education Center. It was created in 2004, when Ron Yasbin took over the deanship. I do not want to go into its background. Initially, I was involved in it too. A funny thing, recently discovered, is about the status of the Center; whether approved or not by the Board of Regents.

3. The professional staff positions of Bill Brown, Joseph Nika and Nicole Booker were all created by dean's executive decisions. The UNLV Foundation shared Bill's position for the first year. There was a spousal consideration too.

4. Prune the Advising Center. Ron expanded its role by taking away the advising of junior and senior majors/minors from the departments. Now, the faculty has no interaction with undergrad majors – whatsoever. Can

a corresponding scenario exist at the graduate level? Advising Center is efficient in freshmen/sophomore advising, holding of college functions, and doing graduation check-ups.

5. Specialized centers. It is kind of corollary to # 2. There is a proliferation of centers at UNLV, and they seem to work like individual fiefdoms. The College centers need to be scrutinized for their financial transactions, contracts and reasons for their creation. Some centers may be like mathematical theorems proved in empty sets, or data on the mountains, stars and viruses that don't even exit. The reference of such a center in official communications may be sending a wrong message to the outside community.

On a somber cosmological plane, we are all sacrificial lambs! (Shakespeare said it so.)

Dec 21, 2009

PS: Dec, 2015: The Number 1 survived, as it was not a part of any budget line; no idea of Number 2; Number 3 and 4 partly held up. Number 5 was not much in a conversation; however, each university center is now evaluated every three years.

66. IN THY NAME – RESEARCH!
"A Study for Women 18-29 Regarding Pain and Sexual Intercourse

"Women 18-29, do you experience pain during sexual intercourse? If so, you may be eligible to participate in a study examining cognitive processes in sexual pain. If you participate in this short study, you will be offered a free consultation with an expert in sexual pain regarding information about the condition and treatment options. Please call Lea at 378-0987 or e-mail her at thalerl@unlv.nevada. edu . This study, under the direction of Dr. Marta *Meana, Department of Psychology, has been approved by the UNLV OPRS (Office of Protective Research Subjects). Lea Thaler* Email: *thalerl@unlv.nevada. edu* Phone: 702-378-0987.»

This announcement, in today's on-line daily publication, *UNLV Today*, stunned me for a while. Every year, the media lists crazy funded research projects. But, the researchers stand by their values and fiercely defend their pursuits. It is an eternal debate! Having lived in Las Vegas, I see raw sex permeating life at every level. My immediate reaction was - like when you suddenly discover one day, that your neighbor has been making his living as a mafia front man or is a registered child molester.

The USA was born after cutting all its umbilical ties with Europe - from political to social structures. In the 1940s, Bertrand Russell ridiculed the US universities for teaching courses like basket weaving. It has become a metaphor. At the same time, look where the US universities stand today, as compared with that of other countries. In a list of top 100 universities in the world, 60 are American including 20 public (state supported) – like, UCLA and Berkeley.

Americans have absolutely added a new dimension to the meanings of education and research. Under the constitutional right of *Freedom of Expression*, the teens in public schools put contraceptives over cucumbers during mandatory sex education classes. The society has no bounds on sexuality and its practices. There is a belief that anything done or understood can be done or understood in a far better manner after some research is conducted on it. This research project may be testing psychological hypotheses on pain during intercourse. In Indian and

Middle Eastern cultures, no one will even talk about this subject openly. What a difference in cultures!

Incidentally, the departments of mathematics and psychology have been in the same building for years. Obviously, my one-time initiative in a joint program in mathematical psychology did not go far, as the faculty interest are either in clinical or counseling – the areas far removed from mathematics. Marta Meana's research has the support of her colleagues and of the university. She has received research grants. The US continues to shock me even after 40+ years and despite having watched explicit radio and TV shows - like that of Jerry Springer and Howard Stern.

The lower age of the volunteers is set at 18, but the majority of the US girls are sexually active by the age of 13. The physiological reasons for coitus pains are often surgically correctable. Talking of surgery, there is a 'reverse' surgery too, of narrowing the vaginal entry dilated due to multiple births and varied piston thrusts. Its purpose is to enhance the pleasure during sexual intercourse.

There is no dull day, when you are on the faculty of a US university. Moreover, Las Vegas adds additional spices in life!

Feb 09, 2010

PS: Oct, 2015: Marta Meana has since moved into administration – served as a special advisor to the President, and is currently the Dean of the Honors College.

COMMENTS

Dear Satish, While I was reading your fine composition it occurred to me that sex here in USA is much more open and exposed than in other parts of the world. And talking about sex at appropriate times and in appropriate places is much more fun than keeping it silent and hushed. Yes, it is titillating and exciting. Fun is the name of the game. **Dutchie**

Dyspareunia has both medical and psychological causes. It is a real medical condition and is not a crazy funded research product. **Rahul**

Dear Satish, I am amazed also. The problem is that the purpose of a US university is to act like a company and make money. We support all sorts of activities, which have absolutely nothing to do with academics such as football and basketball for one. We sell degrees. It does not matter if the client has actually learned anything. The purpose of an American university is to hire as many non-academics as possible and improve the gross national product. We are the land where capitalism is gone mad and nobody knows it, a bad gene pool! Best, **Bob**

Recently, I have been placed as a medical student in hospitals/clinics located in very poor areas with high crime rate. The demographic group I deal with is 90% African American, and another part of town 90% Puerto Rican. The number of teenagers that are sexually active and that have already conceived a sexually transmitted disease is alarming, and they are already seeking advice for planned parenting. What is even more shocking is that many of these teenage patients (age 13-18) seek advice from me about prenatal care, process of conception, and the risks/medical management of their STD, yet still seek sexual intercourse from myself, their doctor.

The culture and way of thinking is really different in these areas. As I have discussed with my colleagues about patient's attempting to develop a sexual relationship with their physician relates to how the patient reacts psychologically. I believe it is because when a male physician demonstrates concern for their patient, they react and feel they have to give back in a sexual manner. It is because in these low socioeconomic areas male sexual abuse and physical abuse is really high, not to mention the increase in prostitution. This study about pain during intercourse disgusts me even more. Research dollars for this could and should go towards something else. **Sundeep Srivastava**

This should raise many a person's eyebrows! **Abraham**

PERSONAL REMARKS

67. PROFESSORSHIP: A BENCHMARK
(Reflective Feedback on the Dean)

My recommendation on Tao Pang became easier after going through the CVs of only two applicants for the position of associate dean. The deciding factor being that Tao has been a full professor since 2002, whereas, Javier was recently promoted to the associate rank in 2008. **Why full professorship is that important?** There are a number of pressing reasons. Above all, tenured (full) professorship, by and large, establishes the academic integrity of the faculty, and it transfers to the department and college.

Expanding on professorship a bit more, UNLV, transitioning into a research university, has been set back by tsunami budget crises. It may take many years to get back to where the university budget was on July 01, 2007. The hiring of new research faculty is nearly out of question. Increased class sizes and teaching loads adversely affect research activities. Unfortunately, over the years, the positions of dept chair and associate dean have been used to get promoted to the full rank. It is time to dispel even its perception from the CoS - the research engine of UNLV.

Currently, Javier is active in research. At this rate, he will be promotable to full rank. In the buzz world of ethnic diversity, Javier is Hispanic. For years, Afro-Americans alone have raised personal issues on the campus. The recent hiring of VP Diversity is a prime example. The Hispanic lobby is growing vocal. Keeping Javier on the track for full professorship is good for the Dept, College and UNLV. Lately, there have been high-level discussions on encouraging associate professors to step up towards professorship. Anyways, you may like to update the ethnic profile of CoS faculty under your watch: in terms of tenure track, tenured, and professors.

Tao, currently being the Physics Chair, also understands the College from different angles. On paper, he stands out, unless he fumbles during the open interview. I have watched Javier organizing the annual Juanita White Lecture a couple of times. It is not easy for him to communicate in front of a large audience. But I never had an occasion to observe Tao. For open interviews, because of my schedule, I had to miss Javier's' QA, but found Tao OK.

Tao may bring in an interesting conduit. During the college dean search last spring, Physics Department remained largely 'indifferent'. I was not on the Search Committee, but I did attend all open sessions and gathered information from other representatives. Perhaps, you too may have sensed it during the campus interviews. So, having Tao on board may help you understand the dynamics of the Physics Department. Who knows, it may be your home one day.

By not selecting Javier, you may be helping him grow further in research. Otherwise, he may 'grieve' in future, if professorship is denied to him. He may grieve on the ground that the AD's administrative responsibilities hurt his research output!?

Nov 02, 2010

68. AN ACADEMIC AMERICANA

Teaching evaluation is a hallmark of American colleges and universities. Someone may like to research into the history of its origin. Broadly speaking, periodic evaluation is an American way of life. Every day in the mail and online, one finds surveys for evaluating various products and services. One may even win prizes by responding to some of them. The underlined thrust is constant improvement of quality.

For instance, three months ago, I attended an NSF course in Cambodia. After its completion on the 10th day, the course was evaluated. Thus, its next offering in Aug, 2011 will be better. Another scenario is closer to home. During this semester, I went on to two hikes through UNLV's division **of Outdoor Adventures**. At the end of each trip, we filled out a short 5-question evaluation form.

This trail of thought struck my mind, as it is time in fall semester when the students evaluate the courses. At UNLV, it is mandated by the Board of Regents. However, it is up to the Administration and individual instructors, as to how to use the data for any statistical analysis. With shrinking attention span, briefer an evaluation instrument and limited in scope, far more effective it is going to be. The current 19-point form applicable to five diverse departments in the College of Sciences (CoS) is tedious. Students are turned off at the sight of it, and thus their feedback is generally hasty –and not very reliable.

Personally, objective evaluation by students is very helpful, provided bias is removed in its administration. Five years ago, as Associate Dean of the CoS, I assisted in the development of a 10-point guideline. On a personal note, in any evaluation round, there is a student who circles F in every evaluating category. Perhaps, it balances out the one who rates me as the best instructor ever! Mathematically speaking, given an instructor, there exists a student who berates his/her instructor. Therefore, I admire the teaching of one or two of my colleagues, who provide a counter example. They have gotten 4.0 on a 4-point scale in classes of size of 30+ students.

Some cultural features are worth sharing from personal experiences. During Spring-2009, I taught at the University of Nizwa, Oman, modeled after a University of Wisconsin campus. The company, that sold online teaching evaluation system to UNLV, sold it in Oman too! However, the teaching evaluation data is not shared with faculty. It may be used to renew or not renew the 2-year contracts of faculty, which are 100 % expatriates. There is no job security of US tenure or Indian confirmed job. However, the higher administration is all Omani.

Whenever, the American universities are contracted to set up colleges/ universities in developing countries, the teaching curricula and evaluation are on the US pattern. I observed it twice (1992, 98), in MUCIA, a consortium of Midwestern universities, when it set up colleges in Malaysia. I was an Indiana University visiting faculty.

However, my experience at my Indian Alma Mater, Panjab University Chandigarh, was different. I taught there during 1980-82. There was/still is a cultural factor - that teachers are above scrutiny, and do no wrong – hence no teaching evaluation! Here at UNLV, as soon as I turn in my grade reports, I cannot wait to see students' evaluation of my teaching. In a way, I may be living at an 'extreme', as I have all teaching evaluation sheets of all the courses taught since Fall-1974. Time has come to dispose them off before the Fire Marshal warns me of the paper piles as fire hazard!

Dec 02, 2010/Sep, 2015

COMMENTS

Oh, never mind the papers on fire, you are "on fire" with your enthusiasm. Hugs from **Dutchie**

I was so happy to see that, in Math 096, we are back to hard-copy instead of electronic. I think we get much more feedback and student participation this way. **Charlie Allen**

69. SELDOM IN SYNC!
(A Reflective Note to the President)

Two days ago, the Trafford Publishing sent me posters, postcards and bookmarkers of my first book, *Scattered Matherticles: Mathematical Reflections, Volume I*. I thought the Lied Library had an exclusive space for displaying the faculty books – instead, it has one for all. As an incidental corollary, it was discovered that a showcase displaying books by campus authors has been discontinued for budgetary reasons! It did not make sense, as some showcases have been there since Lied Library opened up in 2001. At times, functioning of academic bureaucracy remains mysterious. In fairness, let me add that the Lied Library acquired my book as soon as it was brought to their attention.

Today, this saga seems to have converged with other streams. Once I told a friend that publishing a book at age of 70+ gives the same euphoria that a man gets in fathering a child. I felt high when this book was published in Nov, 2010. Naturally, I looked forward to the Provost's reception of the campus authors – a tradition going on for years. Perhaps, this little cheese and wine reception has been axed during a round of budget cuts.

Last spring, while browsing UNLV's Barnes and Noble Bookstore, I glanced over a permanent rack displaying books by the campus authors - mine was absent. On pointing it out to a staff member, I was assured of a copy of my book placed there. A month later, when I happened to browse the Bookstore, it was still not on there! Its absence has nothing to do with the university budget cuts and bureaucracy. Perhaps, it is my luck or that of my book for not getting noticed.

But it really raises a pertinent question of scholarly works bringing name to UNLV at a time, when its programs are going to be more focused on research and scholarship. Each year, the university spends a couple of million$$ for faculty travels and research. Whereas, a book publication adds to the stature of individual faculty, at the same time, it enhances UNLV's image too.

Being in a reflective mood, this line of thought was extrapolated. No matter what - UNLV has been good to me. I have completed 37 years, and all my three kids graduated from it. This book issue would be forgotten when the next book comes out this year. Yes, I am a late bloomer in the field of publication. Recently, I told my grandson, studying in American University, Washington DC: "Do not read or quote books written by untenured professors, as they have caused too much of both print pollution and research dilution."

Interestingly, there is an element of irony between my book and my salary. It was under the Harter Administration, the present policy of giving 10% raises in salary at the time of tenure or/and promotion was adopted in 1996. I missed it out on this 10% raise twice, as I was tenured in 1977 and promoted to the full rank in 1990. Thus, I may be the lowest paid active (full) professor at UNLV. I won't mind this dubious distinction, if it is officially recognized!

July 29, 2011

70. MAKING MAY MEMORABLE!
(A 'Squared' Reflective to the President)

CLOSURE TIME!
PART I

Six years ago, during an administrative workshop (***LEAP***), I heard it said that the presidency of a college in the best job in America. But, at times - like, hiring a Provost, it can become very political and stressful. Being committed to UNLV, it is incumbent upon me to provide you some thoughts on it so that you take a decision that you can look back at it with a degree of satisfaction. Some complexity of this search is a part of a big picture.

Why a pool of 160+ applicants was so weak? The answer is the national image of UNLV - tarnished since 2005-06, when the Chancellor fired both UNLV and UNR presidents, and hurriedly hired their replacements in five months. This saga continues to this date, and no one knows how long it would persist. In this chaos, the only right decision was of President Ashley's hiring you as his Provost.

What is next? If the position were not filled, it would reflect on you. You could have a person of your choice nominated for this position. I sense you did not want to interfere with the section process. Under the circumstances, it is time to look at the internal candidates. I am impressed that Michael has taken himself out of it. However, I told him that he was destined to return to the 7th floor within five years!

In UNLV's 55-year history, internal candidates have done equally effective jobs. In the 1970s, the outsider VP for Academic Affairs (Not called Provost through the 70s) Gentile wanted to leave soon after he was hired. Insider Ray Alden was like a lapdog of the President. On the other hand, the team of President Maxson and insider Provost Unrue was great for the first ten years. Both were thrown out, when they became imperious after ousting popular coach Tarkanian.

Who is the best inside candidate? There may be a chair, but I won't jump over the deans. Amongst the deans, most are interims and raw – except, Jeff and Chris. It makes a decision easy. Jeff must be doing something right to survive for 16 years. Chris will work out equally, but he carries an air of aloofness that may not sit well with some deans and faculty at large.

There is no question that both of them are stronger than the outside finalists. Supposedly, your contract coming for renewal in fall, it then means that the new provost and you will have good reasons to work together and win over the campus community.

On not-a-lighter note, do get input from your wife, but the decision has to be totally yours. Sleep over it for a night before making it public. You will do well as long as you keep the long-term UNLV's image in mind. It is not easy, as you have faced and deflected criticisms over the previous two VP appointments. With focus on UNLV's image alone, you can keep the women lobby, Afro-American lobby and Latino lobby at bay. Luckily, there is no campus API lobby.

Good luck follows sound decisions!

May 12, 2012/Dec, 2015

PART II

You may be fresh to receive anticipated recommendations from the Search Committee this week. You will have a weekend to mull it over – and mull you must, unless pressed otherwise.

In my memories, this was the best provost search in the sense of fairness and openness. Why? Initially, there was no internal candidate amongst the pool of 160+ applicants. As it turned out that only two finalists were generally acceptable, but neither overwhelmingly over the other. At this juncture, it was an excellent decision to include internal candidates.

Since Anna Sosa has withdrawn her name, John White stands out shoulder and above Keith Young. Caroline Yucha exposed her weak spots during open forum with faculty and staff. She and Harold Jones are not too far apart from each other.

In John White, you have an additional legal mind in litigious times. Let me add that earlier, I had discounted the deans of the Dental, Health

Sciences and Law, as traditionally and holistically, they are viewed 'lesser' than the ones in humanities, sciences and business etc. But there is always an exception.

I hear that John White is half White and half Black/Afro-American, but he is not tied down ideologically.

May 20, 2012/Dec, 2015

Epilog: On 05/24/2012, President announced the selection of John White as the next EVP & Provost.

71. FACULTY AWARDS & RECOGNITIONS
(A Reflective Note to the Provost and President)

A human life is measured by rewards and punishments. In academe, there are mostly awards, though smaller and fewer. At UNLV, since the 1980s, the number of awards has increased arithmetically! For instance, when I joined it in 1974, there was not even a single faculty award - whatsoever, in my department, college; and to the best of my memory, none at the university and system levels too. UNLV, founded in 1957, even the Alumni Association had not established its first award then. The 'universal' sabbatical leaves, being no longer automatic in the seventh year, are based on scholarship.

In 1984, the College of Sciences instituted its first award, and it was for distinguished teaching, which I won it in 1986. The College then included the engineering faculty too. Subsequently, College research (1990) and service (2000) awards were added. Again, on a personal note; the Service award came to me in 2004, but the Research award is on a wait list!

The prestige of any award and its awardees are equally enhanced, if the selection process is unbiased, transparent, and its criteria and selectors are fully known in advance. For example, the criteria and process of sabbatical awards are very clear - including the committee membership and its intense deliberations. However, in most university awards, nothing seems open. It does not look good for UNLV aspiring to rise to a Tier One university.

For example, last year, I applied for a senior Barrick award for the first time. It is prestigious enough that generally full professorship follows it, or conversely. It may be viewed as double dipping. In extreme scenarios, the same portfolio may win even 3-4 awards - including merit and sabbatical.

In my case, full professorship is 20+ years old. I thought my record would win Barrick award 'hands down', as I had four books published in four different genres in two years, though in the making for several years. However, utter confusion set in during the application process – mainly between nominators and referees, etc. **Its unheard feature is that the committee is formed after the application deadline!** The bizarre finale was that the committee formation, portfolio evaluations, and intimation of awards by the Provost office were all done **within one week** after the deadline! It is a joke on the awards and awardees - based on my recent experience on sabbatical leave committee - its month-long meetings and thorough deliberations.

Many eyebrows were raised when a college dean (ineligible) and former senior advisor to the President got one of the two senior awards. The other senior award went to an engineering faculty member, who served as Graduate Coordinator - a time consuming position. I know it as my research suffered when I was the Associate Dean of the College (2003-06) and Math Dept. graduate coordinator in the 1990s.

This Barrick award scenario is topped by the 2013 university distinguished professorship conferred upon a department chair serving for over three years. On the other hand, my Department Chair has put his full professorship on hold for at least six years. A distinguish professor being elected as department chair is laudable; but a sitting chair getting distinguished professorship is questionable – if not deplorable. What does it tell all? A lot – including no disciplinic diversity amongst the awardees – based on the examination of all the awardees.

After six months of these thoughts playing over my mind, I felt it was time to share the entire enchilada of awards. The Provost in his first year into the job has already started looking into many 'small', but important things, which were not attended to before.

Do I have an axe to grind? Yes and No. Raising the academic integrity is foremost. Bestowing Barrick Award on me could also herald recognition to interdisciplinary scholarship at UNLV. Likewise, University Teaching award could recognize my unprecedented record of having taught of 60+ different courses and honors seminars. In a current academic culture, faculty retire after teaching only 6-8 different courses in lifetime. There is a statistical 'theorem': For a professor, the sum of the number of published research papers and the number of different courses taught is constant.

By the nature of the academe, faculty thrive in narrow strips of professionalism - as measured by research, teaching and service. Interdisciplinary research and teaching would remain a buzzword, as its very foundation in doctoral work remains narrow. However, it took me 20+ years to break away from the conditioning of doctoral student mindset and discover my potential as a writer of innovative books. Above all, any kind of diversity is strongly linked with recognition of intellectual diversity.

Rounding it up, it is not easy for committee members to think out of the box. Thus, I may be a victim of my uniqueness! At a short end of my professional life, the inner satisfaction of my work eventually overrides any short-term disappointment. At the same time, I do not want any other multi-dimensional scholar going unrecognized in future. It is worth correcting it. These ideas welled up in my mind while attending the Annual Recognition function a month ago.

May 24, 2013/Dec, 2015

PS Dec, 2015: Nothing was heard from the President or Provost. Since then, they have been replaced by both new President and Provost. Turn over at the top administration is very high in the US universities.

72. BRIGHT SPOTS & DARK SPOTS

The merit list of staff, faculty and administrators has been out for a few days now. Over the years, my immediate reaction to it has undergone changes. Mathematically speaking, it has moved away from 'local' to 'global'. Local means that as soon as one gets the list, one looks at the awards of one's colleagues, and then of the so-called friends in other departments and colleges – that is global. It creates a lot of heart burn. But, in the long run, it may be a good neurological stimulant!

This year, I went off the track. Incidentally, I have completed 40 years at UNLV. Yes, I joined it in 1974. I said to myself - let me measure my 'productivity' with respect to the faculty members in other departments who have completed at least 30 years; if there was none in a department, then I took the number closest to 30 – all faculty in the College of Sciences only. Here are eight more faculty members. The administrative faculty are not included:

In **Biology**: Penny Amy (1985); **Chemistry**: Vernon Hodge (1982), Larry Tirri (1976); **Geoscience**: Steve Rowland (1978); **Mathematics**: Sadanand Verma (1967); **Physics**: Lon Spight (1970), Victor Kwong (1984) and James Selser (1981). According to the merit list, my award of $3000 to **nothing** $$ for each one of them seems incongruous – an anomaly!

That raises a few questions: What incentives are being offered to the 'senior' faculty to stop them from turning prematurely into proverbial fossils or deadwoods? For the last 25 years, the pendulum of faculty development has swung to one extreme – focusing on the new hires and young faculty. The new hires get huge start-up funds, various college and university awards (often multiple dipping), and even equity adjustments etc. It must be added that I nearly missed them all!

If this small sample suggests that overall performance does start waning after the age of 60, say, then some incentives and award structure can definitely slow it down – like, giving them consideration for sabbatical and faculty development leave, Regents', University and Barrick awards, etc.

Without such incentives, imagine such relatively 'unproductive' faculty staying on the job beyond the age of 60 for another 15-20 years, then what is their return to the institution, and to the taxpayers? By bringing this to your attention, I hope my sample observations at the Science College level is tested at least across the University. This is my way of re-building UNLV faculty at ground zero level. It surely would help UNLV for achieving Carnegie Tier I status.

Let me stress that this year's data is very unique in a sense that it covered academic records for six long years at least in these nine cases. Its message is loud and clear.

That is all.

Sep 21, 2014

SECTION III
NON-LINEAR EDUCATION

This section has twenty-seven reflections on myriad aspects of education, people and institutions. For example, my participation in the **PAYBAC** program of the local school district and UNLV organizing functions for the high school students and incoming freshmen students has generated several interesting write-ups (73, 78, 79, 82, 83, 88, 90). Again, there is a bit of intersection and overlapping of ideas between the *reflections* in this section and the ones in the other two sections.

Lately, my growing thesis is that education and scholarship can go on beyond the confines of classrooms and offices. I must add that in terms of the desire for public lectures, the US may be leading the world. In general, the US public has an insatiable appetite both for mundane information and for technical knowledge. At times, the visiting scholars are paid up to $25,000 plus expenses (75, 76, 81, 84, 86, 87, 98, 99). The money for such lectures comes from UNLV's private donors and Foundation.

Finally, there are some reflections (92 – 95), which were written when I was a visiting professor at the University of Nizwa, in the Sultanate of Oman. Looking back it after six years, it was an enriching experience personally. One can see how religion, culture and history of a region influence teaching, library collections, communication and professional expectations. The bottom line is that my admiration for the US higher education continues to rise up after each overseas trip. No wonder, the rest of the world tries to copy and modify the US models of education – from schools, colleges, to universities.

73. STEERING STUDENT CAREERS

Clark County School District (CCSD) is the eighth largest school district in the US. Under a **PAYBAC** program, an acronym for **Professional And Youth Building A Commitment**, professionals from various fields volunteer their time for the students. Some banks and companies encourage their managers to participate in it. Generally, there are fireman, cops, men and women in uniform from the US defense forces, engineers, businesspersons and women - active and retired persons. Again, they don't get paid anything for their time.

On a particular day, 10-15 experts visit a school, where they are given a warm reception and brief introduction of the day's activities. An assigned student escorts each speaker to his/her classroom during a particular hour – say, 9-10 AM. No visitor has any prior idea about the class level and subject period. It really does not matter, as one is not a substitute teacher! The mission is to motivate the students for staying in school and do their best to complete it. It is desirable, if a speaker conveys this motivational message from his own examples and experiences.

I have been a participant in this program for the last two years. It is very satisfying to share stories of my life and Indian roots with young minds. The students seem to like it. It is evidenced by the evaluation of each lecture done by the class teacher and students after the speaker has finished the presentation and left the classroom. A couple of weeks later, these evaluations are mailed out to each speaker.

In this article, I want to share a very interesting raw data with the readers of the *Sahi Buniyad*. Each student also fills out information on his **First Choice** and **Second Choice** of profession to be followed in life. For data management, the choices are removed and professions combined. The data that is included at the end is from four schools; two junior/middle schools (Grades 6-8) and two high schools (Grades 9-12). All the schools are public that in India means run by local/state government. Also, one high school is for adults, where the age could be any where from 17 to 71. The other high school is one of the two high schools in Las Vegas for students who after dropping out of the regular schools for a semester or two, decide to go back and finish the remaining course work. Under such conditions on the data, any conclusion should not be generalized too far.

I was really surprised to notice the breadth of the choices that run in the mind of the urban youth in Las Vegas. My thoughts naturally went back to my days in India of the 1950s, and also of Indians of my generation settled in the US, where the pressure on kids to become a medical doctor or engineer is still enormous. I am not drawing any conclusions from the following data. It is left for the readers to do their own analyses.

My personal opinion is that there are infinite number of outlets for human creativity to flow out. The schools are geared towards only for a dozen or so avenues. Both for the parents and teachers, it becomes incumbent to steer the kids, if possible, where the heads and hearts of the students are closer. Moreover, as the teens grow, their vision of future profession is most likely to change.

June 19, 2003/Sep, 2015

Junior/Middle School				**High School**	
1	Actress	2	1	Accounting	1
2	Architect	2	2	Actor	2
3	Ballet Dancer	1	3	Advertising	1
4	Band	1	4	Army	2
5	Band Singer	1	5	Artist	1
6	Baseball Player	1	6	Business Management	1
7	Clothe Designer	1	7	Computer Programmer	2
8	Criminal; Justice	1	8	Cook	1
9	Dentist	3	9	Cosmetologist	1
10	Doctor	10	10	Culinary Field	1
11	Elementary Teacher	1	11	Dancer	2
12	Fire Fighter	1	12	Dentist	1
13	Flower shop Owner	1	13	Doctor	1
14	Football Player	1	14	**Don't Know**	9
15	Hair Stylist	1	15	Electric Motor Repair	1
16	Judge	1	16	Football Player	2
17	Lawyer	8	17	Forensic Scientist	1
18	Marine Biologist	1	18	Garbage man	1
19	Math	1	19	Help Bad Kids	1
20	Motor Rider	1	20	Journalist	1
21	Music Teacher	1	21	Judge	1
22	Obstetrician	1	22	Law Enforcement	2
23	Owner baseball Academy	1	23	Lawyer	2
24	Paleontologist	1	24	Marines	1
25	Pediatrician	3	25	Marketing	1
26	Photographer	1	26	Massage Therapist	1
27	Pilot	1	27	Mechanic	1
28	Police	1	28	Medical	1
29	Politician	1	29	medical Assistant	1
30	Pro Skater	1	30	Medico	2
31	Singer	3	31	Modeling	2
32	Sports medicine	1	32	Mountain Cop	1
33	Starbuck Coffee worker	1	33	Music Composer	1
34	Teacher	8	34	Painter	1
35	Theme Park Engineer	1	35	Pediatrician	2
36	Therapist	2	36	Pharmacist	1
37	Travels	1	37	Physical Therapy	1
38	Vet Assistant	1	38	Psychology	1
39	Veterinarian	5	39	Public Relations	1
40	**Undecided**	14	40	Retail	1
			41	Sales	1
			42	Secretary/Clerk	1
			43	Teacher	2
			44	Teacher 1st Grade	1
			45	US Special operations	1
			46	Veterinarian	1
			47	Writer	1

74. INDIAN DIVERSITY 101

One success leads to the other. On 09/03/2003, I gave a public lecture on the *Monumental Caves of India: Ajanta and Ellora*. In the audience was a university official who contacted me afterwards to give a Diversity Workshop for the professional and classified employees. It pleased me to hear that my passion for the subject had hit a home run!

They are four thematic workshops in the series: Hispanic, Native Indians, Afro–American and Indians (from Indian subcontinent). Mine was the last one, as I was in India for two weeks - till Nov. 15. Today, I ran a workshop that went very well. I opened it with its newfound importance in the context of the **9/11 Attack on America**. Understanding cultural diversity is more than academic. Stories of my personal experiences at UNLV and that of my children were well received.

A workshop, by definition, means some hands-on experience during the period. After 15 minutes, I handed out the following Diversity Quiz. The objective was to have a dynamic and interactive approach. It proved very effective.

A FUN QUIZ ON INDIA AND INDIANS

1. If the US has a 300-500 year **old history**, then how old is India's history?

2. The population of India is **three times** that of USA, how big is India's territory?

3. The US has English as its **only official language**, what about the language in India?

4. Is English the **medium of instruction** in Indian universities?

5. What is the **ethnic and cultural diversity** in India as compared with that of the US?

6. Christianity is the **dominant religion** of the US, what about the major religion of India?

7. What is your **image** of a person **living in India**, and of a person of Indian origin **living in the USA?**

There were about 10 staffers from various units – International Office, Outreach, Student Development and Campus Police. The advantage of this 5-minute quiz was that on each topic I was able to gauge their background and that became a basis for discussion. Essentially, they got a crash course in diversity.

The last point was dwelled upon. The image of people living in India is of abject poverty. Its open sore and sewage melted them. But their eyes popped out when I told that out of nearly 10,000 Indians in Las Vegas, there are 250 physicians, 500 engineers, and 50 owners of motels, businesses, and other professionals. This makes Indians the richest ethnic group, not only in Las Vegas, but also in the USA.

The workshop concluded with a discussion on Indian students at UNLV. I differentiated the ones directly coming from India on student visas from the second generation Indians born and raised in the USA – in terms of their demeanor, accent and attitudes.

Nov 21, 2003/Oct, 2015

75. PROMOTING EXCELLENCE

It is time of the year when every household in the US is inundated with all kinds of charitable and non-profit organizations soliciting for contributions. The solicitation letters tell compelling stories of financial need and the works being done. There is no question that when it comes to giving time, energy, and money to causes of a local community, nation and international causes, few other nationals come close to the Americans. At the insistence of some supportive relatives and friends, I decided to share my following story:

As I was getting closer to my sixty, questions of 'my legacy' started looming over my mind. It also prompted me to think of giving back to the community. Five years ago, I decided to recognize academic excellence in the schools and colleges associated with my family in Bathinda (BTI). It was essentially driven by my entire life of success due to education that has enabled me to help several relatives, friends, and even strangers.

Early on, I realized that such a project in India cannot take off through phone calls and e-mails. During annual summer visits to India, along with local friends, I regularly met the school principals. Resistance encountered, in convincing the staff and principals to identify a distinguished teacher for one of the two awards, was unbelievable. To my dismay, I discovered that in India, if you want to feed 100 beggars for any occasion, it does not take 30 minutes to have them rounded up. But if you want to set up annual memorial awards, the schools and colleges are not welcoming. They simply want the money be handed over and no questions asked.

Anyway, in 2000, we were able to start academic awards in four schools in BTI. This idea, however, has not caught up with the local colleges yet! Two Bal Sarup Bhatnagar Memorial Awards were established in MHR H/S School, Bathinda. He is my maternal grandfather who settled in BTI after retirement in 1930. Four Bhagyawati Bhatnagar memorial awards were instituted in Arya Girls H/S School and Arya Model School. She is my mother who studied in a girls school in the 1920s, when it was not a regular school. Arya Samaj is the first organization in India to advocate for women's education. Arya Model School is a recent addition. Two awards in the memory of my deceased father, NS Bhatnagar were designated in Goodwill High School situated near the BTI railway station, where my father worked for over 20 years.

About the award criteria, the need factor is completely taken out. The Indians are too much hung on poverty. Once, I told in a school assembly, **"Be like an Olympian where a medal may be won or missed by one 100th of a second or by one 10th of an inch."** Thus it has been easy to select a top student. However, the principals buckle down in selecting a distinguished teacher of the year, knowing fully well that the Number Two in one year shall have a good shot at the Award next year.

Two years ago, a similar question possessed me on 'my legacy' at UNLV, which I joined in 1974. UNLV has been good to me, and has directly and indirectly affected the lives of 30 members of the extended Bhatnagar family in Las Vegas. For instance, my brother-in-law, his daughter and son – all three have graduated from UNLV. All three of my kids have graduated from UNLV. Besides, several other members of the extended Bhatnagar family have taken courses at UNLV.

Two years ago, my son, Avnish and I set up a **Bhatnagar Endowment Fund** with the **UNLV Foundation** for the annual **Bhatnagar Awards** in the memory of my father, who often spent more money on the education of his seven kids than his salary was. Since May 2003, the first two cash awards - one instituted for the top graduating **Math Major** and the other for top **Math Minor**, are being awarded – based on sheer excellence in math courses.

This is the ongoing story of my projects that have already touched the lives of some people. Personally, it has been a great journey in life so far. At 75, I am still with UNLV and feel at the top of my profession – having already published eight solo-authored books since turning 71.

Dec 14, 2003/Oct, 2015

76. COLONIAL SCHOLARSHIP PERPETUATES

Yesterday, my wife and I attended a lecture sponsored by the Asian Studies Program of the University of Nevada Las Vegas (UNLV). We were attracted by its title, *Reflections on the Buddha's Bump: Changing Perceptions of the Enlightened One* by Donald Lopez, Carl W. Belser Professor of Buddhist & Tibetan Studies, University of Michigan. Moreover, its abstract read: *"One of the distinguishing marks of the Buddha is the "crown protrusion" atop his head. Over the centuries, its true nature has been extolled by Buddhist monks in Asia and has vexed art historians in Europe and America. The lecture will relate the story of its interpretation and will speculate on its significance."*

While listening to the lecture, my mind kept going back and forth - from Lopez to the 19th century European scholars of oriental studies. Those scholars always had a colonial agenda whether they published books on Indology, translated Sanskrit scriptures into European languages, did archeological work, or brought educational 'reforms' in the colonies. The scholarly mission is only to perpetuate 'superiority' of western thinking.

I used to think that after independence, Indians, in particular, will wise up. Sometimes, political independence is easier to achieve. **Intellectual independence takes much longer, as it has to rise from an individual and flower at an institutional level**. Good academic institutions and think tanks may be started by governments, but unless there are some private institutions to lead and follow them, the process would remain in a chaotic flux.

My intent is not to criticize Lopez's speech, though it furthers the works of the 19th century European scholars. During the question-answer period after the talk, I commented, **"It is not a bump on Buddha's crown, but a hairdo that was popular with the princes and *rishis* of ancient India."** It is a male hairstyle in which a few tufts of hair are knotted at the top of the head and the rest are let to flow down the nape. Even today, during the enactment of Indian epics Ramayana and Mahabharata TV serials, this hairstyle is commonly depicted. However, some foreign scholars are projecting it as some kind of deformation in the Buddha's head! In fact, the Sikhs have taken this hairstyle to a limit by tying up all the hair at the top center of the head and then wear a turban over it.

Another strange thing that Lopez mentioned in his lecture was some anthropological connection between the dark complexioned Indians of Bengal and Bihar with some tribes in Ethiopia! It is ridiculous to even theorize that some Indians are the result of migration from Ethiopia. But that is how a scholarship in humanities is propagated when enough persons from the same school of thought cite a source. Today, the citation index is a measure of scholarly work in academia for promotion and tenure. What the European scholars had in terms of resources, the American scholars have more of it in order to push any scholarly agenda.

I live in two worlds - far apart! Whereas, India nourishes my heart, the US nourishes my intellect. Giving and going back and forth between the two bastions is the story of my life. It has not been easy. Those who came from India to the US during the 1960s, in the first wave of professionals, achieved a lot of professional and personal successes. Since early 1990s, successful Indians have generously contributed in establishing endowed chairs in Asian/Indian Studies in major universities. The dilemma that I encounter is with the faculty hired to promote research in these centers and departments are Chinese and Japanese too. Above all, the administrators are rarely Asian, and their understanding of Asian cultures is minimum.

Let me raise a basic question: **Does an average endowment of 1 million US dollars in an Asian Studies program bring a good scholarly return in the spirit of postcolonial history and culture of India?** My answer is really a No. But how to resolve this dilemma. Those of us who attended great US universities like Harvard, or Indiana, our hearts naturally open out for them. The hiring of a professor directly from India in a US university on a tenure track position is out of question – unless, a person truly has an international stature. Moreover, present Indian scholarship has a long way to catch up with the West. I know this statement may irk some of my Indian friends, but that is what I have seen. I have been visiting India and interacting with Indian scholars for the last 20 years. It is all a matter of a tradition, and that takes time. There are few short cuts to scholarship.

Being a member of UNLV Asian Studies Committee, I was invited to have lunch with Professor Lopez. He did his bachelor's, master's and doctorate in Buddhism, but he believes that the redemption of Buddhism lies in Christian Gospel! Furthermore, I asked, "How come you have written a book of **Buddhism and Science** without ever being a science student?" He had no good answer either. With a reputed publisher, his book may have a worldwide sale. After the lecture, I inquired, "Since you met Dalai Lama several times, did you ever ask him about the protrusion of Buddha's head?" He simply answered, "No."!

The basic question remains - what kind of benefit students get from such a program? It is time that Indians in the US and Indian government come together at least during the next annual *Pravasi Divas* (Jan 9). The 90% of the West still believes in the hocus pocus theory of the Aryans originating from some European region, invading India, and calling the Vedic mantras as shepherd songs, and so on. It is only through joint institutional efforts historical anomalies can be corrected, and new directions discovered.

In my opinion, outsourcing Indian studies program from the US to India is the best way out. With twining programs with the US universities, it is possible to establish attractive Indian Studies programs in major universities in India, where US students would love to travel and attend courses for credits and personal enrichment. Most US universities send their students in foreign countries for specialized programs in languages, art and culture. Last year 160,000 US students went to various foreign countries through home institutions to study abroad. 63% of the students went to western countries. There is a rich market to attract students as well as foreign exchange.

India already has very successful models of institutions in medical and engineering areas. Manipal is famous for medical education and the IITs for engineering. I personally know several US students getting their 2-3 years of medical education in Manipal and then finishing the rest in associated medical colleges in the US. However, they are essentially undergraduate institutions far removed from conducting any fundamental researches worthy of a Nobel Prize.

What disappointed me was the Lopez's choice of only European scholarly sources. I told him that Buddha had a team of monks including his famous disciple Ananda, whose only job was to listen the sermons and memorize each word uttered by Buddha. Later on, the spoken words were transcribed into manuscripts that have turned into a vast literature on Buddhism. Only by digging into these ancient scriptures, one can reconstruct any aspect of the life of the Buddha and understand the global power of Buddhism.

Feb 13, 2004

PS: Sep 2015

This article is a perfect example of education integrity gone amuck or hijacked. It is not done by one individual, but often by a whole gang of scholars. With institutional support and in the name of research, they can create fictional problems in any area from humanities, social sciences and natural sciences – except, of course, in mathematics. For instance, there is a mile-long distorted colonial history of any country and its indigenous people. The tragedy is that it cannot be easily corrected or re-written!

COMMENTS

Bhatnagar Ji: This item is already so well written and can be submitted as such. There is no need to elaborate any further. Your comments are already very clear and make much sense. **Satish Sharma**

I am impressed. Continue the good work! Harbans **Bhola**

I fully agree with your comments on Dr. Lopez which are extremely rational & logical. You rose to the occasion and thwarted his so-called fabricated scientific theories. Bravado. Good action!! **Suresh**

Satish Bhatnagar, From my experience, I would say Indian scholarship has done no better (and in some cases done far worse) as far as coloring its research with "agendas." Now in the post-colonial era, we have Marxist, Hindutvaadi, Dravidianist, Brahminist, you name it sort of ideologies going back and forth. I do not understand how private institutions will fix this 'chaotic flux.' Didn't Lopez say that the story of this 'deformation' originally came from the monks?..Generally speaking, I do not have a high opinion of Indian attempts to construct history.

Dear Inder: I agree with Prof. Bhatnagar on most of the things he has said. Most present day scholars have their colonial agenda and they have been doing everything in their power to perpetuate it. The western scholars have been writing our history – not only India's history, but the history of the East and their religions and languages. Whatever – even rubbish – westerners write is right, because they have power and they have the authority.

Western scholars would not respect what is written in our sacred books, because, in Sir William Jones's opinion, "are hopelessly obscured in the mists of mythology and fantasy." William Jones was a British Judge in Calcutta in late 18th century who became pundit in Sanskrit after only three years of his part time study along with his full time job of judgeship. Jones translated Hindu books with misinterpretations and distortions. They used to hire poor pundits to distort our scriptures.

….. **On the same token, outsourcing Indian studies programs from the USA would not work because of the unfortunate 'Indian stamps' over**

them. Moreover, it would not be cost-effective. But a mediocre graduate from an American university would shine in India. This explains why the Lopez book had a worldwide sale. Would have his book (hundred percent identical to his present book) earned same worldwide recognition if Lopez was associated with an Indian (even best) university?

Satish is right, India has yet to achieve freedom of scholarship (intellectual independence). Unfortunately, most educated elite, not all – living here as well as back in India – would tend to respect western scholarship more than Indian, only because still colonial yoke is shining around their necks.......... Scholarship, in my opinion, can/should not be measured by only its knowledge, but also by the objectivity and readiness to understand what others say. For right interpretation of ancient sacred scriptures, one needs, in addition to his scholarship, a culturally unbiased disciplined mind and a heart sincerely respectful to the culture he is writing about.

The Western scholars have their cultural arrogance to claim that they are always right about the content of their books on Indology, translation of Sanskrit scriptures, and their interpretations of archeological finds of other civilizations. We Indians with colonial yoke around our neck tend to worship them for their arrogance.

But, I tend to disagree with Prof. Bhatnagar if he believes that Indian scholarship is inferior. It is much superior to the western scholarship. .....Indian scholarship has its graceful modesty – a symbol of civilization. Indian scholarship is not considered superior because it does not have authority the West has. Hence, whatever they write, even their ill-based scholarship, is recognized. The West has power. ...

Prof. Bhatnagar is right only if he feels that endowments to India Chairs in universities do not bring a good scholarly return. Reason is clear. Administration is not ours. Universities have their own colonial agendas. It reminds of what I have written in the chapter: **Worldwide Prostitution of History:** Herbert J. Muller (1958: xiii), in his book, *The Loom of History*, has rebuked the historians of the West for their deliberate prejudice against the Eastern civilizations....

Muller, in the same book, has expressed his pain at the intentional mutilation of the history of the ancient eastern civilizations at the hands of Western historians. According to him, superficial, confused, or distorted notion of history is far more dangerous than ignorance of it. History is a Greek word, meaning a search for true knowledge. Ironically, historians are passionately thriving on lies – disguised through omissions, distortions, misrepresentations, generalizations, baseless assertions, and generous use of the words 'perhaps' and 'probably' – which should have no place in any science including history. Some parts of history – particularly ancient histories of the East seem demagogued by tactful use of words/phrases with multiple meanings laced with implicit ethnic bias against ancient Eastern cultures. History needs hard facts.

Inder, I would very much like to talk with Prof. Bhatnagar on phone, if meeting is difficult. He has lot of perspectives I like. I hope I understood rightly what he wrote. If not I am sorry about that.

Good thoughts. This is a human fact that one likes to put other down. One way of showing that you are better is to show that other person is worse. This applies to nations/cultures too and especially if you are the ruler. History unlike mathematics is not absolute. You know Microsoft has encyclopedia on religions and guess who wrote on Hinduism. A white evangelical woman Professor. Her interpretation of Hinduism was as you guessed of a person with bias for Western philosophy. To add insult to the injury the authors of rest of the religions were people of that religion. Hindus did protest it, but I do not know what happened in the end. … Regards, **Rahul**

Uncle, This is a really very well written piece. Your best - so far. **Vicky**

Satish: Thanks for allowing me to read this. I wholeheartedly agree with your comments. I hope that you would forward this to other members of the Asian Studies Program as well. Also, it would be nice to publish this in the Rebel Yell. Hopefully, it would open up some discussion.

In the West the study of Buddhism has become fashionable as a "New Age" thing. Many in the West believe that Tibetan Buddhism is the Buddhism. Dalai Lama achieved publicity and acceptance in the West as an independence activist who fought against the Chinese dictatorship. They think that Dalai Lama is the "Pope" of Buddhism. The West made him a cult figure and used him as a tool to seek their political goals. Now that the West's agenda and relations with China have taken a different form, the Dalai Lama and Tibet have taken a back seat except among the Hollywood types.

I must also add that some higher learning institutions in the West such as the East West Center and some Ivy Leagues do fill a vacuum and provide an important service in the study of Eastern cultures and religions. In that, they have become repositories for some of the original works. Also, they support research and scholarship in these areas of study.

This was apparent to me when I visited the Yale university library collection on South Asia. I think that collaboration in the form of recognition of South Asian scholars to serve on thesis committees would be a feasible solution. One who pursues higher learning in these subject areas in American universities may do well to communicate with scholars in that region, and also to have them serve on their thesis committees. This will ensure an ongoing dialogue. Also, one will have access to resources at both ends. This may be a less expensive or a feasible solution for some who cannot study abroad.

We must get together to discuss setting up some type of a collaborative cultural council to promote understanding and dialogue. Thanks again and keep up the good work. **Karu Hagawate**

Dear Prof. Satish Bhatnagar: Thank you once again for including me in your distribution list for the dissemination of your thoughts and philosophy. I could not agree more with your assessment of indologists in western countries. In the 1960's I was a campus consultant for a yearlong Ford Foundation funded institute, where many indologists from prestigious universities visited and lectured. Except for one Prof. Weiner of MIT (no relation to Norbert Weiner), everyone displayed a "condescending" attitude, at best.

Your suggestion in the penultimate paragraph of your communiqué is excellent. It is natural if students from western countries start their "learning in Indian studies" at a recognized studies program in India. This should be a collaborative venture. One person who can pull this off

235

is my friend Prof. M. P. Singh, who already has established collaborative programs in Computer Science and Business with Coastal Carolina University (sounds familiar?), Clemson University, Tarleton State University, among several others in US and Australia. He is the director of Ansal Institute of Technology in Gurgaon. As such, a copy of this correspondence is sent to him. I do not mean to be presumptuous, as he may not have time for yet another challenging venture. I wish you best of luck! Sincerely, **Subhash C. Saxena**

I read Dr. Bhatnagar's long message forwarded by you. Please tell him not feel disturbed on such falsehoods being spread, as always, by the so-called 'scholars and 'their new research being done in the so-called prestigious institutions. What Lopez says is utter nonsense and only shows his intellectual and academic bankruptcy borne out of highly prejudiced and ignorant mind. He has unsuccessfully tried misrepresenting his meetings with Dalai Lama etc. In India, people will see it as laughable garbage not worthy of any comment.

Br. B is right that this sort of thinking stems from colonial harm done to our great civilization by the East India Company in the eighteenth century when Asiatic Society was formed in Calcutta by them with a colonial agenda to belittle our great heritage with the intention of subjugation. You rob anyone of his history and philosophy, you make him look inferior. They succeeded terribly in implanting many falsehoods, which continue to this day. Unfortunately many of our own great scholars were trained by them and brainwashed who also ended up propagating these falsehoods as they lost their original roots. **Sairam**

77. SHAKESPEARE 101

[**Note**: In the US, historically, education and learning opportunities have never been limited to the walls of the schools and colleges. The classic Chautauqua courses since the founding of the country, free public lectures, conventions and conferences - all enrich life intellectually. With the advent of digital technology, The TED lectures, YouTube and online courses are providing various kinds of skills and training, in addition to traditional courses. They are often free – unless one wants a diploma. A version of this Reflection was included in my book, *VIA BHATINDA* (2013)]

If Shakespeare comes to life today, then he will not be surprised at the immense popularity of his plays. In *Julius Caesar*, Shakespeare confidently predicted the immortality of his work through a character, Cassius: *How many ages hence Shall this our lofty scene be acted over, In states unborn and accents yet unknown*! Last Friday, I drove up north 150 miles to Cedar City, Utah to watch the *Henry IV Part One*.

Neither, I am a Shakespeare fan, nor its avid reader – my interest is limited to a few of his sonnets and plays. Both of my daughters, being English majors, Shakespeare was in the air during their college days. Personally, I can't follow Shakespeare without assistance on the English of his times. However, Americans have a knack to market and commercialize every thing. The plays in the US are rendered in modern English.

A question is why do I go for a play? Its answer is simple: anything surviving for over 400 years must have some universal appeal. Talking of Shakespeare's universal appeal, here are a few things noted from an exhibit in the lobby of the Randall Theater. Shakespeare is more quoted than any other playwright; his plays have been translated, printed and produced in more languages than even the Bible; 1500 films produced on his plays including 20 on *Romeo and Juliet* alone! In all, Shakespeare has created 1289 characters!

During the last two years of college, I studied *Julius Caesar*. Professor Inderjit Manrai taught it by discussing not more than 6-8 lines in a period. He would lead us into Shakespeare's mind and that of his characters in depth and detail. **One need not study psychology and sociology as disciplines, if one has minutely studied a few plays of Shakespeare.**

I am at a point in life, when rarely a book, person, movie etc. holds my full attention for a long time. I quit a book in the middle, but I don't walk out of a theater or a movie. While sitting through, I sift through my own ideas. The play was historical - going back to early 15th century England. Shakespeare lived during 1564-1616. Being patronized first by a knight and then by the King of England. His several plays, on the English monarchy, seems his way of expressing gratitude.

With little interest in medieval European society, while watching the play, my thoughts were constantly ricocheting. I suddenly asked myself as to what was happening in contemporary USA and India then. The name USA did not exist! It was the land of the native Indians, though Europeans had started trickling in. In India, the Mughal Emperor Akbar (1556-1605) had taken controlled over North India. I do not recall any great literary work produced during his era. However, Akbar did patronize a school of music, and Tansen, a Hindu converted to Islam, was a music legend of that era. By and large, Islam is against fine arts in public life.

Shakespeare speaks up through monologues and soliloquies of his characters. Monologues on honesty and unity of nation in *Henry IV* were thought provoking, and have a time immemorial values. Actually, in the gift shop, I did notice a book that contained all the monologues of Shakespeare.

Next morning, I attended three free literary seminars that were very engaging. The first from 9-10 AM was on the last night play, *Henry IV*. There was a gathering of about 75 inquisitive people. The questions, answers, or remarks ranged from history to why Shakespeare or director did it, or did not. **I wondered at how through Shakespeare a cultural unity is created in the nation.**

Is there any indigenous regional or national figure in India who could be a symbol of integration? In North India, Munshi Prem Chand (1880-1936) wrote masterpieces in Hindi under this pseudo name, as the British had proscribed his works. Nearly 50 years ago, the UNESCO included

Prem Chand's novel, *GODAAN* in the list of world classics, and Indiana University Press published its English translation.

From 10:30-11:30 AM, there was a discussion on *My Fair Lady*, an upcoming matinee play on that very day. Yes, the company produces classical non-Shakespearean plays too. There are five this year. Having heard of this play, I said to myself that I would stay as long as it holds my interest. The dialogues were in the open with benches set under a groove of trees. Its sylvan setting added vigor to the mood. A cordless mike was passed on in a very orderly manner from one questioner to the other without any one interrupting the other, or hogging on the time.

This conduct amongst strangers alone defines a cultivated American society. Politeness and mutual respect prevailed in a remarkable manner. It appears those who have a taste in classics also develop such social etiquettes. Needless to say, I never felt like leaving. I am always impressed with American's love for a life long learning! Most people in the audience seemed over 60, but a few teens and young adults were also active participants.

The third session, **Actor Seminar** from 11:30 -12:30 PM was another first time experience. Two poplar character actors of Henry IV ran this seminar. The questions were put on their personal backgrounds, professional training and involvement with the company etc. What amazed me to hear from one actor was that how *Henry IV*, produced two months ago in Washington DC, was radically different from this one. He had acted in both. Different directors can bring out totally different emphasis in the same play. It was during this session that I leant the magnitude of the business acting was in the US.

Theater, filming and acting are integral parts of academic departments in most colleges and universities in the US; unlike India where they are relegated as an extra curricular activities. Therefore, theatrical arts attract the young talent as much as sciences and business do.

My friend in Cedar City wanted me to watch another play before returning to Las Vegas. I said, "I want to relish the experience of only one play at a time. Since I don't watch plays very often, another play may cause a visual indigestion!" There is a lot more in the Festival to inform you, to entice you, and to do anything to do with Shakespeare - like Backstage Tours, Play Orientations, Plays-in-Progress, Productions Seminars, Punch and Judy Shows, besides various literary seminars. It is truly called a Festival, as it enjoins with the city's Art Festival, and Pumpkin Festival.

Above all, there is a week of high school Shakespeare Competition. In Cedar City, names of small hotels, motels and stores are splashed with names associated with Shakespeare. After absorbing only a fraction of it I said: **Shakespeare is a billion dollar business, a life-long university, and a vibrant icon of western civilization!**

July 25, 2004/Sep, 2015

COMMENTS

Hi Satish, I read all your emails and pleased to let you know that you have an excellent talent in writing and your expressions are so good that you don't need editing in any of your writing. You combine all your knowledge and write a book, it will be the best seller in the market, and I guarantee it. **Lem**.

Dear Bhatnagar Sahib, First, your little essays have been so communicative that I have felt always in touch: what could I have said if I did call? Also, I have been busy doing some writing of my own - - though by no means as lively. With all this, I still manage to think of you; especially when I am reading your wonderful stuff! With Love, **Harbans**

3. The British, although coming from a tiny island, were persons of high vision, materialistic planning and management with socio-cultural perception. Even before getting them finally established in India, they started building educational institutions/universities, postal, legal and police services, building a network of canals, roads, railways in Punjab and other parts of the country, set up administrative and judicial machinery throughout the length and breadth of the country, and

so on. They showed the highest degree of modern organizational and management capability in the most modern sense of the twenty first century.

Perhaps, all this can be partially attributed to the work of great poets like Shakespeare which phenomenon is being commercialized by Americans. After all, money makes the mare go and it is through high return-on-investment, more and more investment and consequent innovation sets in. However, India did not lack intellectual and scientific recourse endowment at any point of time. When Akbar was busy promoting music and national integration of Muslims with rest of Indians, our saint poets like Tulsidas, Surdas and Kabirdas were busy in promoting unity of the country through their writings and noble work/followers.

We, as usual, lacked appropriate planning and modern management techniques to boost our country's cultural talent and their work. Even our most learned intelligentsia divested its energy and talent in petty quarrels and unhealthy criticism. In my view, migrants like Europeans (and now Indians) in America, Punjabis in divided India, Jews in Israel, Germans in USA after the second War, have done good work in economic, social and cultural sense and have carved out an excellent place for themselves. They shed laziness and easy going attitude and work culture and take up challenges and cash on the opportunities in their land of settlement. Perhaps, this can be attributed to 'insecurity and fearfulness' in foreign lands at the initial stage of settlement. THANKS FOR THE MAIL/ reflections, which I missed for more than a week. **NIGAM**

Shakespeare is acknowledged to be the greatest author of all times in all languages. Kalidas no doubt touches his heights but is no where near the abundance produced by the former. Shakespeare had spiritual data which is available in Scientology and is far above the bunch of misguided facts commonly labeled as psychology. Thanking you. **Subhash Sood**

For now I just want to comment on your comments about Indian Literature during this period. During this time Bhakti Movement flourished. Bhakti movement gave rise to prominent people like Ramanuja, Ramananda, Nimbarka, Vallabhacharya, Basava, Chaitanya Mahaprabhu, Mirabai, Tulsidas, the Nayanars and Alvars of south, Namdev, Chandidas, Vidyapati and Sant Tukaram.

With them came the rise of devotional literature. Tulsidas wrote Ramacharitmanas. Surdas composed the Sursagar. Not only that Guru Granth Sahib came into existence during that time. All of these people and books helped in integration of Hindus during Muslim rule. I think it helped in survival of Hindus.

These books that I have mentioned had more impact on the masses in than Shakespeare ever had or will have. After all what percentage of Americans or British (not to mention the world population) have read Shakespeare, but in India Ramacharitmanas and rest of these books are household name. **Rahul**

PERSONAL REMARKS

78. TAGGING THE YOUNG SCIENTISTS

Today, I attended the annual poster presentation of undergraduate research projects. Thirty-one students including seven from out of state, worked with the UNLV faculty for **two** summer months. They were paid up to $3000. General research areas with number of researchers in parentheses were Biology (14), Physics (11), Geosciences (2), Engineering (1), Psychology (1), Mathematics (1) and Chemistry (1). It was a pleasant surprise to see five of my former students engaged in research!

My thoughts were very similar to the ones evoked last year. I wish I were an undergraduate in USA! Naturally, it transported me back to my school and college days in India. While in school, during summer months, my father used to put me with private tutors for a few hours a day for studying. I resented a little bit, but it was also too much to play out in the 115 degree Fahrenheit of Bathinda's sandy desert atmosphere.

During college years (1955-59), summer was unsupervised. There was no academic infrastructure. Even today, most Indian colleges and universities are totally closed during summer. It is time to open them up for the gifted students. The fundamental question is what private or/and state initiatives would bring the college professors and students together on creative projects. In India, professors are paid for 12 months vs. the US faculty contracted for 9 months. The US faculty is absolutely free to engage in anything during the summer months; teach in a summer school, do funded research, or even drive a truck that brings in a lot more money.

All major agencies – like, the National Science Foundation, Department of Energy, Department of Defense, National Institute of Health and NASA, have budget allocations for education and research. Selected students are generally seniors. It is the age to explore and investigate. Summer research programs across the country set up a pipeline of thousands of future research scientists. The data tells that 70 % of these students go for their graduate studies vs. 40 % of those who have not experienced research as undergraduates.

Most importantly, the students develop a scientific outlook at a young age. That is where the society in India lags behind. Scientific thinking comes after immersion in a scientific problem for an extended period. By memorization of a few mathematical formulas and scientific principles, one only scratches the surface of scientific approach.

My uncle being an owner of a bookstore in Bathinda, I had access to books for reading in summer months. There was also a small public library near our home. I remember one summer reading the novels (in Urdu) by Jamana Das Akhtar. During another summer, I read all the volumes of *In the Woods of God Realization* (in English) by Swami Ram Tirath (1873-1906), who also lectured in the US after initiation into a monkhood at the age of 25. Incidentally, he was first class first and 1895 gold medalist in MA Mathematics from Punjab University, Lahore!

Individually, it boils to one thing - not to let a time of life go unproductive at a young age. **Harnessing the power of the youth defines the character of a nation**.

Aug 12, 2004/Nov, 2015

COMMENTS

Interesting as usual, uncle! I have a small suggestion; your articles must reach Indian policy-making bodies in Delhi and beyond. Have you explored avenues in this regard? Sincerely,
Shankar, IIM, Bangalore

"The fundamental question is what private or/and state initiatives would bring the college professors and students together on creative projects?" You never answered your own question; simply opening up universities in summer without funding is not the solution. **Rahul**

Americans are highly innovative and professional with their education system; whereas we the Indian are over-wedded to traditions and past. In the context of education and teaching, we are still following the British system and structure given to us (or imposed upon us to serve their manpower needs) two centuries ago. Even that has been distorted a lot and members of the teaching community are more interested in making extra money than in taking care of their students. Tuitions, examination frauds, appointment favor are visible everywhere; parents and youngsters are now reconciled to these and participate in all sorts of dubious practices. Sincerely, **NIGAM**

79. EDUCATION IS SEAMLESS

A remarkable feature of the US education system is its seamless character. In contrast, in India, the hierarchal rigidity of education delivery systems has hardly changed since I attended schools and colleges 50 years ago. For example, in India, a seventh grader has little academic interaction with higher graders. School kids have no extramural activity common with the college students. The system forces the teachers to continue teaching in the preset grooves.

The school teachers seldom visit local colleges and universities for any professional interaction – like, attending seminars or meetings. The college professors in India think that they are sitting on the highest pedestal of a shrine that education enterprise is deemed. In the US, outreach activities are recognizable aspects of institutional mission, and form an integral part of one's professional job.

Here are two recent events that caught my attention for being the Associate Dean of the College of Sciences. On September 11, the **Scholar Day** was held at UNLV. All high school students with Grade Point Average (GPA) of 3.5 and above (out of 4.0), were invited to the Campus. After a brief reception, students were divided according to the college interest, where the directors of college advising centers escorted them to individual departments within the college.

Students get a first hand experience of visiting university labs and meet some professors on one-to-one level. The idea is to turn the students on to higher education by exposing them to the 'frontiers' of disciplines. If a visit is well organized, it is neither time consuming, nor does it seriously interfere with ongoing academic obligations. The rewards are in long term. The kids get to see a different learning environment as well.

Last week, I got a call from the Chairman of the Chemistry Department about a group of high school students coming over to visit the Department. It was a group of chemistry students. In high schools, there are various subject clubs like chemistry club, math club and arts club, and so on. Each student is encouraged to join at least one or two clubs. Not only they learn about the subject beyond the confine of a classroom, but more importantly, they also learn how to run an organization.

An important part of human life is how to get along and move up in an organization. In the US education system, leadership qualities are cultivated at a very early stage - starting even in the elementary classes. The kids, under the supervision of teachers, run for various club offices, make short campaign speeches, and hold proper elections. That is how the foundations of elected democracy are firmed up.

The colleges have individual clubs too. When high school club members visit the campus, they are brought in contact with the respective college clubs. That generates a peer learning and camaraderie. The universities also use such opportunities to recruit high caliber kids from schools.

Going for or after the best things in life is a hallmark of the US culture. In each aspect of life, whenever there is an opening, the recruitment efforts are made to choose the best-qualified person. Currently, in Math Department, out of 20 graduate assistants, fifteen foreign students are from India, Sri Lanka, China, Taiwan, Latin America, and Middle East. Out of the thirty faculty in the Department, twenty are foreign born. That is how education, in the US systems, far from stagnating, continue to grow and improve.

Nov 15, 2004/Nov, 2015

COMMENTS

In India the present educational system, as is the case with most of social and political including administrative wings of the society are hierarchal based and imposed by the British, as part of their colonising process. We are still continuing with that and whatever modifications have come up after 1947, they have made it worse. On account of acute shortage of university/college seats and the system of teaching, examination and evaluation, the interaction between universities/colleges and schools is not at all encouraged. Students have very little choice in selecting the institution of higher learning and the courses.

Dozens of committees and commissions at various levels have been set up and their recommendations have not at all touched the idea you have suggested in the present write up/reflection. Here students and their parents are more interested in getting degrees and go on adding to their formal qualifications, without regard to jobs/profession of their choice. Teachers, although some of them write books, seldom take pains to revise the curriculum or update themselves. In effect, it is one year experience badly repeated for forty and odd years in their life. This is unfortunate for the entire system of education prevalent with us in India. Individuals, who have policy responsibilities, seldom find time away from their files-noting and passing orders to be implemented at the lower level. THANKS. **NIGAM**

(Kindly do not mind spellings and grammatical mistakes in my response, I do not read them, as I am afraid of losing the entire text.)

80. A DAY OF ASSOCIATE DEAN

These days, e-mail is the most common medium of communication - be it a university wide announcement, or a personal memo. Being an associate dean, e-mails have to be checked nearly every two hours. Earlier, I used to do it twice a day. Yesterday, my Dean forwarded an e-mail from an elementary school (K-5) female teacher for prompt action. She is organizing a science fair for elementary kids and needs persons to judge the projects. Certainly, her school does not have any other science teacher. In fact, there is often one teacher in each elementary school in disciplines like music, art and science.

My first thought was how seamless the education environment is in the US. **In India, an elementary school teacher contacting a dean of a university for anything is not in any realm of thought!** Here, the Dean promptly acts on her request. Overseeing all science events in the College of Sciences is one of my charges.

Being Friday afternoon and schools closing by 2 PM, I interrupted the work at hand. First, I called Jane in the College of Science Advising Center, who is actively involved with the College fairs. The faculty has no time to go to elementary schools for judging the projects. Besides, there are over 250 elementary schools in the Clark County School district, though not all organize science fairs.

For the last few years, interest in science has been on decline at several levels. Our effort is to stem the tide, and do as much as possible to promote science. Last year, no high school (9-12) participated in the science fair. Thus, it becomes all the more pertinent on our part to re-seed interest in science at the grassroots level. The curriculum and administrative responsibilities belong to the school district.

I approached the student council of undergraduate students. It is an active group of bright students chosen from each department. They will contact their fellow majors as judges. In the meanwhile, I sent an e-mail to the teacher lauding her enthusiasm in science and the support of the school administrators.

Such calls remind me of the famous money line, 'one investment at a time'. In this process, my thoughts have taken a global turn. It is easy to see why science and math in the US are so far ahead of the rest of the world. It is more than a belief in science. It lies in practice and solving every day problems through scientific and mathematical thinking.

Such experiences are fulfilling, since I can share them with some educators in India. These stories in non-technical jargon are looked forward by the readers of the *Sahi Buniyad*, an educational magazine published from Bathinda. My older daughter being an elementary teacher for 12 years, I am aware of the instructional challenges at this level. This yarn does not end here. Next week, I will make sure that she has the judges for the fair to be held in March.

Jan 29, 2005/Nov, 2015

PERSONAL REMARKS

81. EDUCATIONAL PUBLIC LECTURES
(A Note to William Schlesinger of Duke University)

I was in the audience during your informative lecture under the auspices of the 14th Juanita White Memorial Lecture at UNLV last Thursday. As a mathematics professor and the Associate Dean of the College of Sciences, quite a few thoughts ran up into my mind that I decided to write them down for your thoughtful reply. Let me add that you being a member of the National Academy of Sciences of USA (2003), people listen you.

Any time you showed a graph, my immediate reaction was the reliability of the data that was already more than one hundred years old - whether in world population, or on global warming. The techniques of interpolation, extrapolation and statistical modeling of data are constantly changing with newer mathematical concepts. It was too technical to raise this question in that audience.

The global warming and its catastrophic consequences have been in front of the public and media for almost twenty years. My thoughts also went off to the scientists issuing studies on killer diseases like cancer, AIDS, and so on. The professionals in law and order are always showing the specters of crimes and criminals. The educators are not far behind in projecting declining standards in mathematics and sciences with terrible consequences. The scare tactics have become norms in the US life.

My other thought was to '**label it science**' that created the pollution of the 1960s. In 1970, while driving from Bloomington, Indiana to Chicago, I vividly remember the brownish sky near the industrial town of Gary, Indiana – atmosphere having acidic pungent smell. Would you call the science of the 1940s and 1950s that produced the environmental pollution of 1960s a **bad science** and that of the 1980s and 1990s that cleaned up some polluted waters, a **good science**? Certainly, science is neither good nor bad. What about the scientists and policy makers above them? The irony of science lies in its tunnel vision by its very nature.

That really has raised a question of ethics in sciences during the last 15 years. To be able to stand before an ethical scrutiny, the young scientists have to be trained in that awareness. That makes humanities and social studies no less important. Being in charge of the annual college science

251

fair held at UNLV campus, the high school participation has come down to zero. **The NSF is projecting a shortage of science professionals in every aspect**. The state of the pipeline of future scientists is alarming.

The environmental problems are paradoxical as you responded to a questioner. I remember (1990s) the Malaysian Prime Minister's vehement criticism of the west on the depletion of rain forest of Malaysia. The Malaysians, people in Africa, Asia and South Africa, want a taste of the western prosperity, abundance and comforts of life too, as they see it in the movies and TVs all the time. The right path is always of least resistance!

You know how terrible the predictions of the 19th century British political economist, Thomas Malthus were. By today's standards, his mathematical modeling was hardly of today's college freshman! He predicted India and Africa disappearing from the face of the earth with diseases and overpopulation. One can always defend any scenario. On the one hand, Malthus fathered the study of quantitative economics, but on the other hand, he pioneered the doom and gloom approach in academics and public life.

I really liked your approach of reaching out to the religious groups. Taking science to the people who are farthest from science and getting their support is a way to garner support for a global problem. Current strategy of shocking the public by hitting the media and front covers of magazines and journals has hit the **Principle of Diminishing Return**.

The wise men in every society and age have thought globally. **A man's capacity to do damage to his environment is always matched by his ability to undo it**. After all, man is an integral part of nature. As long as the entire world population is not on a suicidal course, I remain optimistic!

You can see that asking a partial question in the limited time was out of question, and after the talk, I had to rush out. Reception is a time for small talks anyway. I would appreciate hearing from you. Thanks and environmental regards.

Mar 18, 2005/Oct, 2015

COMMENTS

Satish, your note to Schlesinger was interesting but what was more interesting to me was that you letter was labeled 99% Spam by our computer system? Take care. Ciao, **Len**

With the global developments at an unprecedented speed, the database for any presentation, research paper, talk or articles gets irrelevant in two to five years. As such, conclusions and suggestions remain only of marginal academic value. Century old data, gives a picture of present and future scenario which is almost of no relevance to the present society which is transforming at an unthinkable fast pace. I advise my students and research scholars to keep this situation in mind while finalizing their dissertations,

thesis and term papers for formal evaluation and grades/marks. Perhaps this is one of the major reasons why research journals are not of present value to the society at large. Research has to be oriented towards twin objectives: futurity and relevancy. Thanks and greetings. **RS Nigam**

Interesting thoughts here. Do note that many of my slides showing a long-term trend were obtained from ice cores, sediment cores, tree rings etc., analyzed recently using the most modern techniques. There may be errors, but error should be uniform across the record.

I don't regard the science of the 1960s or 1970s as bad science relative to today. We did what we could then, with fewer techniques. Our early understanding of pollutant behavior was instrumental in getting the Clean Air and Clean Water acts passed, and the country is much better off for it. Certainly, we might design these somewhat differently today, but the overall conclusions of the science were pretty good.

I share your regrets about scientific literacy in this country. We are not headed in a reassuring direction. **William H. Schlesinger**

82. SHADES OF EDUCATION

A change in environment is one way for getting a different perspective in life. Eating out is one example, provided one does not go to same eatery. Others are like, hiking on a different trail or terrain, as it opens up new vistas both physically and mentally. In different contexts and situations alone, that one truly understands one's inner drives. My brief trips to India give me new perspectives on life mostly lived in the USA since 1968.

Visiting local schools 3-4 times a year provides a lot to ponder. A couple of days ago, I was a **PAYBAC** motivational speaker in a junior high school. At UNLV, I don't routinely meet groups of preteens. Theirs is a whole new world.

I do remember many a things of my life at the age of 12 in Bathinda. During my school era of India of the 1950s, obedience to the parents and teachers was the highest virtue. In the US, questioning is a birth right, no matter how many times a question has been answered. At this age, the kids do not understand that a real answer to a question would eventually emerge from the quietness of your mind.

As soon as I entered the classroom, both boys and girls went into a brief pandemonium. I was not there to admonish or call them to order. For this reason, the US public school teachers earn my admiration, as they have to use all kinds of communication skills to get their attention. Thus, my challenge as a speaker was to get their attention first.

"Where are you from?" "I have lived in Las Vegas for over 30 years," was my response. But I knew that they were curious about my national origin. Most kids in that school had migrated from Mexico and a few from Latin American countries. In order to dramatize my reply, I said, "If you drill a big hole in the floor of the classroom all the way in our round earth, then which country will be at the other end of the hole?" Twenty-three kids in the class gave nearly thirty wrong answers before one rightly blurted, India. Immediately, I pulled a five-dollar bill from my pocket and awarded it to the kid.

The kid was surprised and held the bill for a while. His classmates were wide eyed too. I knew of the impoverished neighborhood they came from. Having drawn their attention and interest, I briefly talked about India and steered them into my motivational topic. Also, I scored a point by tasting a new perspective on life.

Apr 01, 2005/Oct, 2011

PS: Oct 2015. A variation of their reflection is included in my book *Via Bhatinda* (2003). It is included here for its value in learning from school visitors other than the classroom teachers.

83. STARTING WITH A BANG

Americans do things with jazz and pizzazz. It happened two days ago. The event was named, *The Rebel Connection*, a kick-off for the new academic year, 2005-06. The Rebel in the caption captures UNLV's historic spirit and it is also a part of UNLV's athletics team names and mascot etc. The class instruction begins on August 29. However, this event has been in planning for a year and took place 26 days before the classes are to begin. Were there some students? Absolutely none. Did any professors come? Forget it! The event, held in Judy Bayley Theater, had nearly 200 people. Who were they? They were administrators, professional staff, office workers, and secretaries. All were led by the President of the University.

It was the first event of its kind, but I rarely attended such events in the past. Being the Associate Dean, not only I get all the notifications, but I feel obligatory to show my presence there. In fact, all the deans were in attendance.

As the people were taking their seats, a big screen had Power Point flashes of interesting facts and trivia on UNLV. Having served UNLV for 31 years, it was a double pleasure to be a part of this fun. The President spoke for about 15 minutes with humor and style about the upcoming year and anticipated large enrollment. The hour was taken in explaining various aspects of orientation. A small booklet, *The Rebel Connection* contains every hourly detail of the Orientation Week, to be held on Aug 24-31.

I never encountered such an experience in India neither as a student nor as lecturer. The schools and colleges I attended had 200-3000 students at most. In contrast, UNLV is getting ready to welcome nearly 30,000 students on the campus on the very first day. From my college days of in India of the 1950s, I only recall fuzzy announcements on the day of classes. But there was nothing in the name of orientation to college life. The first three weeks of classes were essentially part of unstructured orientation as the serious studies used to start after nearly one month. Professional colleges - like medicine and engineering, were a little better organized. During the 1950s, the law students in India particularly were known for their lawlessness!

For the next two weeks at UNLV, the recruitment and training of 1000 volunteers is to take place. This involves students, secretaries, staff and faculty. They generally volunteer their time in blocks of two hours. The week of Aug 24-31 is packed with every conceivable activity for students, accompanying parents, friends and relatives. The motto is: *you have a question, we have the answer.*

I love my profession for its new academic years bringing new young faces. It makes me feel vibrant with ideas when I am amidst them. All the strategic entrances to the campus will be manned by volunteers, and information booths set up along paths and academic mall on the campus. UNLV reflects the growth and innovation of Las Vegas, the most exciting city, in the US.

Aug 05, 2005/Nov, 2015

84. LEARNING BEYOND BOOKS

The US college education is a spectrum of compartmentalized knowledge. If high school education forms bricks and mortar of a building that a society is deemed of, then the college education lays a foundation for its structure. It can accordingly bear the weight of several storeys. The strength of American college education lies in the diversity of the course work that students undertake.

But no less important are the opportunities for the US students to gain the latest information and knowledge by attending variety of talks and colloquia given by visitors and scholars on the campus. They are free for the students and some are open to the public. There is hardly a day when an educative lecture or forum is not there in a university campus. It is everyday wrestling of ideas. As a parent and educator, I have strongly encouraged my children and students to attend as many talks as possible. That supplements and integrates with what is learnt inside the classrooms.

A week ago, two distinguished scholars visited UNLV. On Thursday, there was a lecture on *Creativity is a Decision* by Robert J. Sternberg, a well-known Yale university psychologist and the President of the American Psychology Association. Several academic units besides the Arthur C. Clarke Foundation sponsored this lecture. The Foundation encourages creativity in many ways. Clarke - now 87, is an author of nearly 100 books. In 1945, as a young student of math and physics, he determined the orbit in which the communication satellites are to be launched. It is named as Clarke Orbit, which is crucial to modern cellular technology of communication.

The audience in the hall overflowed onto the floor and hallway. Sternberg factored thirteen steps towards creativity and wrapped them with real stories. Working in a right environment and loving what you do with conviction as well as humor are conducive to new ideas. Some people in the audience must be thinking that Sternberg was going to give a mathematical formula for becoming creative overnight. He stressed that creators are not born, but cultivated. The adults and children are at par in creativity! One can unravel at one's unique strength by hiking off a beaten trail and take calculated risks as much as possible.

In a mathematical sense, there was nothing new for me in substance except, new phrases and stories weaved around each bullet point. Yet, periodic listening to such talks keeps the mind focused about innovation even during mundane activities. It is like having an occasional good drink and gourmet dinner for sensory delights.

I often measure my life of 65 years with a yardstick of creativity. It then boils down to creativity that is publicly acclaimed. Any claim on creativity has to have some public acceptance! By calling oneself creative is just not enough. My own hesitation to publish my ideas has been a glaring obstacle. It goes back to 1963, when I declined to get my solutions of very difficult problems in solid geometry published! Incidentally, at a New Year party in Bangalore last year, I declared that my New Year resolution is to get the first volume of my *Reflections* published!

The next day, on Friday, was a lecture on *Enterprise: Chemistry 2015* by William F. Carroll, the President of the American Chemical Society (ACS). The ACS is claimed to be the largest professional organization in the world with a membership of over 150,000. The audience of nearly 100 was mostly of professionals besides a few science students. My students earn extra credits for attending such lectures and writing a 200-300 word critique. These exercises eventually bring out an overview as well as depth to the book knowledge. They are like enzymes that help in the digestion of food.

As President of the ACS, this was his 53rd lecture delivered in various special interest groups of chemistry! A sense of humor and organization are common characteristics of American speakers. Dividing the contents into three streams of public perception, secondary education and future through 2015, Carroll delineated them through his remarks on industry, R&D (Research and Development), transfer of jobs and technology to other countries. He specifically touched the problem of declining number of foreign students coming for the US PhDs, and shortage of academic faculty, as more PhDs are joining the industry.

The concept of commoditization of specialties impressed me. He remarked that a point has reached in science that research can be divided into **Formula Research** and **Original Research**. All the hoopla about the US companies setting up R&D in countries like, China and India is for the **Formula Research**. He was least concerned about its negative impact on the US economy. It has been politicized and blown out of proportions in the media.

The lecture also tied chemistry with the political climate, immigration, homeland security and global economy. His most important observation was on the buzzword of interdisciplinary research. He cautioned that unless individuals involved essentially have breadth in their graduate work in various areas, interdisciplinary research at the fundamental level might not fructify. In India, the limited curricula, at the bachelor's levels, puts its graduates at a disadvantage for collaborative researches.

In Indian colleges and universities, such popular lectures are still non-existent. The professional organizations on the lines of the US have been in existence, but they are non-functional and ineffective in outreach activities. I have been a life member of Indian Mathematics Society for the last 25 years, but nothing has been heard from the Society for years! In contrast, the annual US Joint Mathematics Meeting held in January is the largest worldwide assembly of mathematicians.

Underling the importance of such lectures on a personal note, I still remember a lecture on subconscious mind and dreams by Professor JR Puri. It was held in an open lawn of Government. Rajindra College, Bathinda in 1958. I was a math student, and yet the lecture was so well delivered that it sparked my interest in modern psychology forever.

Sep 28, 2005/Nov, 2015

COMMENTS

Hi Satish: Both this one and the one before this are good 'reflections.' I am glad you are bringing into focus those topics that remain unexplored. The current one touches on specifically the significance of talks and lectures beyond the classroom. I believe both the universities and the University Grants Commission should encourage and support talks by prominent and well-known scholars in their fields. American higher education system promotes such talks. **Moorty** (Professor of English)

The education system of India is not creating thinkers or those who can observe. You are right there, but still a number of Indians are filling the academic positions abroad. The Americans inculcate love of learning among its student population. Recently I found out about a book called, Theory *of Intelligence*. It was interesting that it was published in Ahmedabad. **Subhash Sood**

85. LANGUAGE IMPLIES DIVERSITY

Everyone is sentimental about one's mother language. A language can unify people into one nation, as English did it in the United States. Languages can be divisive as a 1000-year history of India provides a testimony. The attack on one part of India by a foreign invader was never taken an attack on the country since Alexander's invasion of India in 326 BC.

My parents, coming from Lucknow and Agra, were settled in Bathinda, the heartland of Punjab. Our mother firmly instructed all us - her brood of six then, that we always communicated with each other in Hindi inside and outside the home. Imagine as a teen, I speaking with a friend on my left in Punjabi, but with a brother on my right in Hindi. It used to be embarrassing! Today, I have full command over both the languages. It extended our horizon on the language issue. In fact, I learnt Urdu and English at home from my grandfather before it was taught in the school.

Last week, while speaking before the 8th graders, I exhorted them to learn English. In that school, majority of students speak English as their second language. It was a week when the protests were taking place all across the US in support of illegal/undocumented immigrants through Mexico. However, I stressed that one must never lose pride in one's parents, food, language, and religion, as they all define a deeper individual identity.

For me, languages have several components. I had to demonstrate reading proficiency in French and Russian for my doctorate from Indiana University. German, I studied myself for fun. Twenty years ago, during my travels in the Tamilnadu State of India, I was shocked to see the Hindi signage painted black in order to remind the future generations of their opposition to Hindi, as enforced by the Central Government in the 1960s. During that very trip, my brother-in-law learnt to read Tamil from Hindi in 72 hours! The converse is also true. Politicization of languages is damaging to the intellect.

Our openness towards language is transferred to our children. Learning even the rudiments of a language means the working out of different brain cells. Languages are also like various body-building machines in a gym. Working only one muscle of a body eventually backfires on overall health.

Our 10-month old grandson stays with us for 6-7 hours on weekdays. My wife and I expose him to Hindi and Punjabi. Our daughter speaks in English and son-in-law in Spanish, as that is his mother language. It is so fascinating to see this baby already responding in all these languages!

Diversity is a buzzword in the US today. It means hiring and admitting certain percentages of ethnic groups to reflect the demographic distribution of the region. It only widens the gaps in the hearts and minds. But learning any aspect of a language also brings an appreciation of some history and culture associated with that language. It truly broadens the outlook, and tolerance becomes its corollary.

April 03, 2006

COMMENTS

Yes, people, such as me, are severely hampered having only one language. A new philosophy of actively speaking in another language to children is an excellent idea in my opinion. The mind is vigorously expanded and refined with more than one language. I think I'll learn Hindi. But, more importantly, my second language should be American Sign Language for an easier and smoother day. **Dutchie**

Younger a child is more languages it can learn. If one learns more languages, one gives exercise to one's imagination. People who are averse to languages are generally pygmies intellectually. Bengali and Tamil are very rich and richer than Hindi. Hindi is hardly 50 years old. Both Tamilians and Hindi speaking people are to be blamed for the problem you have stated. India was never a country as it is now. Many show Afghanistan, Sri Lanka and Burma as part of India. Sri Lanka and Burma were part of the administrative unit not too long ago. Hindu Sikh problem is basically language problem. Our ideas at least on this issue are very close. **Subhash**

86. WHEN ENOUGH IS ENOUGH?

Those who never break the rules, bend the laws, or stretch the principles can never be creators, entrepreneurs and leaders of men and ideas. This thought swelled up my mind on just hearing a saga of punishment meted out to my granddaughter. In two weeks, she will be 18. What is her crime? During a 9-day trip to Costa Rica, she took one sip of beer along with her girlfriends - no binge drinking, no wilding, no cussing etc.

On coming back to their hotel, the girls ran into a teacher who casually inquired about their outing. My granddaughter was the first one to admit of having tasted alcohol, which was a violation of their trip policy. The immediate punishment was their grounding for the remaining trip (2 days) and no participation in any group activity.

The trip-in-charge teacher forced those students to call and tell the story to their parents. The upset parents scolded the kids. The adults forget that if the kids will not pick up the courage to taste the forbidden fruits at 17 or 18, then when? I am not for the celebration of these unforgettable moments, but this humiliation is uncalled for. When my daughter told me about this incident ten days ago, I suggested her not to be over-reactive.

The matters did not stop there. A report went out to the Principal and was placed before the Student Council. The parents were called in to the school. Since it was a breach of a signed conduct contract, my granddaughter was now taken out of the Student Council. It remains to be seen whether she is debarred from participation in a recognition function. Moreover, it becomes a part of her school record.

My granddaughter is in the top 0.5% of her class. She was on a tennis team, elected officer of the Student Council, member and founder of clubs, and involved in community service. I always encouraged her to go beyond academics, and got her into tennis five years ago. The punishment exceeds her folly. In all serious ness, a sip of alcohol is no less educational!

Her first taste of beer reminds me of my first taste of cigarettes. At age 19, in Oct. 1959, I wrote my mother the day I decided to smoke a couple of cigarettes a day. She wrote back of its negative impact on my five younger brothers. At that time, I was more concerned with my conscience being free of any guilt. Later on, I read of identical experiences of Gandhi with cigarettes and meat (considered a taboo in his family). Gandhi's whole life was based on truth founded deep during his teen years with full faith in/ of his parents.

Being in education for 45 years, my wife and both teacher-daughters often wonder when they find me critical of present system of over schooling. This is inimical to the individual growth. The anti-religious public schools in the US do not teach forgiveness! They teach weird zero tolerance policies. Instead of appreciating her truthful behavior, the administration wants to scar her career. But her living up to the name *Sherni* (lioness) that I gave her makes me proud of her conduct. She is destined to soar higher in life!

April 22, 2006/Oct, 2015

COMMENTS

And, higher and higher and higher for Anjali. She is so special and so deserving of better treatment by the administration. How silly. A non-school sponsored function in a foreign country. Flexibility is an imperative in our lives. Flexibility is kindness, consideration and recognition of humanness in all of us. Why be so punitive and cruel? Why? You said it best, "They teach zero tolerance." We little people can't win. It is becoming so discouraging. My confidence stays with Anjali. **Dutchie Dutch**/Henderson

Without barrier, life does not exist. If you have a guest in your house, he also faces some barriers, which must not be violated. There are barriers even between sexual partners. Without barriers, any activity becomes meaningless. There are conventions, social conventions. One can break these. But these are not moral values. If a group of students goes on a trip, in my view they should follow the restrictions imposed. It is a different matter what or how much is punishment. But a value should not be broken. Progress in science occurred when someone went against common beliefs. But these are not values. In my humble opinion, your granddaughter violated a code. This is only my opinion. You are not bound to follow it. There is also a meaning and message in your letter, which is noble as well as challenging. If we do not question what has been told to us there would progress which is equal to zero. Only an Army can survive with these instructions. **Subhash/Ambala (Physician)**

You have a great granddaughter about whom you should be mighty proud. Truthfulness is a rare quality. I agree she will soar to great heights. Smartness and straight forwardness are rare combination. Having said that you think religious schools teach forgiveness. I studied in parochial school all my life and no transgression went unpunished. Small offenses led to caning by our Irish six-footer principal. I remember once we were forced to forgo breakfast, as nobody in class was ready to rat on a class fellow. As for punishment, that is a consequence of breaking law. Nature is very unforgiving too. Try putting hand in fire and see the results. But a smart kid like Anjali will also incorporate this experience to achieve more. In long term, this will be small bump. **Rahul/Austin (physician)**

I am appalled beyond doubt about the school policy. Is not honesty the best policy? Punishment beyond the bounds of so-called 'violation' school policy? Sherni stuck to her guns. She needs to be applauded; the school needs to be chided. **Moorty/Cedar City, Utah (professor)**

Amen. Encourage the lioness for me…**Steve/Henderson (Pastor)**

I am simply shocked at the treatment meted out to your granddaughter in the land universally acclaimed as the world leader for liberalism, human dignity and a long democratic tradition. I only hope and wish that this was an aberration, an isolated old-fashioned institution and would not in any manner adversely affect your granddaughter's personality or her normal growth. If you apprehend any adverse effect, just send her to me in India. My wife and I shall adopt her as our granddaughter and look after her studies by staying with us or in a hostel, as she may like. **SR Wadhwa/New Delhi (Tax consultant)**

I found your essay, "When Enough is Enough" very thought provoking. Reading this piece as a parent reminded me of how I struggle to maintain order without squelching initiative and creativity in my children. As a teacher and a concerned citizen, I pondered the connection between the penal and education system, how there is no room for growth and reform, but only for punishment. In such an extreme situation, how can one learn if one is afraid to take risks? Thank you for such a stimulating piece. Are you sending these out, even to the local papers? My best wishes for your granddaughter, your lioness! **Maria UNLV English Lecturer**

87. BALANCING ACTS OF EDUCATION

Two years ago, my daughter cautioned me, "Dad, you won't say a word of advice to Anjali about her attending college after high school!" Anjali is my granddaughter. It was tough on an active educator to stay quiet while listening all the time the talks on her taking scholastic exams, admission applications, choice of colleges, campus visits, scholarships, and so on.

Yesterday, at Anjali's 18th birthday celebration, my daughter asked me to say a few words at a family gathering. Only a day earlier, a friend had e-mailed me the commencement address of Subroto Bagchi to the 2006-class of the world renowned, Indian Institute of Management, Bangalore. Bagchi is a co-founder of an international consulting company, *MindTree*. The well-written address must have been effectively delivered too - as it is posted on many websites.

Bagchi distilled out the moral values that he imbibed living at home with his parents. They became the guiding principles of his life and ethical standards in his business. In his own words, "My parents set the foundation of my life and the value system, which makes me what I am today and largely defines what success means to me today. Success to me is about vision. It is the ability to rise above the immediacy of pain. It is about imagination. It is about sensitivity to small people. It is about inclusion. It is about connectedness to larger existence. It is about personal tenacity. It is about creating extraordinary success with ordinary lives."

Bagchi must be a good storyteller, as there are touching and poignant incidents behind each moral in the quote that ended his address. In my brief birthday remarks, I combined it with my own story of sacrifice for my family.

Undergraduate (BA/BS) education is the biggest business in the US today. It involves over a million college bound kids. Multiply it with $10,000-50,000 for the annual expenses. There are a number of reasons-including, parental push, unchallenging free and compulsory high school education, which perhaps, drive the kids, at the age of 17-18, to 'run away from homes'. It does not matter how good the colleges and universities are in their own backyards. Independent living and learning from one's mistakes define American life. It is catching on abroad too.

I strongly oppose to taking loans for undergraduate education. The marketing by the loan and credit companies is so powerful that young kids go under huge debts for the rest of their lives. It is a modern bonded slavery- worse than the indentured labor of the 17th century! On the other hand, it shocks me to see millions of dollars in private scholarships remain un-awarded every year, as the students are seduced to apply for loans with interest than search for scholarships and fill out applications. It reminds me of my college days in India, when for only a couple of scholarships in the entire country, thousands of students used to apply! Personally, I hardly missed any opportunity.

The ultimate purpose of a college degree is to serve the society at large, and the families are central. If the kids are disconnected from their families at a young of age, they are going to miss the daily immersion in family belief systems. With growing number of broken homes, every one is fending for oneself. Certainly, each home is not ideally prepared for a set of human values. Children can also learn the art of any unsocial behavior by watching their warring parents. Mafia is an example of crime culture in some families.

I told my son during his 1986 'shopping' for college, "You still have a lot to learn on emotional aspects of life from the home environment. On the top, you can even study basic calculus and physics no less rigorously at UNLV." His mind was set upon Stanford University. As a sidebar, UNLV put money in his pocket while Stanford would have dried us out!

Every one forgets formulas of math, principles of sciences, theories in social studies, and other data that are pushed down in the college curricula. To be able to think independently and work in teams are only incidental virtues in colleges. However, they are not in the exclusive domain of any one class of institutions. By and large, the character building qualities ingrained at home complement college education.

Like a typical kid in the US today, Anjali has been watching for the last two years her parents going apart in different directions. Objectively speaking, this family saga of litigation, financial quagmire, counseling of pre and post divorce can be looked in two ways. Send Anjali away to an out-of-state university and pretend that she would remain focused in her studies. A girl at 18 in the US or India may herself have her own family.

Learning from this family drama without leaving Las Vegas is also a first-hand educational experience for Anjali. She can live in a dorm while attending UNLV (She did apply at my suggestion). Education comes in many packages and most of them have no labels of their contents. This idea has been in my mind for a year, but it has yet to be shared with Anjali and her pre-divorced parents.

The popular inspirational books – like, *All I Wanted to Learn from Life I Learnt from Kindergarten,* periodically tilt the balance away from the structured education delivered in schools and colleges. The graduate education (MA/PhD) in the US is an entirely different story - reserved for another *Reflection,* if Anjali ever decides to go for it!

May 03, 2006/Oct, 2015

COMMENTS

First of all, thank you for sending your reflections. I shrink from becoming in the middle of family differences. It is not a black and white issue from my vantage point. The distance from the turmoil at home may be what she does need to get some perspective and peace away from the stresses and strains of the processes of the divorce.

Becoming an independent person with confidence is a process that comes much smoother away from home under another kind of protective environment. The mistakes she might, but not likely make, will not be serious and the protection of the university is there to help her pick up the pieces. From what I see, Anjali does need to get away for a while. Maybe she will transfer back to UNLV next year. It is true that you will not change your mind and goading you to change your mind is not feasible in any way. Another point of view is here. Hugs, **Dutchie**

A very good article indeed. I strongly agree with most of the content and your thoughts in context of US educational system. I believe, coming from an Indian educational background (both formal and otherwise) puts us in a unique situation where we have a different (and sometimes a better) perspective towards defining a "Quality Education System". **Gaurav Sharma**

88. GRADUATION HERE AND THERE

Yesterday was the high school (of 12 years) graduation of my granddaughter. The venue being only 100 yards away from my office, I had no excuse of not joining ten other members of my extended family. The graduation ceremony was held in the partitioned basketball arena of UNLV. In the US, everything is done on a humongous scale with associated fanfare and pageantry. The huge TV screens and various size monitors are installed in strategic locations so that no matter where you are in the arena, you don't miss a beat of an action.

For the graduating class of 550 students, there were over 5000 cheering grandparents, relatives, parents, neighbors and friends. There was a special entrance and seating for the sick and wheel chaired. A few came with tubes inserted and oxygen cylinders attached. The flowers, candies and small gifts were on sale at every turn. High school graduation events make a billion dollar industry. My one student flew 2000 miles to attend her brother's graduation by missing her three classes and hurting her course grade.

In India, the word **graduate** means someone who has done bachelor's, and **graduation** means the finishing of only a bachelor's degree. For many years in the US, my wife and I would be confused at the graduation announcements and invitations. Finally, we understood that in the US, graduation means the successful completion of any program of any duration, at any age, or any stage. We have attended graduation ceremonies of our kids of 3-4 years old when they finished their nurseries. No matter what the level of graduation is, the glitz and glamour of caps and gowns, foods and drinks, the presence of friends, parents and grandparents make it a joyous occasion for so many. That is great!

Having been brought up in a different culture in my adolescence, my initial reaction still continues to be out of a lack of understanding of the US traditions. My high school was of 10 years. Students used to be drained during a month of preparation for the final comprehensive exams. Taking a series of 6-7 three-hour exams for another two weeks was most stressful. The worst was the six-week wait for the results! We felt physically and mentally scattered for a while.

In the US system, literally no one fails, if a student is 'well-behaved' and does not miss the classes. The pass percentage from KG to the 12th grade in US public schools is nearly 100%. The school funding is driven by the number of students. In the high school exams that I took in 1955, only 60% of the students passed out of over 100,000 students. The same exam that my daughter took in 1981, the pass percentage in Ambala District amongst the private students was only 38%! One has to wait for one year for taking the exam again!

In the US, there is hardly any teaching for the 12th graders during the spring semester. It is all fun and lax due to an entirely different philosophy of high school education. In India, high school education, by and large, is geared towards colleges and universities. I often remark that if a kid has to pursue higher education, then do high school of India, bachelor's of the US; master's of India and PhD from the USA.

June 15, 2006/Oct, 2015

89. IT IS MORE THAN TEACHING

Sometimes, it takes too many dots to make a connection between two events or concepts. A month ago, my Department Chairman, while working on my annual evaluation, inquired about the students' evaluation of 2.91 (on a 4-point scale) in one of my courses. He knew that it was seldom less than 3.0. He being a statistician, I jokingly said it was a bad data. Two months ago, my daughter told me that she was going to send her son to a private tutorial center for mathematics, as I was not very helpful! These scenarios have been on my mind for a few weeks, but they have only resonated recently.

Teaching an academic discipline or coaching an athletic activity involves more than competency on the part of even a seasoned instructor or coach. Assuming, they know their trade, the results could be different in similar societies. In authoritarian cultures, the fear factor brings the best out of the students and players. In free and affluent cultures, the rewards are taken for granted. Thus, it is challenging to motivate them.

Stakes being much higher in athletics, successful coaches like Bob Knight can yell at their players. Jimmy Johnson, the winner of two Super Bowls with Dallas Cowboys, could not turn Miami Dolphins around. In a free society, (its limit is lawlessness), freedom has taken a new dimension - challenging the authority, bending, or breaking the rules with impunity. It is a new norm.

Teaching in the US high schools is filled with horror stories. During the last 33 years, I have watched teaching taking dive in the colleges too. UNLV may top it, as nearly every student works for 30-40 hours a week, while carrying fulltime course load. This semester, in an upper division course, three students told me straight on my face that they had no time to discuss a problem before or after the class. Last semester, I provided several extra credit opportunities for students to learn beyond the textbook and make up for any poor performance. At the end, in the course evaluation, not even a single student appreciated it. The alarming feature is that they are all mathematics and science majors!

My grandson has 4.0 GPA in high school. Three months ago, he came up to me with 6-8 challenging math problems, which the teacher gave for extra credits. I tried to 'teach' him - how to analyze a problem, parcel a problem into smaller ones, and 'play' with them. Consequently, only 2-3 problems could be finished. Sensing his restlessness, I told him that my doing his problems would not help him in a long run. In trying to raise his conscience, I even added that it was 'unfair' for me to do the problems, as other kids may not have such an advantage.

A few days later, I called him for discussing a homework problem on the phone. In fact, when he was 5-8 year old, we used to play 'phone' jeopardy by finding right answers of varied questions. But, a 15-year old kid, in the US, lives in his/her own world. In India, I learnt in high school out of fear of punishment from the parents and teachers; in college, with sheer hard work and without any encouragement! However, I have taught my US kids and students with various incentives and motivation. Perhaps, it is time for me to figure out the latest in motivational psychology and new instructional techniques!

March 07, 2007/Oct, 2015

PS: 10/10/15. A variation of this **Reflection** has also appeared in my book **Converging Matherticles** (2015). Here the emphasis is on motivation and tutoring, an extra-curricular component of classroom teaching.

COMMENTS

When a student is learning how to write, sometimes it is best to take someone else's words to find your own. I do not have a strong background in math or any discipline that requires problem solving with numbers. However, I have learned in math or any other subject that observing another person's technique of tackling a problem illustrates how you should go about it on your own. As a result, after practicing for long hours, nights, and months, one may find their own method of attacking a problem. I feel that utilizing my own methods of learning and combining it with the techniques of others, allows me to absorb more. The problem today with teenagers, myself, and some graduate student's sometimes is if we have the will to do all this.

In addition, I have learned in education that not all students can meet at the same wavelength as their instructor. At the collegiate level and high school level today, this might be due to a lack of effort. On the other hand, I have noticed those who put in so much effort but cannot for some reason meet half way with the instructor. Sometimes, the answer to this might be that it just is not the right time for them. They may require a certain foundation that has not developed yet, or they just simply learn in a different manner. This presents a prolonged discussion in education today, which relates to learning by implementing "fear."

In the medical school I attend, a Pakistani instructor believes learning is not achieved by creating fear for the student. She feels all too often instructors instill this fear in their students and in the end; it slows down the students' performance. While I agree, you probably do learn more not being stressed, yet if you are too relaxed then this is not an exemplary way of learning either. This discussion might be different in various disciplines, but in medicine, I believe there should be fear because physicians must be able to provide short concise answers and be able act quickly. Today, we might need a combination of fear and relaxed learning.
Sundeep Srivastava

It is unfortunate for the new students that they cannot see the advantage of learning, even when encouragement and incentives are given. Challenge that if we do not perform, we will be out of school and perhaps without a future made us work hard. However, even more so, we thrived on challenges. We wanted to show ourselves as well as to others that we could achieve. Unfortunately, this generation thinks they should be handed out everything...and even with that, they are always complaining about working hard. **Prafulla**

My experience exactly. Most if not all students in Las Vegas work from 20 to more than 40 hours a week and their freedom to pursue academic interests suffers. On the other hand, there is much to be said for working and studying as an entree to the working world. I found that a handful of my students were exceptional as "students" despite the workload they carried. But to my knowledge, few of them enjoyed promising academic or 'real world' careers. Now that I live in a more traditional academic town, I can see the difference. Oregon State is heavy in engineering, the sciences and agriculture and the students seem to come from a different planet than those in Las Vegas. As I am fond of saying, we escaped to reality. **Robert W Moore**

90. UNIVERSITIES & PARTTIME FACULTY

UNLV prides itself in being known as a metropolitan university. It is the only comprehensive university situated in Las Vegas, which is currently the fastest growing city in the US. Ever since my participation in a university planning retreat last August, off and on, I have been trying to identify the metropolitan characteristics of Las Vegas.

In 1974, when I joined UNLV, Las Vegas was not on the map of the retired communities. Florida was the national destination. In the 1960s, Arizona became the second choice as water and power brought greenery and central air conditioning to its desert. It was in the 1980s that Las Vegas came up on the seniors map. Since then, it has now surpassed Florida and Arizona in attracting senior citizens from all over the country. Seniors bring their time-tested talents and savings, which boost the local economy.

For instance, I still recall Leo Schumann, a retired engineer, who 'got sick of puttering around the house'. He joined UNLV and became one of the best math graduate students of his class (1976) at the age of 68. He taught part time for the Department for another 10 years. Leo's contemporary, Art Bell, at 80, took graduate math courses in order to 'keep his mind sharp'.

UNLV, realizing a potential in senior resources, started a Senior Citizen Program under which the Nevada Seniors over 62 pay no tuition fees during the academic year and 50% during summer. As the senior population grew so did their academic interests. **EXCELL, Elder Hostel** and **Senior Adult Theater** programs, offered through the Division of Extended Education, are so successful that they have brought national recognition to UNLV.

As part-time instructors, senior citizens can make significant contributions to UNLV. The Dance Department, amongst its adjunct faculty, has a large number of seniors. However, UNLV needs to tap this resource systematically. I have encountered retirees with graduate degrees including PhDs from top-notch schools with distinguished professional careers. Most are financially well off, but they want their minds engaged in challenging outlets. The benefits of their association with UNLV are far reaching, if such contacts are properly tapped. They are potential donors too!

Look at McDonald's and Wal-Mart, the two most successful business houses in the world. Before 3 PM, most employees at any McDonald's are senior citizens. In Wal-Marts, senior employees are seen as workers, greeters and helpers. There are remedial and lower division courses in every department that are cost effective, profitable and quality controlled, if part-time instructors teach them. Research/PhD faculty have no aptitude for these courses. Moreover, it is the under-utilization of their research expertise, if they routinely teach lower division courses.

"Mind is a terrible thing to waste" is a famous ad line of the **United Negro Fund**, when applied to the teens' potential wasted for lack of educational resources. However, it also applies to the communities that let the capabilities and expertise of their seniors go untapped.

Nov 23, 2007/Nov, 2015

COMMENTS

Another interesting article! I have expended all the hours, my retirement will allow this year, by working for the Graduate and Engineering Colleges. I not only enjoyed it, but believe I contributed to both assignments. At 69, I feel that I am still "worth my wile" and can keep up with the 25 year-olds! Have a wonderful Thanksgiving! **Margie**

As the graying of baby boomers is occurring, there will be more availability of this brain fund. **Rahul**

Thanks Satish...I have forwarded this to outreach college and the academic success center, who are actually organizing elder activities through OLLI and other activities.

Neal Smatresk/UNLV Provost

Satish, this is a very interesting idea. I recently discussed a similar approach with others. There are creative examples at other colleges/

universities, including some private colleges that have been able to develop a substantial campus-based housing and education program for seniors, and develop a strong, steady revenue stream. We should explore further.

David Ashley/UNLV President

PERSONAL REMARKS

91. TESTING TIME IN OMAN

At UNLV, I give the first class test at the end of the third or fourth week of a semester. The University of Nizwa (UN) has turned out to be different, as during the first two weeks hardly any instruction is done. No one shows up except one or two half-hearted students. The first test is pushed at the end of the sixth week. Suddenly, it clicked on me that there is a parallel track of my coming to Oman. How do I test myself out on this? It is time to roll back. Being at the shorter end of life, I must optimize my time on Planet Earth. That is my driving point in life now.

My curiosity about Middle East is, indeed, very old. Mainly, there is historic fascination. This region has been a crucible of Islam since the 7th century, and various empires have flourished here. Some regional adventurers went as far as India and won its territories. Over the years, I had explored short assignments in a few countries of this region. This one materialized after a chance meeting with Raju Abraham in Las Vegas. He has been an English Professor at the UN since 2007.

My overseas visits are coupled with my periodic itches of getting away from the US life. The two are closely connected, and that has been a story of my life. Though I had returned to the US in Dec. 2007, after a four-month sabbatical leave in India, I accepted the UN offer in July, 2008. The US economic crises had also hit UNLV, and drastic budget cuts were being discussed. The Administration gave me leave without pay and saved my salary. I was not on a firing line, but the feelers were being thrown to the faculty for an early retirement.

I joined the UN after spending two months in India and attending a history of math conference at Manipur University. Climatically, Nizwa has been perfect from health point of view. It has been five weeks of no problem, though; I eat out 2-3 times a day. However, I also credit it to one hour of yogercises (*Pranayama* & *Aasans*) every morning. A sip of whiskey at night, 4-5 times a week, keeps the internal system disinfected.

Am I getting professional satisfaction? Not yet. The biggest rub, on the top of three different upper division courses, is my convoluted schedule. I have to be on the campus on all five days of the week. I badly miss my UNLV schedule of two courses, two days a week. On the remaining three days, going to the campus is at my own accord. The worst scenario of academic life is one week of spring break – when all the students are gone and campus is deserted. But faculty are expected to attend some lectures and do research, which is only spelled correctly.

Do I enjoy the students here? The answer is really iffy, as the tuning is still going on! The UN, being a 'private' university, either the students **(95% females)** seem to come from rich families, or getting good scholarships. The UN fees is double that of UNLV! The students' English, being hardly equal to that of the US 9th graders of high schools, it obstructs their overall learning, unless it is mixed with Arabic! The UN follows an American model - from the textbooks used to the administrative model. The situation is complex.

The UN library isn't exciting, and the campus life is void of any public events. Its campus (new, under construction), being 40 KM from *Souq* (city center), makes UN, an 8-5 university for the staff, faculty and students. In contrast, UNLV's Lied library is nationally ranked, and campus buzzes with activities. However, Nizwa is an oasis for my *Reflections*!

Feb 23, 2009 (Oman)/Oct, 2015

92. A SLICE OF EDUCATION CULTURE
(Reflective Note to the UN Chancellor)

I thought that my letter of appointment had an error in stating that '*Your suggested appointment will be on 15/1/2009 or as soon as possible thereafter.*' I booked my flight for Jan 15. Later on, an e-mail from the Dept Head stated that the classes would begin on Jan 31. Since a flight change costs up to $250, I arrived on Jan 15, assuming that there may be a week of orientation for new students and faculty. However, there were no social events. We are learning about the UN and Omani cultures by fumbles and tumbles.

After two weeks, when students got their textbooks and started trickling into the classes, I was surprised to see all females. Their walking late to classes, asking for early dismissals and chattering etc. are sensitive issues. I needed to check **students' manual** for which I asked some colleagues, the Dept Head and Human Resources. It is not ready yet, or not available. I tired to have my own Ten Commandments for the sanctity of the classroom-learning environment, but that is also in the making. How different can I be at the UN?

At the UN, the staff is nice and polite in listening to the problems, but no one wants to/or can solve even minor problems. When you find out that these problems being faced by other colleagues seem to have been accepted by them, then either you also follow suit, or do your bit to make the place better. Let me quote what I wrote to my colleagues in a March 14 memo: "**We may have come from different parts of the world, but our common mission is to make this newly 'born' (2004), University of Nizwa (UN) a better place than we found it**." That is the essence of my professionalism.

I am not suggesting any executive actions by you to bring about the changes. But I fully know that the new universities like the UN may be paying in thousands of dollars to foreign consultants for the types of recommendations that you are getting from me. In fact, I could be a consultant of any accreditation bodies, but my heart is not in that work.

To be on a safe side in a totally new culture, I also looked for a **faculty handbook** on the privileges and responsibilities of a professor joining for a semester. Amongst the nuts and bolts, I wanted to know if I was entitled to 30 days paid leave, since 60 days are to be given even to those who joined in Oct/Nov 2008. As a matter of fact, I personally spoke with the College Dean about it, and gave it in writing. It has been more than a month. My research projects have suffered for not being able to go to Egypt and Jordon during the break. But I have to be in India during April 12-17, making sure that my classes are covered.

The No-Response approach may make the problems disappear from one mental screen, but they continue to simmer on the other. Let me lighten you with a funny scenario. The staff IDs and generic business cards are also the billboards of a university, when professors go out at the meetings. It has been ten weeks and I have no UN identity to show off while introducing myself!

March 31, 2009/Oct, 2015

PS; 04/04/09: Met the Chancellor at lunch for about 20 minutes. He marked my points to various offices for action - liked faculty orientation before the semester and a handbook based on faculty inputs. Told him about UNLV's strengths: College of Hotel Administration's Dubai and Singapore centers; Entertainment engineering and Nursing programs; Sending the UN students to UNLV for summer courses.

93. ACADEMIC CULTURE OF A KIND
(Reflective Note to the UN Chancellor)

This is urgent from the perspective of a faculty member who is concerned about laying the solid foundations of academic standards at the University of Nizwa (UN). Yesterday, an e-mail from the Dean directed the faculty for not holding any exams during the Cultural Season on the campus from April 06-22, 2009. It really took me by surprise! Faculty was not consulted directly or indirectly. After all, it is the faculty in the trenches that sweat with students.

After 10 weeks, it is clear that the UN, set up on a model of a US university, has a long way to go in polishing its academic standards. Yes, the Omani students should be encouraged to participate in cultural and intramural activities for stretching their intellectual limits, but not at the cost of the academic courses. On my part, early in the semester, I declined to go Sultan Qaboos University during the semester, as it meant canceling my classes.

You know it well, that in a typical US university, on a given day, there are literally scores of stimulating lectures(unlike the 03/21 at the UN), seminars, and performances, sporting events, intramural activities, Greek clubs etc, but the students and faculty keep academics first; never ever allowing any disruption of their classes.

One faculty member observed that the cultural period is the end of the real studies at the UN. The Department Head told me that the total number of real instruction days add up to eight weeks - not fifteen weeks. Here is a picture that as a Chancellor you have to reconcile it with one in the books. Any syllabus from Week/Day #1 to Week/Day #15, is not telling the true picture.

The dates and number of tests/quizzes are carefully fixed for each course. It is a challenge to keep these students, mainly females, focused on their studies. They miss classes for 'fake' reasons of health, family, or even tests in other courses! Talking of fakes, I have heard calls of fake doctorates and fake full professors here! It may be tip of an iceberg.

Is there a better recourse? Yes, if a student brings a genuine proof of time-consuming participation during a scheduled exam day, then he/she should be given a make-up test/exam. It is a win-win-win scenario for the students, faculty and administrators.

I have given extra classes this week for the pre-scheduled exams next week, arranged colleagues to administer the exam while I am gone to India from April 12-17. This memo is written in the same spirits in which I wrote to my math colleagues on March 14: *"We may have come from different parts of the world, but our common mission is to make this newly 'born' (2004), University of Nizwa a better place than we found it."*

Therefore, an exception should be made for my exams during this cultural week.

April 07, 2009/Oct, 2015

PS: Neither I received any response, nor any student came up to the classes on the exam days!

94. A PACKAGE OF INTELLIGENCE

Intelligence is a word whose equivalent is found in every lexicon. However, it does not have one meaning, but has many shades of it. Presently, intelligence is equated up with formal education. Let me very briefly straighten up the difference between modern education on mass scale and classical education on relatively small scales, particularly in the light of Indian subcontinent. The objective is not to draw any superiority of one over the other, but to point out some complementary features in the ultimate development of a person.

Modern education, through high schools, essentially drills facts and disconnected pieces of knowledge into the young minds. Those not attending schools imbibe 'functional' education through interaction with people in daily lives and travels; also, by listening to discourses in churches and temples, by discussing in bars and cafes, by reading in the libraries, internet, listening to TED lectures and YouTube, etc. The phrase "Three R's" is only 100 years old. The printed word being rare then, the question of reading and writing did not arise. Relevant arithmetic can be picked up off the street. People get more applied wisdom, on the top of moral values, which are totally absent in today's public education.

These thoughts erupted like volcanic lava yesterday. I was at the Ruwi Bus Terminal located in the busiest area of Muscat, Oman's capital. Noticing fresh coconuts at a stall, I ordered for one. While I was waiting to pick up my order, an Omani, in white *dishdasha* and cap, pulled an empty chair and invited me to sit over. He was with two other Omanis, all in their 50s. Taking off my sun hat as I settled down, he asked me in clear English, "How are you professor?" Naturally, I was surprised. His friends looked just casual.

On my complimenting him for his human judgment, he went on a step further and inquired about my subject. I said, "Since you correctly guessed my profession, so try guessing my subject too." Lo and behold, he confidently uttered mathematics and physics - in this order! I waived my hat off for his 'intelligence'! As I was sipping coconut water, he observed a few other traits while sipping his tea. It was a very nice chat. Here is a bottom line: the man drives a cab in Muscat.

He is one of the ethnic Omanis who, centuries ago, migrated from Africa, very dark as compared with the native Arabs, who have fair complexion. He told me how his children eat, drink and play around all day, but no studying. He frankly added that was the way when he was a kid, never listened to his father's advice on studies. Then, I explained how the Omanis are intelligent, though they may not have received even high school education. The Arabs are the best managers of expatriates - whether brought in Oman as unskilled labor or highly educated professionals – like, accountants, doctors, professors and engineers, from all over the world.

In Oman, as in all Gulf countries, every business has to be in the name of an Omani. I have met a Hindu dentist from Bangalore happily working for an Omani for the last 26 years in downtown Nizwa. He told me that had not seen the owner for the last ten years! Having spoken with individual Indian barbers, launderers, construction workers, all are happy to work for 12-14 hours a day - for six days a week! A laborer is provided good free food and clean accommodation. Full salaries are saved to support families in India, Pakistan, Bangladesh, Philippines etc.

Finally, education is not the monopoly of the schools, colleges and universities. It is free and is in the air!

May 01, 2009/Oman/Oct, 2015

95. EDUCATION MASKS PEOPLE

I could not believe a professor of computer science not owning a personal computer or having access to one. It was yesterday that I encountered this anomaly by the grace of IT goddess, when I re-connected with a lost friend. Incidentally, such a scenario can only be experienced when you have lived long enough into your 70s. Though known since 1958, we lost contact over the last 20 years. During the phone call, when I asked for his e-mail ID, he did not have one. For a regular communication, I suggested him to visit cyber cafes that in India are very convenient, fast, and inexpensive (25 cents/hour). But he feels insecure walking or driving, though living in a small town. Having been good friends in youth, I partly understood his deeper thinking.

Suddenly, my reflective mind took a flight into the depth of this Indian mindset. In India of the 1950s, a popular joke on the relevance of education was that a person with a science master's could not fix an electrical fuse in the house. It still happens every other day due to variable power surges. In fact, my brother-in-law with physics PhD has no practical skills in handling minor electrical chores. Education is not at all geared to daily needs. On the top, the Hindus gulp down anything in the name of 'education'.

In contrast, an average American can take care of many house problems. American home garages are equipped with tools needed for fixing problems in carpentry, electrical and garden related works. Actually, majority of the US patents are tinkered and music bands are formed and developed in the home garages. High school and college labs only complement work started in the garages. At UNLV, no student, irrespective of a major, can graduate without a solid science course with lab.

Musing over my two years (1955-57) of science in a Bathinda college, the lab work was just not taken seriously. Most students fudged and cooked up the experimental data. Science was only a vernacular word; it had no curricular meanings before India's independence in 1947. A few years ago, when I visited this college, I was shocked to see the same old lab building, and so did it appear nearly the same lab equipment!

But the deeper reason of this disconnect is everyday Hindu way of life. The Hindu mind, being largely philosophical, abhors the sweat of the brow and brain. It indulges in talking in circles. This is antithesis to scientific thinking, which is linear, and it relies on demonstration of identical results under identical conditions. Paradoxically, India abounds with highly superstitious science educated persons!

During my 2-year (1980-82) stay in India, I was surprised at the introduction of BS/BA in computer science at Kurukshetra University without any access to computers. It was all theoretical. This friend of mine was the first (full) professor of computer science. A question may be posed - what good did it do? As a matter of fact, after another 10 years, the colleges and universities in India turned out legions of software professionals that took over the IT dotcom of the western world! No one ever expected it.

Ironically, India, that educated them, had no jobs for them. The western countries hire them cheap. **Bottom line**: If one lives long enough and is good at something, then one shall fit in somewhere.

April 30, 2010

COMMENTS

Thanks, Satish. Yes, the anachronisms of people are astonishing. Maybe it's a lack of attention and the skill of extrapolation to fit into daily, mundane activities of daily life. Hmmm???

Please add Jane, my daughter's e-mail address to your list. Thanks. **Dutchie**

Hi Satish, while I was reading your reflection, I was thinking of the late Sir Fred Hoyle. He was quite a whizz with computers back in the 1950's and '60's. He taught many computer courses related to astronomy at Cambridge University where he was Plumian Professor of Astronomy. He developed ways by which astronomical data could be analysed by computers. Yet, he never took to the desktop. When he went to live in Bournmouth where he spent the remaining years of his life, he had to have his arm twisted to have even a fax machine installed in his home! Best wishes: **Francis**.

Namaste Tauji, After reading the Reflection "EDUCATION MASKS PEOPLE" The same thing has happened with me in the Thermal Office. I had to pass some bill, but the officer surprised me by saying that he was quiet busy. But, with 2-3 officers, he was talking about share market. After doing some another work, I came back after lunch at 3:00 pm, but they entered into office at 3:35 pm and said that Ankit Ji *aab to 4:00 baj gaya* now whether I sign the documents, it doesn't make any difference, as now no one will forward it *kyonki 5:00 baja to off ho jaata hai.kal aana. aaram se kehe diya*. officer our there as they are EDUCATED JUST A DEGREE HOLDER NON THEY HAVE THE HUMANITY LEVEL NOT THE PRACTICAL TRAINING OF HOW TO DEAL WITH THE PERSON THEY ARE COMING FOR THEIR WORK TO THEM. "JUST DEGREE & RISHWAT" THEY ARE OFFICERS. After this incident I gone through: Bottom Line:- Government Employees think. But do that the office time is 9:00 am to 5:00 pm, It means that they leave the home for office at 9:00 am & reach home at 5:00pm. *Aapka Matakdin.* **Deepu**

I applaud you! If you assume each one desires to "fit in" then what you say is a "truth." However, there are some who never want to fit in, e.g. Ted Krzinsky (misspelled his name) the "Unabomber." Oh dear! Now what? Best regards, **Mannetta**

96. EDUCATIONAL HOOPLAS

It is a reality of life that the rich individuals, families, societies and nations have their hi-fi styles of celebrating their special occasions and events. They are in sharp contrast to the ways of the poor. Normally, any comparison is a non-story. However, it becomes a reflective scenario when a person is caught between these two layers, or has lived through the two diverse worlds in one lifetime.

This line of thoughts has been triggered by the 'graduation' season (mid May through mid June) in the US. It is probably a billion-dollar entertainment industry. Studying in India of the 1950s, the very word, graduation had only one meaning – completion of a bachelor's degree. That is what the British introduced in India. I don't know what exactly graduation meant in the UK - then and now. After moving to the US, we eventually realized that graduation means completion of any course, be that of a day's duration, and in any walk of life - not necessarily academics. It used to irritate me, as it turned over the entire graduation image that I grew up with for the first 30 years of my life.

Graduation is a US fanfare - from the commencement day to subsequent celebratory parties. Again, another nomenclature contrast. In India, commencement is still called convocation. In the US, the two are quite different occasions. Their dictionaries meanings depend upon the dictionary one chooses -whether Oxford or Webster! I am not against parties and celebrations, though the limits are being pushed out in the US. But, I can't stand the trivialization of achievements behind it. That is where I am caught up in my perspectives.

This year, my two older grandkids are graduating - one from a Las Vegas high school and the other from University of California, San Diego. In the US, graduation is a big family event. My daughter has meticulously planned a joint party in a glitzy hall of a hotel casino. There is, perhaps, a touch of vengeance, as we did not publicly celebrate her passing of the high school and college. In fairness, she won diamond ear tops on passing high school exams. It was during our two-year stay in India. The toughness of Indian high school exams can be gauged by the pass percentage of only 38%. In 1985, she finished her BA from UNLV in three years, at age 20-.

I often reminded the kids that in our family, bachelors are expected. For decades, our families have lived off education. It reminds me of a sign, seen at the training facility of Oakland Raiders (NFL team) - *Excellence is Expected Here*. As it happens in the life of every parent transplanted from India to the US, all kinds of upbringing norms and restrictions begin to change with the younger kids. Subsequently, we had graduation parties for 40-50 friends and relatives, which were held at our home, or in the open parks.

Again, putting it in perspective, the US graduation has two parts. First is the commencement ceremony that sets the US really apart from rest of the world. Once, I attended a graduation ceremony of my 4-year old granddaughter from her day-care center, wearing beautiful regalia and decorum around. Multiply it by a factor of 100 for a high school or college graduation.

Even in today's India, there are no high school graduation ceremonies. College ceremonies are somber events. On a personal note, the only ceremony that I have attended was for my bachelor's degree, exclusively for those students, who passed BA with Honors (no comparison with typical US honors!). In a 180-degree contrast with 'immediate' commencement ceremony in the US, I passed BA (Honors in Math) exams in June 1959, but attended the convocation held in Dec 1959! Moreover, it was held only in one city, Chandigarh, for the selected students from 200+ affiliated colleges in the entire state of Punjab!

Later on, I did not care to attend the convocation for my master's from India, nor commencement for the doctorate from Indiana University, Bloomington. Reason: attending the commencement meant spending about $50 for it, but cost nothing for getting the diploma by mail. With wife and two kids, I could not afford time and money from my monthly stipend of $400.

Again, the word, diploma has driven me nuts. In the US, diploma means a piece of paper proclaiming the completion of the requirements of a course, be that passing an electrician's course or a doctorate in mathematics. In India, diplomas generally meant some academic qualifications between a high school certificate and college degree.

On the occasions of kids' passing of their exams, parents used to send *ladoos* (popular Indian sweet) in paper bags to the homes of close friends and relatives. On my passing days, I opposed even that. Now I realize that it was depriving my parents of moments of filial pride and happiness. My reason was simple, as I considered my performance below my expectations. That is for another occasion. The point is how much US hoopla can I accept in the context of my past?

Everything changes with time, except some hardened habits. I have tried to support and encourage celebration of excellence. But driving for 5-6 hours or flying to San Diego to attend commencement ceremonies, does not simply jell with my person. In the age of smart phones, Facebook and YouTube, what is the point of sitting in a crowd of 20,000 people for 2-3 hours, and watch for hardly 20 seconds your graduating kid go up on the stage, accept the diploma, shake a few hands, and get off the stage to disappear in the crowd again?

In 1992, we did drive to Los Angeles for our son's commencement (master's). Nothing of that event stands out. I don't even recall the commencement speaker's image, which the USC, and the like, pride in inviting one. It was an organized crowd of revelers, and it may have moved one notch up in 20 years! Above all, the old-time fun in driving, flying and staying in a hotel room for a night or two has been largely replaced with fear and stress in the post 9/11 USA. Despite all this, ten family members are set upon traveling from LV to SD for this event.

May 23, 2010/Oct, 2015

COMMENTS

Couldn't agree more with you on this. There is a big commercial/business angle to this as well in US. Check out the local branch of Big Box stores. They all have some kind of merchandise on sale related to "Graduation Fanfare" every year around this time. I still remember growing up in India ... parents used to promise an "hmt" wristwatch to their wards, if they stood, first in their class ... those were simpler days I guess. –**Gaurav**

Hello Uncle, I agree with you point of view here. Maybe it is because I am from India too and got my Bachelors in Engineering degree there (trust me it was more of a sigh of relief to be done with it rather than any joy). Back in India, everyone is expected to get a degree and it's not a choice after high school. In stark contrast, here in the States these lazy bums have to be coaxed/encouraged a lot to attend college, and I think that's why it's a bigger deal.

To me, it's a pretentious display of some kind of joy, because in this day and age. a degree will not get you anything. Some people who have lived in the States side long enough forget where they came from and are selective in their habits/traditions/celebrations, that's my only remorse. I am glad to read that you are not one of them; you still question things to find a deeper meaning. I admire you because you have core values/ principles and are not afraid to say your mind even if it is contrary to popular thought of the time or the place.

I feel I can relate to your writings. You write a lot about the contrast in the life that you once had long back and what it is now. I enjoy your writings about things that have helped you personally, and about how to keep the mind invigorated, and have a good laugh reading about your idiosyncrasies. Your writings also encompass real life stories about people who have worked hard selflessly, but do not get their due and you try your best to bring such subjects in the foreground that would have otherwise been never known to me at least. I think in the past 2-3 years, I have read reflections on a wide variety of topics, but the ones I enjoy the most are the most basic and simple daily life reflections about things most of us consider mundane, you put it down in simple words and make me think about what I thought was trite otherwise. That gives my brain a good dose of stimulation.

I fear I might sound naïve above and it may sound ironical, since I have mostly told you- the author about what you write about. LOL!! But if I were to sum it up then what stands out the most to me in your writings is the simplicity of the matter presented in a rather un-opinionated way, which is still up for a good healthy debate. **Rohan**

"But driving for 5-6 hours or flying to San Diego to attend my granddaughter's commencement ceremony, does not just rhyme with my temperament. In the age of smart phones, Face book and YouTube, what is the point of being in a crowd of 20,000 people for 2-3 hours, and watch for a minute your graduate going up on the stage, take the diploma, shake a couple of hands, and get off the stage to disappear in the crowd again?" I agree with this Nana!!! But I also agree with what you said about doing it for the happiness of your parents and family. Nikhail and I have succumbed to every want of Mommy's because we realize the party is more for her than us. **Anjali**

Dear Satish, This one I really like with enthusiasm. Not only do I agree about not attending graduations the way that you explained, your opinions were very satisfying. Thanks. My two children did not go to their high school graduations and Jane didn't go to her college graduation. Jesse went to his Cal Tech graduation mostly for my Mom who was so pleased and happy to go to California with us to help celebrate. We had no party. None, nada, nothing was done about a party. But, any excuse for a party is noteworthy. Let's party, party, party with happiness for these two young people, Anjali and Nikhail. They both were diligent and successful. Congratulations to the family also. Hugs from **Dutchie**

Dad, I note at least two glaring inaccuracies: First, rest assured, there is not an ounce of vengeance behind kids' graduation party plans. As I travel down *my* memory lane, I recall ALL of my birthdays and major milestones (before, during, and after marriage) celebrated with much pomp & circumstance by my parents! I›m sure mom was able to conduct her children›s events with such passion, only with your support. For instance, my B-day parties were always more lavish than Avnish's- which I constantly taunted him about. You & mom gifted me with diamond earrings for passing my Indian exams and I received an emerald/diamond ring for Bachelor's degree. I had a lovely graduation party, for Bachelor's AND Master's degree with many guests and mom's

297

tasty homemade food (her labor of love). In comparison, for Anjali/ Nikhail's upcoming party, I will be simply writing a check for ready-made food and showing up at same time as other guests. Each generation tends to take fun & glamour to another level, as mine will do for their kids one day!

Second, I was 19 years old when I attended my B.A. commencement ceremony at Thomas & Mack. Then married at 21, blessed with two kids and M. Ed degree by 27, with divorce by 40. What's next? Hope to retire from drudgery of work by age 55. Ha-Ha....**Gori/Archna**

I wrote: Well, your second point, note, it is written 20- that means close to 20. You were three weeks short of before turning 20. So 20- years is like 19 years + 9 to 11 months, 19+ means 19 years + 4 to 8 months and 19 means 19+ 1 to 3 months. It is more accurate, and gives a touch of grades - my creation!

On working in life, I remain inspired by two legendary football coaches --**Joe Paterno** (84 Years) and **Bobby Bowden** (82). Both kept their teams in top ten. Bowden often said that the only thing after retirement was death. That is why some active people come out of retirement to resume their 'passion', which in actuality one never leaves. I am sure, you will identify a passion in life much before you retire at 55. By the way, I plan on being around when you turn 55, though may not be working full-time!

Dear Satish, Wonderful reflection.....for those who studied in India in the 50's. Others who have been raised in the hoopla environment won't understand what we are complaining about!! I found so many of your observations and remarks **SO TRUE** !! We are caught in a '*Trisanku* paradise" Regards. **RAJA**

Yes, I think you were spot on. Graduation seems to have become a devalued currency in the US, as people seem to "graduate" from every level of education. In Britain, when someone is referred as a "graduate", it means they have completed a three or four year university course. Your reflection again reminded me of Hoyle. When he had finished studying for his doctorate in 1940, all that was needed was a simple ceremony in the senate building. He did not go ahead with it, as this would have placed him in a higher tax bracket! So for a long time he simply remained "Mr. Hoyle"! All the best: **Francis**.

I agree with you, especially about the "vocabulary" differences between American and British English. They are going to construct a "roundabout" in the University Boulevard in our campus to relieve frequent traffic bottlenecks. Some folks questioned what the term "roundabout" was about? I told them that road-wise it was like the DuPont circle in Washington, DC! **Subhash Saxena**

PERSONAL REMARKS

97. RE-FIXING A SPOT LIGHT

During the last five years, 2007-2012, UNLV has undergone several rounds of horizontal, vertical, and transversal budget cuts. By and large, it has become lean so that it can run faster! Already, some restorative efforts are underway, particularly in the hiring of five-star faculty. They are the signs of renewed health. Of course, there are persons who are critical of such hires, because of the layoffs and buyouts of the staff and faculty, which were done to meet the budget deficits just a year ago. To me, it is all creative book keeping!

In the spirit of restoration and revival, let me share a healthy academic tradition that has been supposedly taken off in the very first round of the cuts. It is the annual recognition of the campus authors. A year ago, I wrote to the then Provost about its discontinuation. It may save peanuts. Let us do its simple math for ten authors in a given year. A wine and cheese reception won't cost more than $250. This event complements the annual honors convocation held generally in the lobby of the Ham Hall. I am glad it has survived, though cuts in foods and drinks were noticeable last month.

Last Friday, I spoke with the manager of UNLV bookstore about my two books not being on a particular bookshelf marked for the books of the camps authors. The response, I got was, "I have no way of knowing the faculty who have published books. My source used to be the annual recognition of the authors held in Lied Library, and that has not taken place for a while!"

A few months ago, I also checked with the library, as to what happened to a showcase displaying faculty books? The answer was budget cuts! Would you take it? The library can have an entire wall of showcases displaying the books of the faculty - until they retired! Where is the cost? There are still too many showcases for various other displays.

Of course, I have a personal interest in its revival, as my two books are out. I am 72. Around this age, professors become deadwood; they lose interest in the affairs of their department, college, university; their lecture notes turn out yellow; and nothing is published for years together.

Recognition functions generate positive vibes and delay the onset of mental rust.

When people say that UNLV has grown big - and such things, no matter how reasonable they are, cannot be corrected quickly - I do not agree with it. The administration is too distracted, wrapped up and bogged down in various compliance rules and regulations – externally forced upon – like, accreditation, assessments, federal, fire and asbestos regulations, etc.

Adding a touch of salsa to this scenario, here is a last bite. Until a year or two ago, the colleges did not have directors for its publicity and development/fund raising. Without spotlights on the creative work of five-star faculty, how can they do their jobs or justify them? Needless to say, periodic recognition of scholarly achievements alone distinguishes a university from a college.

May 28, 2012/Dec, 2015

COMMENTS

I agree we should celebrate authors on campus....perhaps the incoming Provost can cook something up with Patty.... **Neal Smatresk/President**

Satish and Neal; Thank you for your interest in the Libraries Author event, now defunct. Allow me to provide some additional information concerning the decision:

1. The libraries lost 15 Percent of its staff over the past three years, and the events coordinator was the first to go.

2. Contrary to what you might think about how easy it is to plan such an event, it was a 9-month process involving many people. Attached is the last spreadsheet we used for planning.

3. The process was especially complicated because we had no way of identifying books published by UNLV authors except for a continual haranguing to get the information from faculty themselves - or their department support staff. (Perhaps Digital Measures will help with that process once it is up and fully functioning for all faculty)

4. We really didn't have a space....the space used is a study space, which we reconfigure ..Also, work to do. And then students are kicked out during the busiest time of year. (This will also change once we get our new event space created)

5. Once we had the list of books and authors and the celebration we ALWAYS had complaints... From those whose books were overlooked because we didn't find them.. From those whose books we couldn't get on time from publishers despite rush orders... In addition, mostly from the larger majority of faculty whose scholarship is NOT books. But journal articles.

6. It seemed increasingly ironic to celebrate books when the libraries has cut its monograph budget by 60 percent.

I agree that we should celebrate the scholarly accomplishments of our faculty. I think it should be for all forms of scholarly endeavor. I look forward to partnering with the office of the EVP&P to determine what that might be. **Patricia Iannuzzi**/Dean Libraries

I am sure we can. **John White**/Incoming Provost and EVP

PS Dec, 2015: Neither the tradition of annual reception of the campus authors revived nor their books displayed in the Library. It is partly due to transiency in the office of the Provost and President. I picked up this 'campaign' when my first book was published and now on my way to the ninth book!

98. MAS PROGRAM: MY FOSTER BABY!

After reading a couple of forwarded e-mails on the possible resurrection of the moribund MAS program, I am prompted to write on it. As an 'in-house' historian, let me add that Dean Ernie Peck created the program in 1990. It was an extension of a post-baccalaureate joint program with the College of Education on professional development for the teachers in the school district. However, the post-baccalaureate program was eliminated in a round of 'cuts' of academic programs and units 3-4 years ago.

Roberta Williams (biologist) chaired the MAS committee since its inception, and I was its founding member - carried over from a School Relations Committee. When Roberta died in the spring of 2004, Dean Ron Yasbin 'threw' MAS into my lap. I was then his Associate Dean (2003-06). He gave me an additional title of Acting Director of the MAS program, but no financial compensation! Immediately, I revamped this program. Reason, in the previous 10-12 years, it had morphed into a diluted MS program in biology. Biology faculty were unhappy, as the students could not handle 700-level courses and theses.

Also, three were deeper problems – some MAS students unadvised or misadvised were taking 3-5 years for finishing it - normally a 2-year program. There was no recourse, if a student and supervisor did not get along, and other interpersonal issues were there. Consequently, a new course based option was added - a major and two minors for a total of 36 credits.

However, Dean Yasbin suddenly 'stopped' admission of the new students into the program after I returned to full time faculty. That is one of the reasons that no one has earned an MAS degree recently. Earlier, the average graduation rate was of 2-3 students per year. Faculty from Geoscience (Steve Rowland) and Chemistry (Vernon Hodge) actively contributed into the program. However, Mathematics and Physics remained on sidelines!

A question may be raised: Does this program have a future in the College? Unqualified Yes! Since its birth, the pogrom has been administratively housed in the Dean's office. That is the right place for it. However, the program needs to be re-cast for one last time to make it truly belong to all the five stakeholders of the College.

Here is my suggestion: a student must take at least one 700-level course from each of the five departments of the College - no major, no minors, and no concentration whatsoever! The MAS will then truly reflect its name, Master of Arts in Sciences! The remaining 15 graduate credits may be completed with courses in the College, 15+ 0 or 12+3 (3 credits for a professional paper) - no six-credit thesis option. Such an MAS program is simple to implement, simple to administer, and simple to oversee – no demands on any one department.

A twin question is: who will pursue it? Based upon my 40 years of interaction with academic community – on campus and off campus, the clientele will come from prospective science teachers in schools, teachers seeking alternative to soft degrees in the College of Education, and employees of a dozen of federal agencies. In 1989, there was no PhD program in the College - now each department has at least one. In many graduate schools, 20-30 % of the students admitted in PhD programs are separated for a number of reasons. Some of them may opt for the MAS in addition to an MS degree from the respective departments.

This duo of graduate degrees would strengthen their employability in 2 and 4-year colleges, and in areas that we do not know. Moreover, some students may pursue highly popular and paying PhD programs in math education, physics education, chemistry education, biology education, or in overarching science education! Incidentally, universities like UCLA have a PhD program in Science education, but UNLV does not have any bachelor's or master's program in science education. Above all, the MAS degree would meet the present buzz of the STEM mantra.

What is the bottom line? For years, the MAS program has remained fiscally viable without any severe demands on a department's resources. It involves designing of no new courses. Presently, the graduate courses are not over-populated with students. For instance, there are hardly ten students in MAT/STAT courses at 700-level. Let each department list a few 700-level courses that the MAS students can take without more than one prerequisite course. In mathematics, I roll out the dice by listing the following courses: MAT 711, 712, 714, STA 713, 715.

I hope this email, a bit long though, does engage all the interested parties.

Nov 11, 2013/Dec, 2015

COMMENTS

Dr. B., This is the first I've heard of the MAS program, and my opinion is that it has real merit. My master's at UW-Madison was in science education, and the EDD that I didn't finish at IU included a minor in science education. I'm not looking for another degree program at my age, but I know one guy currently in an EDD program in curriculum and instruction with math emphasis who might be a good candidate.

I heartily agree with your characterization..."soft degrees in the College of Education." I still have a copy of an open letter to the faculty that I wrote in the sixties while teaching at what now University of Northern Iowa is. (It was Iowa State Teachers College when I started there.) I suggested closing the School of Education, doing away with the eight or ten education courses that kept teaching candidates from taking real content courses, and making the licensing of teachers dependent on successful teaching as a novice or intern working under master teachers in a real school situation. It never got any traction where it counted, but many of my colleagues liked my ideas. I'm reminded of a statement attributed to an administrator at one of the state universities in New York. "Bringing about change in a School of Education is very much like trying to move a graveyard." **Owen Nelson**

COMMENTATORS & ANALYSTS EXTRAORDINAIRE

Sixteen years ago, I started writing **Reflections,** a reincarnation of my life-long passion of writing all kinds of letters in a long hand. The big difference was that that my reflective writings went public – from one to many, as I started sharing them with my friends and relatives. And, from there, these reflections go to their friends and relatives, and so on. Years ago, a student of mine created a blog, viabti.blogspot.com, but only a few months ago, I posted the reflections regularly. I don't have a website yet. It is mostly emails in a bcc - electronically old-fashioned mode in social media.

I have several mailing lists and I am used to this inefficient mode of communication. I have Facebook and Twitter accounts too, but they too have remained unused. That is my approach to communication. Naturally, some of my readers write back and give comments. At times, a small dialog takes place. It has added clarity, expanded the topic, and sharpened my intellect – must at this stage of life.

For a number of reasons, not all the comments and commentators are included in the book– only those comments, which are concise and strong. In reflective style of writings, inclusion of comments adds a new flavor. Initially, I never saved the comments. Also, sometimes, no comments were received. That is why the spaces following some **Reflections** are blank.

It is not merely a time to thank them, but also share a piece of 'immortality' that this book may bring! When I look at the credentials of these persons, I am myself awed and wowed. These comments have come out of their incredible rich backgrounds. I don't think any other author can easily match this list. Here are the names:

Raju Abraham, 66: Known for ten years. English professor – has taught in Baroda/India, Sana/Yemen, and presently in Oman with University of Nizwa, where I was a visiting professor during Spring-2009.

Francis Andrew, 66 is professor of English in the College of Applied Sciences, in Nizwa. His knowledge of Christian theology, astronomy and science in general is very extensive. He uses them effectively in the writing of science fiction books – nearly dozen. We met in 2009 and have been in regular touch since then.

Anand R. Bhatia, aged 72, is a retired professor of business from California State University, San Bernardino. We have known each other for 30+ years mainly for our common ideas and values, though we grew up extremes cities – he, in Mumbai and me, in Bathinda.

Avnish Bhatnagar: My son, age 47, working at Google since 2006. His comments are fewer, but deep.

Rahul Bhatnagar, 56: Distantly related - physician by training in India. He has an interesting job of medical director of drug safety with a pharmaceutical company; very astute commentator and analyst of nearly all my *Reflections*. He can refine and dissect an issue to a state that becomes undistinguishable from the one it started from.

Harbans Singh Bhola, 83: Emeritus professor of education, Indiana University, known since 1971. He had his bachelors with Math A and B courses from PU that I had too. He has sharp intellect and a robust Punjabi sense of humor.

CS Chen is one of the few faculty who left UNLV in 2005, after 17 years on getting the chairmanship at Southern Mississippi, Hattiesburg. However, he realized that his not getting the deanship is due to his Asian factors. He is a very productive researcher, collaborator and successful grant writer.

Irma Dutchie is our next-door neighbor, that I call her, our angel now after 13 years. Both physically and mentally, she can challenge any 60-year old. She has a Bostonian aura about her life style. Her love for life is as phenomenal as helping friends, strangers and charity organizations with her time, money and energy. She is my inspiration for life. At 85, she says that she can't be without a boyfriend!

Aaron Harris, 36 was the best student in both the graduate courses that he took from me during 2006-07. He is about to get his PhD in Mathematics Education from UNLV - while teaching mathematics full time in a high school and raising four kids with his wife of fifteen years.

Owen Nelson, 83 year old, has been a part time instructor at UNLV for over 15 years – hired for the sole purpose of teaching remedial math courses. He got his MS in science education from UW- Madison and ABD (All But Dissertation) from Indiana University. Owen is one of the rare individuals whose intellectual growth has not been limited by formal college degrees. He has extensively commented on most of my mathematical reflections. Owen stands out in contrast with many PhDs who seldom see, smell, talk or think out of a box of their narrow specializations.

RS Nigam: Retired Professor of Commerce and Director of Delhi School of Economics – known since 1986. He died in 2014 at the age of 79.

IBS Passi, 76 years old is working as an honorary professor of mathematics in IISER while continuing to do researches in algebra. He was a year senior to me during our maser's from PU Chandigarh, and has the unique distinction of topping the examinations both for BA and MA. After PhD from UK, he taught at KU before moving to PU. We have been directly and indirectly in touch with each other ever since. He is a member of Indian Academy of Science, and has served as President of the IMS.

Subhash C. Saxena, 79: known for 20-30 years – all due to our common participation in the national and international math meetings - retired from Coastal University in North Carolina.

BhuDev Sharma 78: Known since 1990, math professor - taught in India, Trinidad and several universities in the US. He organized World Association of Vedic Studies and its biennial conferences in India and the USA. He is an able educational administrator. For several years, published the *Vishwa Vivek*, the first Hindi monthly magazine in the US.

Ved P. Sharma, 77: friends since 1964, when we taught in Panjab University, Shimla. Twelve years of chairing the Department of Economics in Mankato State took a toll on his back and knees. He is still working fulltime, but going one semester at a time.

Harpreet Singh, 40: A rare combination of computer science, finance, active spirituality, and creative writing – always stretching the limits of his body and mind. He has been known for 15 years – initially through his parents.

Sarvajit Singh, 76 and I have been known to each other since 1965. He is a solid researcher. After years at KU, he moved to MDU Rohtak, where he served as Professor & Head of Math Dept. and Dean before retiring. He is a member Indian National Academy of Sciences, and was President of the IMS.

Subhash Sood: Physician by training in India, UK and USA - studied other systems of medicine too. He went so deep into Scientology that he established a center in Ambala Cantt, and translated several scientology books from English into Hindi. He died in 2007 at the age of 73 - in a 100-year old dilapidated mansion in which he was born to a well-known physician father. He was my most passionate reader and critique for 25 years.

Len Zane, 71: Emeritus UNLV physics professor, who also served as the founding Director/Dean of the Honors College for ten years. We often chat and exchange ideas – an avid hiker and engaging conversationalist.

NOTES